States of Separation

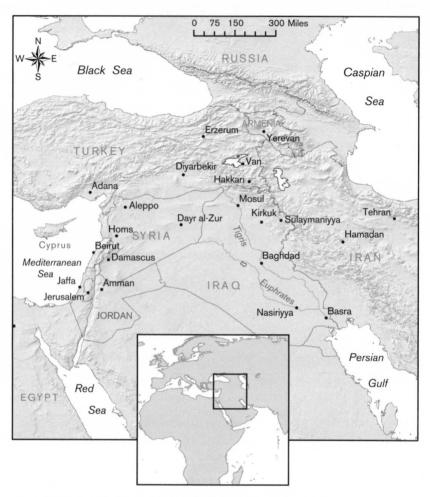

MAP 1. The Eastern Mediterranean and its borderlands. Map by Sachi Arakawa.

States of Separation

TRANSFER, PARTITION, AND THE MAKING
OF THE MODERN MIDDLE EAST

Laura Robson

UNIVERSITY OF CALIFORNIA PRESS

University of California Press, one of the most distinguished university presses in the United States, enriches lives around the world by advancing scholarship in the humanities, social sciences, and natural sciences. Its activities are supported by the UC Press Foundation and by philanthropic contributions from individuals and institutions. For more information, visit www.ucpress.edu.

University of California Press
Oakland, California

© 2017 by Laura Robson

Library of Congress Cataloging-in-Publication Data

Names: Robson, Laura, author.
Title: States of separation : transfer, partition, and the making of the modern Middle East / Laura Robson.
Description: Oakland, California : University of California Press, [2017] | Includes bibliographical references and index.
Identifiers: LCCN 2016043342| ISBN 9780520292154 (cloth : alk. paper) | ISBN 9780520965669 (ebook)
Subjects: LCSH: Forced migration—Middle East. | Middle East—Population policy. | League of Nations. | Middle East—Politics and government—20th century. | Middle East—History—20th century. | Iraq—History—20thcentury. | Syria—History—20th century. | Palestine—History—20th century.
Classification: LCC HV640.4.M628 R63 2016 | DDC 325/.210956—dc23
LC record available at https://lccn.loc.gov/2016043342

Manufactured in the United States of America

26 25 24 23 22 21 20 19 18 17
10 9 8 7 6 5 4 3 2 1

For Tam

These are the conditions and these are the sacrifices and we therefore pray the Allies . . . to return our people to Urumia.

        J. M. YONAN AND PERA MIRZA, *letter to British government on Assyrian position in Iraq*, 1918

At a time when thoughtful persons are dreaming about some form of co-operation to replace national conflict, it is reassuring to feel that France, England, 'Iraq, Syria and the League of Nations have been able to work so well together. . . . The Assyrian Settlement is a striking example of what might be accomplished in the world as a whole if social justice could become a guiding principle of national affairs and if international competition could be superseded by a new spirit of team work.

        BAYARD DODGE, *"The Settlement of the Assyrians on the Khabbur,"* 1940

Under the most diverse conditions and disparate circumstances, we watch the development of the same phenomena—homelessness on an unprecedented scale, rootlessness to an unprecedented depth.

        HANNAH ARENDT, *The Origins of Totalitarianism*, 1951

CONTENTS

ILLUSTRATIONS

FIGURES

MAPS

ACKNOWLEDGMENTS

I am very grateful to the many people and institutions whose support helped make this book a reality. I received research funding for this work from the American Council of Learned Societies/Mellon Foundation Recent Doctoral Recipients Fellowship and from a Faculty Enhancement Grant at Portland State University. I thank the Department of History, the Friends of History, and the Middle East Studies Center at Portland State University for their support, as well as the many archivists and librarians at institutions in the United Kingdom, Switzerland, Israel/Palestine, Jordan, France, and the United States who assisted me in locating relevant material.

Other scholars also contributed generously through discussions, comments, and suggestions on various parts of the work. I would like to thank Benjamin Thomas White, Akram Khater, Ussama Makdisi, Jennifer Dueck, Heleen Murre-van den Berg, Sargon Donabed, Dina Khoury, Joel Beinin, Keith Watenpaugh, Andrew Patrick, and Patricia Goldsworthy-Bishop for acting as thoughtful and generous interlocutors at various stages in this project and for including me in conferences, workshops, and other professional venues where I could test my ideas. My colleagues in the history department at Portland State have likewise assisted in a variety of ways, and I thank Jennifer Tappan, Catherine McNeur, James Grehan, Joseph Bohling, Chia Yin Hsu, Natan Meir, and Desmond Cheung for their thoughts and suggestions. I am also very grateful for the thoughtful and incisive critiques offered by the four anonymous manuscript reviewers. Niels Hooper at University of California Press has been an exceptionally helpful and farsighted editor, and I thank him for bringing the project to fruition.

My greatest debts are to my family. My children, Andrew and Silje, have provided delightful relief from the often grim topics at hand. Most of all I thank my husband, Tam Rankin, to whom I owe the title of this volume, and a great deal more besides. This book is dedicated to him with love.

Introduction

In 1933, following a brutal massacre of Assyrian Christians in northern Iraq, officials at the League of Nations in Geneva began discussing what one representative called a new "means of solving the conflicts of race and religions at present occurring in the Near East": removing Assyrians from Iraq altogether and shipping them en masse to some distant territory.[1] Potential sites included Brazil, South Africa, Timbuktu, and British Guiana—where, one official report noted hopefully, "Apart from the Indians . . . the population consists of only a few settlers and ranchers," among whom the Assyrians could easily be reconstituted as a national bloc.[2] The idea of a mass removal of Assyrians to some far-flung location halfway around the globe quickly became a cause célèbre across Europe as a pragmatic solution to an intractable problem of Middle Eastern ethnic and religious conflict; and this apparently bizarre proposal was by no means exceptional. Within its first two decades, the League involved itself in several other plans for ethnically based mass transfer: forced population exchange between Greece and Turkey, large-scale Armenian resettlement in the border areas of Syria, redistribution of territory by ethnicity in Palestine, and the relocation of European Jews to any available empty space—"whether this be in America, Africa, or Australia does not really matter," as the president of the League's Office on Refugees declared, "as long as they can be *together on their own*."[3]

When the First World War ended, the Eastern Mediterranean's multiple and mixed ethnic, linguistic, and religious communities were in the midst of an intense internal negotiation over what kind of states should emerge out of the wreckage of the old Ottoman Empire. But following the peace agreements, most of the former Ottoman Arab territories were immediately occupied and subdued. Under the aegis of the brand-new League of Nations, Iraq,

Palestine, Syria, and Lebanon were declared "mandate" states: British and French colonial holdings that were, theoretically, being supervised on the road to national independence by their European overseers. Responsibility for recasting these new nations' multiplicity of ethnicities, religions, and languages into a modern state order would rest with the League of Nations, an "international" authority run primarily in the interests of the victorious Allied powers (and longtime empire-builders) Britain and France. The British, the French, and the League aimed jointly to envision, shape, and institutionalize a new regional order in which state organization would reflect ethnic and national identities in newer and neater ways than in the messy recent past—a task that could legitimize European intervention in the Middle East as part of an emerging practice of international governance, while simultaneously serving as a practical mode of colonial population control on the ground.

So over the protests of those on the ground slated for displacement, the British and French mandate governments collaborated with the League to propose, fund, and in some cases actually implement a series of dramatic plans for ethnic engineering. Removing the entire Assyrian Christian community of Iraq to Brazil or British Guiana, creating Armenian buffer zones in the hard-to-control border areas of Syria, drawing new ethnic borders and enforcing mass population exchange between Jewish and Arab territories in Palestine—the League and its allies marked such varied tactics of demographic manipulation as "solutions" whose benefits, remaking the region as a series of identifiably modern and fundamentally controllable ethnonational blocs, would ultimately justify the human costs.

·   ·   ·

The preceding decades had seen the emergence of several disparate precursors to this idea that would eventually converge in the specific geographical space of the former Ottoman Arab provinces. In the late nineteenth century, Britain and France almost simultaneously laid the groundwork for tying religious and ethnic identification to political representation, both at home and in their respective empires. At home, Jewish assimilation (and resistance to it) sparked vigorous public debate about the relationship between ethnoreligious affiliation and political belonging in London and Paris, leading toward a new interpretation of European Jews as "minorities" within their home countries.[4] Nineteenth-century European colonial practices repeatedly sought to push particular indigenous populations out of colonized territories, sometimes with genocidal violence, in the interests of creating racially specific landscapes.[5] In this context, the French granted special citizenship rights to Algerian Jews and settled Europeans on land appropriated from Muslim Algerians; the British created communally based franchises in India and Egypt and dispossessed indigenous inhabitants in parts of Africa and Australia to create white settler colonial enclaves. Such practices of articulating political rights via communal identifications, alongside mass displacement of indigenous populations to create ethnically specific settler spaces, reflected a shared British and French strategy of making ethnicity, religion, and race central to both citizens' and subjects' relations with the state.

The new Zionist movement that emerged in nineteenth-century Europe—like other European nationalisms of the time—embraced this vision of ethnonational citizenship. Beginning in the late nineteenth century, Zionists proposed to solve Europe's "Jewish problem" by removing Jews (who had already begun emigrating in large numbers) and placing them elsewhere as a national bloc, an idea that caught the attention in particular of British officials who could imagine imperial uses for European populations relocated to remote corners of empire. In an important conceptual leap, Zionism's advocates began to present mass removal and resettlement as a humanitarian strategy to deal with the problems of pluralism, one that could simultaneously benefit relocated communities and their imperial patrons. Zionism was not the only global example of a movement seeking validation and political authority for a disenfranchised, mobile population via the "remaking" of an ethnic homeland; in the American context, for instance, the immediate postwar period saw a revival of the idea of a "repatriation" of African Americans to an African homeland spearheaded by the pan-Africanist Marcus Garvey, who founded a shipping line intended to transfer both goods and people from the African diaspora to the African continent.[6] Such appropriations of the ethos of removal and resettlement as a mode of minority empowerment further entrenched the idea of ethnic separatism on the international stage.

In the Ottoman sphere, this emerging European emphasis on an ethnonational identity that was supremely relevant to citizenship and political participation began to mingle with older Ottoman notions of community and subjecthood to produce new and often toxic visions of national belonging. In the decades preceding the First World War, the brutal fracturing of the old Ottoman political order in eastern Europe led to massive expulsions of Muslim refugees out of the Balkans and the Caucasus into Ottoman territory. Such dislocations encouraged concomitant Ottoman expulsions of Christians from Anatolia, and gradually led the Ottoman Empire to develop formal and informal modes of ethnic differentiation—not infrequently shading into ethnic cleansing and eventually, in the Armenian case, genocide—as a way of resisting military defeat and territorial loss. These practices of ethnic violence would contribute both ideologically and practically to the postwar construction of a regional regime of ethnonational separation.

The First World War and its immediate aftermath advanced these ideas further. The bloodshed of the conflict itself helped sculpt new and powerful ethnic loyalties across the Balkans and central Europe. At the peace talks, Woodrow Wilson's so-called Fourteen Points endorsed the concept of homogenous nation-states as a necessary precondition for democratic self-rule, without successfully answering—or perhaps even acknowledging—the question of how to disentangle the multiple ethnicities, religions, and languages of regions like the Balkans. Following the war, the treaties signed at Versailles provided state attachments for sixty million people formerly under the Habsburg, Ottoman, and Russian empires but left twenty-five million more as "unclassifiable" under the new system of nation-states.[7] Among them were stateless survivors of the Ottoman state's genocidal campaigns who now became wards of the international community. Camps housing Armenian and Assyrian refugees in Iraq and Syria soon became spaces for the nationalization of ethnicity and religion and experiments in international population management. As the scale of postwar mass displacement became clearer, the Allies and the League began to consider mass resettlement and population exchange as ways to stabilize a fragile global order and protect their own interests.[8]

As Britain, France, and the League of Nations claimed control over the Arab provinces of the old Ottoman Empire through the new "mandates" system, their officials began to imagine ways to reorganize these spaces via the dual strategies of transfer and partition. Drawing simultaneously on the ethnic cleansings of the recent Ottoman past, European colonial practices of population control and management, and Zionist concepts of removal and resettlement, the League and the British and French mandate governments mooted a number of schemes for ethnically based population exchange and transfer in the interwar Middle East.[9] These campaigns ranged widely in scope, ambition, and extent of implementation, from the execution of a brutal compulsory exchange of Muslims and Christians between Greece and Turkey to encouragement and support for mass European Jewish resettlement in

Palestine to a series of unrealized proposals for resettling Assyrians out of Iraq and Syria to spaces as far-flung as Brazil, British Guiana, and Timbuktu. These decades also saw a number of more local transfer plans, moving Assyrian and Armenian communities around Iraq and Syria with the purpose of propping up British and French colonial control in difficult border areas. Such schemes, though they differed substantially in specifics and extent, shared a basic vision of "minority" (i.e., non-Muslim) Jewish, Armenian, and Assyrian communities as potentially useful tools for constructing internationally sanctioned forms of imperial control across the Levant.

It soon became clear that the British, the French, and the League had all underestimated the extent of local resistance to such plans, on the part of those undergoing resettlement as well as those impacted by their arrival. On the ground, many Assyrians and Armenians vigorously resisted transfer, instead promoting alternative visions of their political future sometimes partially derived from Ottoman models. Their Arab neighbors were no more enthusiastic, often vocally condemning the transfer of refugee populations into new areas of Syria and Iraq as a scheme to introduce colonial collaborators into Arab territory—objections echoed in even stronger terms as the British mandate government oversaw the entrance of thousands of European Jewish settlers into Palestine. All these local actors made extensive use of the legal language and bureaucratic mechanisms of the League itself to press their cases against the machinations of mandatory authority. Further, the imperial concept of "empty" land to which whole communities could be conveniently removed—a particularly cherished idea in the British empire— began to recede as the global anticolonial movements of the 1930s stretched resources and shrank imperial imaginings.

In the face of these difficulties, a different idea for restructuring the Middle East began to take hold: partition. Ethnic divisions of territory had previously been discussed (and partially implemented) in Syria and Iraq, but reached a new apogee in the late 1930s as the Peel Commission formally proposed the division of Palestine into separate Arab and Jewish states. Palestinian Arabs responded to this plan with a major anticolonial revolt that seriously challenged British rule; but important supporters of transfer and partition had emerged internationally. Across Europe and the United States, Armenian, Assyrian, and Jewish diaspora groups proved anxious to demonstrate their belonging in the ingathering of civilized nations by supporting the project of a national "homeland," however remote it might be from their actual lived experiences. Their lobbying in support of projects of mass resettlement and ethnically conscious state building lent legitimacy and support to British, French, and League visions of ethnic nationhood in the service of empire.

By the end of the 1930s, the Middle East had become a space for a massive experiment in demographic engineering. In Iraq, Palestine, and Syria, European colonial modes of establishing land claims and controlling populations via racial, ethnic, and religious categorization converged with a recent Ottoman past featuring desperate and violent efforts at nationalization and a newly empowered racialized settler colonialism in the form of Zionism. These threads came together to create a dystopian vision in which ethnonational separation served simultaneously as a practical method of controlling colonial subjects and a rationale for imposing a neoimperial form of international governance, with long-standing consequences for the political landscape of the modern Middle East.

ONE

Origins

The idea that physical separation could serve as a solution to the problems of building a new world of nation-states arrived swiftly and dramatically on the global stage after the First World War. Transfer, resettlement, partition, ethnic engineering of various sorts became the solutions of the hour, as an international grab bag of diplomats, bureaucrats, nationalists, and refugees grappled with the astonishing collapse of the old empires and the problems of creating putatively representative systems of governance in the violently forged new nation-states of the Middle East.

Though its rise and broad acceptance seemed to happen rather suddenly, the concept of ethnic separation had some crucial precursors. Three major earlier iterations of protoseparatism arose almost simultaneously in the context of the late nineteenth-century encounters between the expanding British and French empires and the struggling Ottoman state: British and French communalizing policies in their colonies; the Zionist movement and a new discourse of Jewish ethnicity and nationhood; and ethnoreligious violence in the Ottoman-Balkan wars of the early twentieth century. All three of these phenomena, apparently disparate as they were, converged in the Arab Middle East as it was drawn into the spheres of European colonialism and Zionist ambition.

The peace agreements articulated and institutionalized these nascent concepts of ethnic separation. The new League of Nations was charged with overseeing and administering two major new international structures: the minorities treaties defining the rights of "minority" communities in the new nation-states of eastern Europe, and the mandate system giving Britain and France temporary right to rule over the former Ottoman Arab provinces. Both frameworks assumed ethnic nationalism as the basis for citizens' relations to the state and assigned the League the responsibility of policing the relationship between ethnicity, religion, and citizenship in the supervised territories of eastern Europe and the Middle East. By the mid-1920s, these earlier precedents had helped shape a new set of international structures that emphasized ethnic belonging as a fundamental aspect of modern statehood.

ETHNICITY AND CITIZENSHIP IN THE EUROPEAN EMPIRES

The rise of race science interacted with the massive expansion of European empire into Africa in the late nineteenth century, bolstering concepts of inherent, unchanging racial identities and feeding into political decisions to tie ethnicity and race to citizenship and nationhood.[1] The pseudoscience investigating the biological basis of race concerned itself not only with colonial subjects but also, centrally, with the question of Jewish otherness. As Jews took an increased role in public life following the process of legal emancipation unfolding in nineteenth-century Britain and France, the question of racial and biological formulations of Jewish identity became a major topic in an emerging science of race, and many Jewish as well as non-Jewish scientists accepted the premise that there was a biological basis for political and social group characteristics.[2]

By the late nineteenth century, this premise constituted one of the primary assumptions of late European imperial politics in both the colonies and the metropole. Public conversation about Darwin's theories of evolution unfolded alongside increased contact with Asian, African, and Middle Eastern populations understood as "primitives," particularly in the form of popular public exhibitions of racial and ethnic types.[3] At the same time, a rising sense of white solidarity emerged from settler colonies from Australia to South Africa, as politicians and the public alike began to internalize the failures of eighteenth-century projects of cultural and political assimilation among colonized peoples.[4] As the empires expanded, race consciousness became not only a legitimization of imperial rule but also a mode of governance in itself, structuring and limiting indigenous peoples' access to the colonial state.

British and French colonial officials accepted similar assumptions about the centrality and immutability of race, ethnicity, and religion, but created different political and legal systems around these ideas. First in India and then in Africa, British officials developed what they called a "status quo" policy: essentially, that imperial rule should seek to avoid major changes to cultural practice and particularly religious or ethnic difference, both because "native" forms of cultural practice were innate and unalterable and because such changes might unnecessarily raise resistance to colonial rule. As the noted Orientalist Sir William Jones, founder of the Asiatic Society of Bengal and an important early figure in academic "Orientalism," wrote to the governor-general of India in 1788, "Nothing could . . . be wiser than by a legislative Act, to assure the Hindu and Mussulman subjects of Great Britain that the private laws, which they severally hold sacred, and violation of which they would have thought the most grievous oppression, should not be suppressed by a new system, of which they could have no knowledge, and which they must have considered as imposed on them by a spirit of rigour and intolerance." [5] Such views combined new modern conceptions of race (Jones was the originator of the "Aryan Theory," which posited the shared origins of Indo-European languages and gave rise to the concept of the "Aryan race")[6] with practical strategies for governing large numbers of resistant colonial subjects.

In the nineteenth and early twentieth centuries, British imperial law in India approached the problems of governing pluralistic populations by enshrining purportedly traditional communal divides in formal legal terms. Beginning in 1909, a series of laws governing legislative representation established separate electorates for Muslims and Hindus.[7] In so doing, they created a new political landscape, making rigid new political categories out of previously more flexible social ones and defining Muslims and Hindus as essentially different, politically and culturally.[8] In Egypt, British officials (and some Coptic nationalists) developed a similar concept of the Copts as the only true descendants of the ancient Egyptians—"uncontaminated by intermarriage with Arabs and negroes," as one enthusiast put it.[9] Some imperial propagandists explicitly compared the Copts to India's Muslims, presenting them as a subjugated group requiring protection from a potentially oppressive majority and promoting the idea of separate Coptic representation. These concepts of colonial "minorities" often made explicit reference to European Jews, demonstrating how metropolitan unease over Jewish political participation could make its way into unrelated colonial contexts. The Copts, Egyptian high commissioner Eldon Gorst told Edward Grey, were unfit for executive administrative positions because they "played towards the [Muslim] peasant, the same part as does the Jew in Russia." [10]

This presentation of the Copts as a separate race akin to the Jews and requiring different imperial treatment soon expanded to include other non-Muslim communities. In particular, British imperial officials began to view Ottoman Armenians and Assyrians as examples of "original" Christians whose protection was incumbent on the European Christian powers. As an increased missionary presence across the Middle East coincided with a number of archaeological excavations of the ancient ruins of Nineveh and Babylon, and especially with the discovery of the Nimrud palace of Ashurnasirpal II in 1848, British enthusiasts drew on these recent discoveries of pre-Islamic Assyrian greatness to promote the idea that Assyrians were direct descendants of this ancient empire just as Copts were descendants of the pharaohs. "The present Assyrian," one missionary wrote in 1929, "does represent the ancient Assyrian stock, the subject of Sargon and Sennacherib. . . . The writer has known men who claimed to be able to trace their own lineal descent from King Nebuchadnezzar."[11] This racialization of religious difference, drawing partly on metropolitan interpretations of Jewish otherness, was becoming central to the nature of colonial rule across the British empire.

In the French empire, indigenous Jewish communities in North Africa became a particular focus of colonial efforts to establish the relationship between communal identity and political rights. Following the invasion and occupation of Algeria in the 1830s, the French government embarked on a systematic program to encourage French settlement on a mass scale. To attract *colons* (settlers), the colonial government appropriated 2,700,000 hectares of territory—nearly a quarter of Algeria's arable land—from indigenous Algerians and reallocated it to settlers for agricultural development. This ethnically based mass displacement, accompanied by mass murders of civilians that some scholars have viewed as essentially genocidal, foreshadowed the further development of a highly (and violently) ethnically conscious colonial policy.[12]

In 1848, Algeria became the only French colonial space to be incorporated into French territory; settlers were recognized as French citizens and the government of Algeria reenvisioned as part of the metropolitan administration.[13] Algeria's integration into the French metropolitan bureaucracy in the second half of the nineteenth century institutionalized settler privilege by imposing French law, ending indigenous legal practices, and formalizing French citizenship rights for the *colons*. In 1865 the metropolitan government declared that French citizenship would be open to indigenous Algerians who were willing to convert to Christianity, declare their adherence to French cultural values, and publicly reject Arab or Berber ties. In practice, of course, few Algerians took up this option, leaving French citizenship and its attendant political, legal, and economic privileges almost entirely to the European settler population.[14]

The newly formed Alliance Israélite Universelle now sought to apply this idea to Algerian Jews. Founded in 1860 by the French Jewish lawyer Adolphe Crémieux, the Alliance was initially intended to promote the cause of universal Jewish emancipation, particularly in the territories of eastern Europe now emerging as semi-independent nation-states.[15] Almost simultaneously, the Alliance began to move in the imperial sphere as well, opening Jewish schools across French North Africa and Turkey and promoting acculturation to French metropolitan secularism.[16] Its members—mainly highly educated French Jews committed to the principle of assimilation—advocated for extending the principle of Jewish emancipation to Sephardic communities under French colonial rule in the Maghrib. In 1870, the Alliance successfully pushed through what became known as the Crémieux Decree, which gave French citizenship to approximately 35,000 "native" Jews in Algeria without altering the second-class "indigenous" status held by Algerian Muslims and Berbers.[17] The Crémieux Decree's redefinition of North African Jewish identity as carrying specific political rights thus legally differentiated Algerian Jews from their Muslim compatriots.

This development foreshadowed decades of colonial decision making across North Africa and the Middle East that would tie religious community to political rights and representation—often through violent dispossession, reallocation of territory, and forced evacuation practices developed with reference to race, ethnicity, and religion. It also suggested how in both the British and French imperial experience, anxieties surrounding Jewish assimilation and emancipation at home contributed to emerging concepts of race and governance in the colonies. As the nineteenth century wore on, these discourses gradually translated into structural enforcement of racial and religious difference in colonized spaces from Algeria to India, setting the stage for the international acceptance of geographical separation for different races, ethnicities, and religions. Indeed, such practices had important parallels in other settler colonial projects, including American expansion westward in the nineteenth century, German colonial settlement in southwest Africa, Dutch colonial policy in Indonesia, and British colonization in Australia and New Zealand.[18]

Such ideas were not the purview of British and French colonial officials alone. By the turn of the century, the emerging Zionist movement had not only begun to superimpose a politicized nationalism on European Jewish communal identity but also to propose physical separation as a solution to Europe's "Jewish problem," in ways that reflected and interacted with colonial concepts of ethnic geographies. By the time of the First World War, Zionism had developed a small-scale but concrete ideology and practice of removal and transfer that spanned the European and Ottoman spheres.

The idea of mass European Jewish transfer to Palestine originated in Russia and eastern Europe as a response to the often violent anti-Semitism of the tsarist regime. As Jewish emigration out of Europe—particularly to the United States—became a tide, some Jewish thinkers began to consider the idea of collective relocation to Palestine, with the idea of manifesting some form of Jewish nationhood.[19] By the mid-nineteenth century, even before leaders like the Viennese journalist Theodor Herzl had begun to formulate Zionist goals for a Jewish state, French and British Jewish activists had already begun to discuss financing for mass settlement in Palestine for persecuted Russian Jews.[20] By 1897, when Herzl convened the First Zionist Congress in Basel, Switzerland, a small group of Zionist activists had begun to articulate the goals and approaches of the new movement in more specific ways. They sought to solve Europe's "Jewish question" through two primary tactics: a nationalization of Jewish identity and a literal, physical repositioning of that nationhood elsewhere.

Herzl argued that this nationalization represented the natural outcome of Jewish emancipation: "It could not have been the historical intent of emancipation that we should cease to be Jews, for when we tried to mingle with the others we were rebuffed. Rather, the historical intent of emancipation must have been that we were to create a homeland for our liberated nation."[21] Removal from Europe was as central to his vision as resettlement in Palestine. Writing privately in his diary, Herzl was already considering other options for the transfer of Europe's Jews: "I am thinking of giving the movement a closer territorial goal, preserving Zion as the final goal. The poor masses need immediate help, and Turkey is not yet so desperate as to accede to our wishes. . . . Thus we must organize ourselves for a goal attainable soon, under the Zion flag and maintaining all of our history claims. Perhaps we can demand Cyprus from England, and even keep an eye on South Africa or America—until Turkey is dissolved."[22]

Following a failed attempt to interest the German government in intervening with the Ottoman state on behalf of Zionist interests, Herzl turned his attention and energies to looking for allies in Britain. Zionism had already attracted some interest and sympathy there, particularly among evangelical Protestants; the *Jewish Chronicle,* based in London, was the first to publish Herzl's major proposals, and Herzl had good relations with a number of Jewish leaders there.[23] So in 1899, the Jewish Colonial Trust (the Zionist bank founded to fund settlement efforts) established itself in Britain, and the following year the Zionist congress was moved from Basel to London. Diplomatic efforts to interest the British government in the project of Zionism slowly started to bear fruit.

British interest in Zionism rested on three principles: unease with the Jews as an element in British political and economic life, evangelical Protestant interest in claims over the "Holy Land," and—perhaps most crucially—a sense of the possibilities Zionist settlement opened up for imperial expansion. The turn of the twentieth century saw many Britons expressing a discomfort with Jews as prominent actors in the British political sphere, viewing them as a potential threat to the racialized hierarchies of the liberal imperial order.[24] The well-known critic of imperialism J. A. Hobson gave voice to this anti-Semitic feeling in his description of developments in South Africa in 1899, suggesting that the whole of the mining industry there had fallen into the hands of German Jews coming into South Africa via England: "Many of them are the veriest scum of Europe. . . . These men will rig the politics when they have the franchise. Many of them have taken English names and the extent of the Jew power is thus partially concealed. I am not exaggerating one whit."[25] Anxiety over the possibility of impoverished eastern European Jewish refugees flooding into Britain also contributed to this unease, leading in 1902 to a "Royal Commission on Alien Immigration" to investigate Jewish migration and, three years later, the passage of the "Aliens Act" introducing restrictions on immigration to the United Kingdom.[26] Anti-Semitism of this nature overlapped with a rising evangelical Protestantism that viewed Jews as potential targets of mission activity and was fascinated with the "Holy Land," where biblical archaeology and early mass tourism were beginning to intersect to make political claims for Western Christian interests.[27]

But there were other and potentially more important incentives for British support for Zionism as well. These became particularly apparent in the first years of the twentieth century as Herzl entered into negotiations with the British government for Jewish settlement somewhere, even if not Palestine. In discussions with Foreign Secretary Joseph Chamberlain in 1902, Herzl and his associate Leopold Greenberg (later the editor of the *Jewish Chronicle*) proposed a plan for Jewish settlement in El Arish in Egypt's Sinai peninsula. Facing opposition from Egyptian politicians and Lord Cromer, Britain's consul general in Egypt, the plan was eventually declared impossible due to practical concerns around irrigation. But the following year Chamberlain, recently returned from an expedition to East Africa, suggested to Herzl that this territory—which he described as bearing "considerable resemblance to the Sussex Downs"[28]—might represent a suitable arena for Jewish colonization. Though initially reluctant, Herzl eventually agreed to consider the possibilities for what came to be called the "Uganda plan": a mass resettlement of eastern European Jewish communities in East Africa under the auspices of British imperial protection.[29] Zionist advocacy and British support for these ideas demonstrated a shared hope that mass transfer of Europe's Jewish "minority" could simultaneously solve the problem of Jewish integration, create a new modern nation, and develop as-yet-unclaimed space for empire.[30]

This "territorialism" quickly became a mainstream aspect of Zionist thought in these early years, when the parameters of Zionism were still under negotiation. Later Zionist historiography would treat territorialism as a disastrous thought experiment that sought merely to provide a temporary haven (*Nachtasyl,* or "night shelter," as the Hungarian Zionist Max Nordau described it) for persecuted Jews and succeeded only in diminishing European Jewish claims to Palestine in the process.[31] But at this moment, Herzl took the proposal seriously and saw considerable support for the idea within Zionist ranks. It had precedents in Leon Pinsker's work, which explicitly declared that the creation of Jewish nationhood was much more important than the location of the state.[32] Chaim Weizmann viewed the turn toward Uganda as "the logical consequence of [Herzl's] conception of Zionism and of the role which the movement had to play in the life of the Jews."[33] Following the worsening violence against Jews in Russia beginning with the Kishinev pogroms of 1903, territorialism gained considerable support not only among British-oriented secular Jewish figures like Greenberg but also among local Jewish communities in eastern Europe.[34] Like Herzl, many of these communities considered physical removal from the horrors of European anti-Semitism a key aspect of the Zionist platform and, as historian Gur Alroey writes, "did not see any contradiction between their membership in the Zionist movement and their aspiration to establish a state for the Jews outside the Land of Israel."[35]

At the same time that Herzl and Greenberg were in negotiations with the British government over Jewish colonization in Egypt or Africa, small groups of Zionists were already setting up tiny communal settlements in Ottoman Palestine. Although the Ottoman government allowed Jewish immigration from Europe on an individual basis, it feared the creation of monolithic enclaves that could present a challenge to its multiethnic state and forbade large-scale settlement of ethnic or national groups in any single location, especially Palestine.[36] Though Ottoman officials did not generally regard Ottoman Jews as a threat, they were cautious about Zionism, which they viewed as a European ideology backed by the same states that had posed economic and military threats to the Ottoman Empire for generations. As the Ottoman parliamentarian Ahmed Riza Bey declared in 1909, "If the Jews are moderate, the government will not oppose bringing them into the empire. But we should not forget that if the Jews make out of Zionism a political question . . . then a Jewish question will be created in Turkey and its outcome will be very bitter."[37] So though they allowed individual settlement in Syria and Mesopotamia, Ottoman officials refused permission for mass migration of Russian and eastern European Jews to Palestine multiple times in the late nineteenth century, citing decades of commitment to their principles of ethnic pluralism and stating that Palestine no longer contained significant unoccupied land.[38]

Nevertheless, European Jews (mostly Russian and Romanian) did begin to move to Palestine in small but significant numbers, with many entering Palestine illegally. The Jewish population in Palestine doubled between 1868 and 1882 to about 25,000 people (including both European immigrants and local Jewish communities), roughly 6 percent of the population. By the turn of the century, some figures put the Jewish population at as much as 50,000— nearly 10 percent of the population.[39] The Ottoman state watched this development with some anxiety, noting the insular nature of the settler communities at places like Jaffa and aware of foreign support for the endeavor from British, French, and Russian representatives both inside and outside Palestine.

By the early twentieth century, then, Zionism had begun to provide a small-scale but concrete example of an ideology and practice of ethnonational separation in both the European and the Ottoman spheres. The British government's acceptance, in principle, of mass Jewish transfer out of Europe rested on the premise that some form of Jewish settler colonialism could operate for the benefit of the British empire. But it also served as a legitimization of the principles of ethnic removal and resettlement, a point that was not lost on the Ottoman state as its officials began to think about their own non-Turkish, non-Muslim communities in this new era of the nation-state. In 1890, the Ottoman sultan 'Abdul-Hamid demonstrated his grasp of the situation: "Why should we accept Jews whom the civilized European nations do not want in their countries and whom they have expelled? . . . It is not expedient to do so, especially at a time when there is Armenian subversion."[40] And this link between Zionism and Armenian nationalism as parallel separatist narratives was not purely an Ottoman official discourse. Zionists in Palestine participated in it too, as when the Jewish journalist Avraham Elmaliach, writing in Jerusalem's Sephardic press in 1909, declared that Zionists wanted "to establish in Palestine a gathering of citizens as loyal to Turkey [sic] as the Armenians and the Greeks"—perhaps not, at this moment, the best mode of reassuring the Ottomans of Zionist loyalty to the crumbling empire.[41]

Generally, though, Zionism did not look like a rising movement in the years leading up to the First World War. It had failed to convince large numbers of Jews anywhere in Europe, and was riven by internal disagreements over the East Africa scheme. In 1905, when the Seventh Zionist Congress finally voted the plan down, a group of "territorialists" led by the English Zionist Israel Zangwill split off to form the Jewish Territorial Organization to advocate for Jewish settlement somewhere other than Palestine. The split clarified a distinction between those hoping for immediate Jewish removal to anywhere as a means of saving as many victimized Jews in eastern Europe as possible, and those (mainly Russian and led by Menachem Ussishkin) determined to advocate for nationhood in Palestine regardless of how long it might take or how unlikely it seemed. Herzl's premature death in 1904 at the age of forty-four contributed to the movement's shift toward the Russian perspective, as the backing from a major European power for which Herzl had worked so diligently appeared increasingly unlikely. As the war approached, national divides also became more salient; the small Zionist movement suffered from a split between pro-German and pro-Entente adherents, which the German leadership's move to Copenhagen did nothing to heal.[42] From Copenhagen the Zionist office primarily concerned itself with organizing relief for Jewish refugees pouring out of eastern Europe, while the pro-Allied Zionist leadership based in London continued to lobby a British imperial government that still seemed potentially sympathetic to its cause.

This lobbying paid off in spectacular fashion when, in November 1917, the British government officially accepted the principle of Zionism in a letter from Arthur Balfour, now serving as foreign secretary, to Lord Rothschild, declaring Britain's support for the project of a "Jewish national home" in Palestine.[43] The Balfour Declaration bridged the gap between proremoval and pronational Zionists; now, under the auspices of British imperial protection, they could have both. On the eve of the British invasion and occupation of Palestine, the British government had come to view Zionist settlement in the "Holy Land" as bringing the same potential benefits to the British empire that they had previously envisioned in Egypt or East Africa, along with the romantic fulfillment of the "restorationist" vision beloved of many British evangelical Protestants.[44]

The formal acceptance by a major European imperial power of the principle of mass transfer as a political solution shocked many Jews in western Europe who viewed it as a betrayal of assimilationist ideals.[45] In a famous statement, secretary of state for India Edwin Montagu—the only Jew serving in the British cabinet—expressed his dissatisfaction with the Balfour Declaration's interpretation of religion as a determinant of political and national status:

> If a Jewish Englishman sets his eyes on the Mount of Olives and longs for the day when he will shake British soil from his shoes and go back to agricultural pursuits in Palestine, he has always seemed to me to have acknowledged aims inconsistent with British citizenship and to have admitted that he is unfit for a share in public life in Great Britain, or to be treated as an Englishman. I have always understood that those who indulged in this creed were largely animated by the restrictions upon and refusal of liberty to Jews in Russia. But at the very time when these Jews have been acknowledged as Jewish Russians and given all liberties, it seems to be inconceivable that Zionism should be officially recognised by the British Government, and that Mr. Balfour should be authorized to say that Palestine was to be reconstituted as the "national home of the Jewish people." I do not know what this involves, but I assume that it means that Mahommedans and Christians are to make way for the Jews and that the Jews should be put in all positions of preference and should be peculiarly associated with Palestine in the same way that England is with the English or France with the French, that Turks and other Mahommedans in Palestine will be regarded as foreigners, just in the same way as Jews will hereafter be treated as foreigners in every country but Palestine. Perhaps also citizenship must be granted only as a result of a religious test.[46]

It was indeed a crucial moment, for the reasons that Montagu had identified and more. The idea of tying ethnicity or religion to citizenship had already been enshrined in the colonies in legal and political terms; the Balfour

Declaration now institutionalized the idea in an international context. Further, while population expulsion, removal, and transfer had all been enforced in colonial contexts before, this represented something new: the acceptance of mass transfer as an internationally sanctioned strategy for creating a new global order characterized by ethnonational homogeneity.

OTTOMAN MODELS OF ETHNIC SEPARATION

Since its massive expansion from Anatolia into Arab territory to the east and European territory to the west in the fifteenth and sixteenth centuries, the Ottoman state had been marked by an enormously pluralistic subject population in linguistic, religious, ethnic, and national terms. Its rulers were thus faced from an early date with the questions and problems of ruling over a highly disparate population spread over a vast expanse. Until the loss of most of its European territories in the nineteenth century, the Ottoman Empire included many regions in the Balkans and the Caucasus where Christians constituted a numerical majority, as well as other areas, particularly in the Arab provinces, where Jews and Christians represented demographically significant communities. Though Ottoman authorities ruled their empire as an Islamic state, with their claims to legitimacy resting in part on specifically Muslim conceptions of religiously sanctioned power, they found it politically and militarily expedient as well as theologically justified to create spaces within the empire for these large non-Muslim communities to operate on a semiautonomous basis.

To do this, Christian and Jewish communities in the empire were categorized as *dhimmis* (protected peoples) and organized into millets, a word indicating a non-Muslim community allowed to maintain a degree of communal autonomy (in particular, separate courts for questions of personal law like marriage, divorce, and inheritance) in return for certain institutionalized disadvantages like special taxes.[47] There was no broad impetus on the part of the Porte to convert these *dhimmis* to Islam.[48] The specifics of the system varied dramatically through the empire in earlier periods, but underwent a degree of institutionalization and centralization in the nineteenth century as the Ottoman government sought to reshape the empire through a series of political, economic, and military reforms.[49] The move toward institutionalizing the millet system meant that the Ottoman state now identified and differentiated certain religious communities in increasingly formal (though still locally variable) terms. It did not, however, correlate such communal distinctions with specific rights to collective political representation within a national framework, as was beginning to happen in certain European colonial spaces in North Africa and South Asia.[50]

This formalization of the millet system took place alongside new and, for the Ottomans, ominous political developments. From the eighteenth century onward, the British, French, and Russian governments all imposed increasingly draconian "capitulations" treaties on the Ottoman state in the aftermath of military victories. As well as exempting foreigners on Ottoman soil from adherence to Ottoman law and bestowing preferential tax status on foreign investment projects, the capitulations enshrined the principle that these European powers could enforce "protectorates" over the Ottoman Empire's Christian and Jewish communities: the Russians over the Greek Orthodox, the French over the Latin Catholics, and the British over the tiny Protestant convert communities and, more importantly, the empire's Jews.[51] The European powers now began to increase their political and financial investment in these "protected" communities, creating new forms of economic and political separation between Ottoman Muslims and Christians. Further, in the late nineteenth century, American and British Protestant missions began to establish relations with local Armenian, Greek Orthodox, and Latin communities in the Balkans, Anatolia, and the Arab provinces. Though their rates of conversion to Protestantism were infinitesimal, the educational institutions these missions established targeted and benefited Christians in substantial numbers. Mission schools increased the social, economic, and political distance between Christian communities and their Muslim neighbors, as well as reducing Christian subjects' reliance on Ottoman state institutions for economic opportunity and social advancement.[52] This infusion of European interest, money, and ideas into Christian and Jewish communities in the Ottoman sphere also contributed to the rise of a new consciousness of European concepts of representation, citizenship, and nationhood among a growing and disproportionately non-Muslim middle class.[53] In this context, another possible definition of millet—as meaning "nation"—became increasingly relevant, especially for Armenian and Greek communities exposed to the political tumult of the nineteenth-century Balkans. By the early twentieth century, the Ottoman government was allowing the term "millet" as a legal description for some sociolinguistic communities as well as longer-defined religious denominations.[54]

These developments coincided and interacted with a series of multilateral uprisings that resulted in territorial losses for the Ottomans and the emergence of new, unstable, and often irredentist nation-states across the Balkans. Beginning with Serbia and Greece in the early nineteenth century, the British, French, Austrians, and Russians provided assistance to what were essentially local insurgencies, allowing small and often divided local movements to challenge Ottoman power and occasionally each other. Greek and Serbian elites sometimes described these revolts as nationalist, but most of the peasant participants were driven by more parochial motives; few of them would have articulated national sentiments as an explanation for their participation in the insurrections, instead citing religious, familial, or regional loyalties—or simply economic opportunity. Much of the actual fighting was carried out by local brigands, a military class present throughout the Balkans who in the early nineteenth century served as mercenary bandits in a wide variety of small-scale conflicts.[55]

Strategic support from the so-called Great Powers, alongside Ottoman military disarray, allowed Serbia to claim internal autonomy in 1829 and a small sovereign state of Greece to emerge in 1830.[56] In neither case did this result in a polity that could independently mount a challenge to the economic, cultural, and political power of the still-vibrant Ottoman Empire—not least because, as one scholar has put it, "the inhabitants of the new states were as viciously divided among themselves in peace as they had been in war."[57] Indeed, as the number of new states expanded to include Romania and Bulgaria, the major beneficiaries to this new regional order appeared to be not the new nation-states themselves but their imperial patrons, particularly tsarist Russia and the Austro-Hungarian Habsburg empire.[58]

Both in the new states and in the Ottoman imperial center, the violent fracturing of the Balkan political order created new, confused, and contradictory perceptions of the relationship between ethnicity, religion, and national identity. This became especially clear in the conflict over the last bastion of Ottoman power in Europe, Macedonia, which featured an enormously diverse population even by Balkan standards.[59] Its disposition had been a topic of intensive international negotiation since 1878, when the Treaty of San Stefano ended the Russo-Ottoman War and assigned most of the territory to a newly autonomous Bulgaria—a decision reversed a few months later in Berlin, where Macedonia was restored to Ottoman control. By the late nineteenth century Macedonia had become the target of both Greek and Bulgarian expansionism, with Serbian and Romanian nationalists also making claims over Macedonian territory. A schism within the Orthodox church between Greek and Bulgarian elements and the emergence of two revolutionary organizations advocating for some form of Macedonian autonomy complicated the situation further. In 1903, these revolutionary organizations organized a general revolt against the Ottoman military. Though it was put down within a month, the insurrection created chaos and opened the door for further military activity from a variety of points on the political spectrum. By the next year, Greek and Bulgarian militias were operating across Macedonia and seriously disrupting peasant life.

Bandits from both sides used the church schism as shorthand for national affiliation, threatening locals to force declarations of loyalty to either the Bulgarian "Exarchate" or the Greek Patriarchate of Constantinople—a meaningless question in terms of religious practice, but an important indication of how denominational affiliation could stand in as a mark of ethnonational difference in the absence of discernable national feeling among the Macedonian peasantry.[60] The Ottoman government took this moment to conduct a Macedonian census and issue identity cards stating religious denomination. The census committee's question about affiliation with either the Exarchate or the Patriarchate had provoked little comment when asked during the previous census twenty years before, but now elicited passionate opposition from villagers who protested the classification options, complained of the harsh tactics of pro-Greek Ottoman census officials, and refused to participate in the identity card system.[61] Such local resistance clearly demonstrated how religious categories were now taking on new and politically charged meanings.

These violent encounters and territorial challenges had another consequence that would further redefine ethnicity, religion, and nationality in the Ottoman sphere: mass dislocation. As the Balkan wars disrupted peasant communities from Greece to Bulgaria, violence along the Ottoman-Russian border also uprooted huge numbers of people. Following the Crimean War of 1854–56, earlier flows of people out of Russian and border territory became a flood, with as many as 900,000 people fleeing the Caucasus and Crimea regions for Ottoman territory.[62] The next decade, Russian efforts to subdue recalcitrant Chechen and Dagestani Muslim populations in the North Caucasus caused further exodus. By 1914, as many as two and a half million refugees from the North Caucasus would be living within the confines of the Ottoman Empire.[63] This huge and sudden refugee influx from both the Caucasus and the Balkans forced the Ottoman state to establish a formal refugee regime of sorts, dealing not only with strategies for resettlement but also with the construction and enforcement of a statewide policy on ethnicity, religion, immigration, and citizenship.[64]

Initially, the influx of refugees caused chaos; thousands died in overcrowded and disease-ridden transit camps. But with the establishment in 1859 of a "General Administrative Commission for Migrants," Ottoman officials were already beginning to think about how refugee resettlement could serve their interests as they planned centralization, pacification, and sedentarization campaigns in the hinterlands. The commission, assigning government personnel (including translators) to assist with the practicalities, mapped out regions of settlement in Anatolia where refugees would be collected and placed.[65] The commission's workload and authority increased following the Russo-Ottoman War of 1877–78 and the mass displacement of mostly Muslim expellees from the lost territories of Serbia, Montenegro, Romania, and Greece.

Balkan and Caucasian refugees thus became participants in Ottoman efforts to establish greater control over some of the most difficult political territory in the empire. North Caucasians, in particular, were recruited into military units (which were allowed to retain Caucasian leadership and sometimes distinguished by Caucasian dress) loyal to the Ottoman state and deployed in largely Christian regions in which Ottoman control was perceived as insecure; such forces played a major role in a number of massacres of Armenian communities in the 1890s.[66] Refugees were also deployed to encourage sedentarization in largely nomadic areas. Historian Resat Kasaba points out that early resettlement efforts placed refugees in *muhajir* (immigrant) villages in central Anatolia, carefully positioned in "ribbonlike patterns around the lower reaches of the mountain, so that the migration routes of the local tribes would be blocked and the tribes would have to alter their nomadic lives."[67] In 1901, the commission resettled refugees from Bosnia in and around Ankara, providing them with such amenities as newly built villages, hospitals and other medical infrastructure, starter farm animals and seed, and food provisions.[68] And the Ottoman state also used the influx to think more systematically about issues of citizenship, nationality, and immigration. The 1869 Law on Nationality, enacted in part as a response to the refugee crisis, granted Muslim refugees immediate citizenship rights and established detailed ethnonational parameters for immigration into Ottoman territory.[69] By the end of the nineteenth century, the Ottoman state was in the main refusing to accept non-Muslim refugees and had formally forbidden Muslim emigration out of the empire.[70]

By the time of the Balkan Wars of 1912–13, this sort of informal violence had reclassified populations into nascent nations successfully enough to produce organized state armies intent on ethnically based nation-building and -expanding projects. In the spring of 1912 Bulgaria, Serbia, Greece, and Montenegro, with Russian assistance, agreed on a collective effort to detach the Balkans from Ottoman control. A relatively quick victory against an Ottoman military already challenged in other directions, particularly by its simultaneous entanglement with Italy in Libya, resulted in the loss of nearly all the Ottoman Empire's European holdings. The Balkan allies, unable to agree on the subsequent disposition of the territory they had won, engaged in a second war among themselves, allowing the Ottomans to regain control over western Thrace.

The Second Balkan War, in 1913, represented the first large-scale military encounter among Balkan Christians in which conscripted armies carried out most of the fighting.[71] This more state-oriented approach to nation building meant the enforcement of national identity through army-enforced ethnic cleansing, not only of Muslims but also of other Christian "nations." Deportation and massacre of Muslim villagers, coupled with the starvation and disease that accompanied the siege of cities like Edirne, reduced the Muslim population to almost nothing in many areas. The sources also record cases of forced conversion to Christianity, particularly in the context of the Bulgarian conquest of Pomak villages in the Rhodope Mountains.[72] But this enforced Christianization of the battle territories was not the only form of homogenization taking place in the context of the wars. In the name of these newly constructed national identities, Bulgarian troops massacred Greeks at a number of locations in Macedonia, matching Greek attacks on Bulgarian civilians in Bulgarian territory. The earlier violence had drawn new ethnoreligious boundaries; the Second Balkan War gave newly formed national armies a venue to reify and enforce them.

This war gave rise to an even more dramatic refugee influx and a significant expansion of the Ottoman state's interest in using refugees to engage in demographic engineering. Initially, Muslims fleeing the violence in the Balkans gathered in three main points: Albania and the urban centers of Edirne and Salonica. Those who found themselves in Albania, about sixty thousand strong, fared worst; stranded in an already impoverished country, with no access to relief efforts coming from either the Ottoman sphere or western Europe, many of them starved.[73] From Salonica and Edirne, by contrast, many refugees found their way into Anatolia with the assistance of private relief organizations like the Salonica Islamic Committee or the Greek government, which shipped refugees out to Ottoman territory following the wars. The Ottoman Refugee Commission estimated that a total of 414,000 refugees were settled in the empire following the Balkan conflicts.[74] The crisis not only intensified refugees' own sense of ethnicity but also strengthened emerging concepts of Turkish national identity. As the Turkish nationalist intellectual Halide Edip noted, "The vast number of Balkan Turks, refugees who poured into Constantinople and Anatolia with their lurid and sinister tales of martyrdom and suffering at the hands of the Balkan Christians, the indifference and even the apparent joy of the so-called civilized outside world at their sorry state, aroused a curious sympathy for everything that was Turkish in those days."[75]

The enormous numbers of refugees and their need for immediate resettlement sparked a series of demographic engineering projects—targeting Greek communities in Istanbul, along the Aegean coast, and in Thrace for replacement—that were unprecedented in scope and ambition. Boycotts, intimidation, and occasional violence combined to force 150,000 Greek Ottomans out of the empire and into Greece. As Balkan and Caucasian Muslim refugees flooded into Anatolia, the concept of removing particular communities to ensure a more desirable ethnic profile took on another justification: the property of the deported could be redistributed to incoming destitute Muslim refugee communities, one of the initial rationales behind the first deportations of the Armenians beginning in 1915 and a development that would become a theme in removals and resettlements across the Middle East (and elsewhere) through the twentieth century.[76] The Ottoman-European encounters of the late nineteenth and early twentieth centuries had turned the Balkans, the Caucasus, and Anatolia into an enormous arena of experimental demographic engineering.

RACE, NATION, MINORITY, MAJORITY: THE LEAGUE OF NATIONS AND THE NEW INTERNATIONAL ORDER

By the time of the First World War, then, the inhabitants of the Arab provinces of the old Ottoman Empire had already witnessed three disparate precursors of ethnic separatism: communalizing colonial policy in Egypt and Algeria, European Zionist settler colonies in Palestine, and waves of Christian and Muslim refugees fleeing ethnic and communal violence in the

Ottoman Balkan sphere. Following the war, they would also see the creation of a formal international legal and political system that assumed and enforced ethnonational identifications as the fundamental building blocks of a new state order—an idea applied with especial enthusiasm in parts of the world now coming under new forms of "international" authority. The postwar treaties of Versailles, Sèvres, and Lausanne collectively created two related frames for ongoing Allied control over unreliable territory: a system of "minority protection" (and its corollary, population exchange) in the new and fragile states of eastern Europe, and a neocolonial regime of externally monitored "mandate" nations in the Levant, both under the jurisdiction of the newly constructed League of Nations based in Geneva.[77]

On paper, the League of Nations was envisioned as the world's first intergovernmental organization dedicated to the maintenance of global peace and security. In practice, it most often sought to protect the interests of its most important constituents, the British and French empires, cloaking an agenda driven by nineteenth-century liberal imperialism in some new Wilsonian language about self-determination and nation building.[78] Given its lack of military backing and its members' deep reluctance to make use of economic sanctions, the League had very limited powers of enforcement. Nevertheless, it developed extensive although perpetually ill-funded bureaucratic institutions dedicated to upholding international agreements and monitoring the rights of threatened groups. As the dust of the negotiations settled, overseeing "minority" protection in eastern Europe and monitoring the mandate system in the Middle East came to represent central rationales for the League's continued existence.

The use of the words "minority" and "majority" to describe ethnonational communities within states represented a relative neologism at the peace talks, not only in terms of the former Ottoman territories but also with regard to central and eastern Europe. The concept of national "minorities" requiring special forms of collective protection from majoritarian states had come to the fore in Europe only in the late nineteenth and early twentieth centuries. It initially emerged in three contexts: Marxists proposing the formulation of some kind of Habsburg federalist system, internationalist Jewish organizations advocating for specific collective Jewish rights and representation in eastern Europe, and new international organizations promoting pacifist and reformist agendas. None of these had succeeded in making the idea central to European diplomatic thought.[79] Its emergence as a primary feature of the postwar order at Paris was somewhat unexpected, and was largely the consequence of the unanticipated and total collapse of the Habsburg state and the rising Bolshevist movement in the Russian sphere alongside the emergence of Woodrow Wilson's peculiarly American vision of "self-determination."[80]

The emergence of a violent Polish-Ukrainian struggle in 1918 and the multiple anti-Jewish pogroms in Polish cities in the closing days of the war caused Poland to emerge as a test case of the dangers of nationalism in a postimperial world. At Versailles, European leaders who had failed to predict the dramatic and total collapse of the central European empires worried that Poland would be, as Arthur Balfour had it, "a perpetual occasion of European strife" for decades to come.[81] The subsequent debate over Poland's future became a debate over the League's role in policing the protection of the "minorities" created by the collapse of the central European empires.

Jewish internationalist groups were well positioned to influence this discussion, both because of the prominence and immediacy of questions about the fate of Jewish communities in Poland and because many had been articulating "minority" claims to guaranteed communal rights and representation for some decades. But at the peace talks, bitter divisions emerged among Jewish representatives over the nature of their political claims. The Paris talks saw a major dispute between assimilationists, represented by the Alliance Israélite Universelle and Lucien Wolf's Joint Foreign Committee, and the Zionist faction, represented primarily by Menachem Ussishkin, Nahum Solokow, and Chaim Weizmann and supported by most of the American Jewish representatives at the Paris peace conference.[82] The Zionist-American coalition, describing Jews as one of the multiple "national, religious, racial and linguistic minorities" in Europe, requested recognition as "distinct and autonomous organisms" in their host states, including the right to run their own schools and cultural institutions and the right to proportional representation in any state-level legislative bodies. They also demanded some form of enforcement, with the League of Nations acting as arbiter.[83] Wolf and the assimilationists had some of the same desiderata: forbidding economic boycotts against Jews, allowing for Jewish religious and cultural institutions, using British legal models to deal with the question of Sunday trade, and structuring electoral law to give Jews something close to proportional representation.[84] But in bitter opposition to the Zionist position, Wolf declared that he would not support any minority treaty clause that referred to the Jews as a "nationality."[85]

The question of minority rights was further complicated by broad uncertainty among the Allied powers about which of the nationalities in the former Habsburg, Russian, and Ottoman empires should be awarded their own states. Among the Allies, a general accord eventually emerged supporting recognition for Poland and Czechoslovakia, leaving the question of how to deal with the non-Polish and non-Czech populations within the new states' borders. (The fate of the enormous ethnic German populations—now reenvisioned as "minorities"—found across the Baltic states, Poland, Czechoslovakia, and the Soviet Union represented a major issue, with ominous signs as early as the 1920s that the nascent Nazi party was ready to make use of the concept of minority rights to support irredentist territorial claims.)[86] Eventually, these negotiations resulted in the Allied acceptance of the idea that these newly identified minorities possessed collective rights that could be guaranteed only by an authority outside the state. The introduction of this particular vision of minority rights tied to external minority "protection" was, as historian Eric Weitz points out, "a fateful move with profound policy implications, because it presumed the domination of one population in the state, and others who would be wards of the international system and therefore subject to all the hesitations and contradictions of Great Power politics."[87]

In the end the first "minority treaty"—signed with Poland in June 1919 and serving as the basis for a number of others—made fairly modest demands. In early drafts, the Polish government had been required to "accord to all racial or national minorities within their several jurisdictions exactly the same treatment and security, both in law and in fact, that is accorded to the racial or national majority of their people."[88] But the final version required more simply that the signatories would "not prohibit or interfere with the free exercise of any creed, religion or belief . . . and that no person within their respective jurisdictions shall be molested in life, liberty or pursuit of happiness by reason of his adherence to any creed, religion or belief."[89] Minority communities had no way to complain directly to the League of any violations of their rights; they had to induce a third state or the League itself to lodge a protest. The final documents called for equal rights for all citizens, the free exercise of religion and cultural practice including language, and some mechanisms for protecting cultural distinctiveness, but stopped short of guaranteeing any form of political autonomy for minorities. As French prime minister Georges Clemenceau wrote to the Polish nationalist agitator Ignacy Paderewski, "They do not constitute any recognition of the Jews as a separate political community within the Polish State"[90]—though their recognition of "minority" communities as permanent collective entities with externally guaranteed civil rights inevitably carried political implications, not least in its suggestion of the impossibility of full assimilation.

In many ways this new minorities regime represented not innovation but continuity, applying long-standing British and French approaches to controlling territory and peoples within and outside their empires to the postwar nation-state system. (The same could be said of the League itself; as historian Mark Mazower has noted, "Although organizationally the League was a radical departure from the past, in other ways it fitted squarely into an earlier Victorian tradition of Great Power paternalism ... that coexisted comfortably with both liberal Christianity and racism.")[91] The minorities treaties were limited to the new states of eastern Europe; their protections did not apply in other European states, much less colonized spaces where British and French colonial officials routinely moved against particular ethnic and religious groups with impunity. The architects of the Polish treaty rejected the idea of universal protections for minorities on the grounds that they would impinge on national sovereignty in places like Britain and France. As one negotiator noted, such a plan would have given the League "the right to protect the Chinese in Liverpool, the Roman Catholics in France, the French in Canada, quite apart from the more serious problems, such as the Irish ... such a right could only be recognized in the case of a new or immature state of Eastern Europe or Western Asia."[92] Minorities, then, were to serve as a site for western European intervention and a reminder of the limitations of sovereignty in territories labeled less civilized—just as they had in the nineteenth-century "capitulations" regime.

Further, as the Information Section of the League noted, the treaties were not intended to establish "a general jurisprudence applicable wherever racial, linguistic or religious minorities existed.... [but to offer assistance where] owing to special circumstances, these problems might present particular difficulties."[93] In other words, the appellation of minority was not intended to describe every ethnic, national, or religious group outside the majority; it applied only to groups with an already established history of national or protonational consciousness developed in the European diplomatic exchanges of the late nineteenth century.[94] In the Middle East, only a few specific communities would be explicitly recognized as minorities in this sense: non-Muslims with nineteenth-century histories of ties to western European "protector" states.[95]

The application of these requirements to only a few states caused immense irritation among targeted nations, who viewed the treaties as extensions of the old capitulations agreements that had long used minority rights as a fig leaf for external political and economic intervention. As the Romanian representative to the League quite correctly protested, the treaties "implied the establishment of two categories of countries—countries of the first class, which, in spite of having small groups of minorities, were placed under no obligations; and countries of the second class, which had been obliged to assume extremely onerous obligations."[96] The minorities treaties, then, enshrined two already well-established imperial principles: that ethnicity and religion were potentially relevant to citizenship and should be institutionally defined with a view to state stability, and that minority communities represented a legitimate site of external intervention into the affairs of theoretically sovereign but less "civilized" nations.[97] The minorities treaties thus fit into a much longer pattern of international law, begun as far back as Westphalia, which negotiated relations among the "three elements of the international legal order" identified by legal scholar Nathaniel Berman: "(1) a substantively grounded international community (Christendom of the 17th century, Europe of the early 19th, Civilization of the late 19th, all the way to today's Liberal Democracies); (2) sovereigns, whose 'potency' and 'serenity' are periodically reimagined; (3) those viewed as not full participants in the community of sovereigns, those 'Vassals, Subjects, People,' whose rights and subordinate role are variably conceived and reconceived."[98] An early assessment of the success of the minorities treaties demonstrates how clearly this point was understood at the time, noting that "in the Versailles peace system, the minorities provisions constituted a corollary and corrective to the principle of national self-determination."[99]

That said, it was equally evident that the League's powers of enforcement of the minorities treaties would be limited. The postwar agreements set up a petition system whereby complaints about violations would be accepted and filtered through "committees of three," ad hoc groups including the acting chair of the council and two other members from countries unmentioned in the petition. If the committee of three deemed a petition valid, it sent the complaint on to the relevant state's government and requested a response. In the event of a disagreement about an appropriate corrective measure, another committee of three would review the case further. Beyond that, it was not clear what the League might be able to do to prevent violations. The committee appointed to deal with minority protection was clearly aware of this difficulty, declaring that it would ordinarily limit itself to "benevolent and informal communications" with affected governments and emphasizing the responsibility of protected minorities to "co-operate as loyal fellow citizens with the nations to which they now belong."[100] If the main consequence of the minorities system was the clear delineation of the affected states' limited sovereignty in the new international order, it also inadvertently pointed out the almost total inability of the "Great Powers" to enforce their own rules.[101]

Partly because of this evident weakness, by the time the Lausanne treaties were negotiated a few years later, mass deportation and population "exchange" had emerged as central modes of dealing with minority problems. Whereas the negotiators at Paris had broadly decided on a system of minority protection that might also accommodate a degree of voluntary population exchange as an ancillary tool, the delegates at the 1923 Lausanne conference decided that transfer should be an initial and primary mode of engagement. "First," as the legal scholar Catriona Drew has noted, "they would reach agreement on the scope of the population exchange; then, they would legislate minority protection for those not to be 'turned out.'"[102] Minority protection and minority expulsion had become "two sides of the same coin"—an approach that made use of a Wilsonian concept of self-determination, privileging the rights of theoretical nations over the rights of individuals, to legitimize forms of external intervention that carried a much older imperial pedigree.[103]

ETHNONATIONALISM AND THE MANDATE SYSTEM

If the minorities treaties were applied to the new states of eastern Europe with the specific purpose of marking their subordinate status within a nineteenth-century-style global hierarchy, the mandate system did the same thing in more overt fashion for the former Arab provinces of the Ottoman Empire. And just as the existence of "minorities" had constituted a major part of the Allies' argument for continued supervision of the Balkans and eastern Europe, the League of Nations now began to develop a narrative of ethnic, religious, and national difference in the Middle Eastern mandate territories that sought both to legitimize mandate rule over Arab populations and to define the League's supervisory capacity over the British and French mandatory authorities.

Britain, France, and Russia had agreed on the basic outlines of a European division of Ottoman Arab territory some years before the actual fall of the empire. With Russia's withdrawal from the proceedings in 1917, Britain and France were left free to implement a modified version of the 1916 Sykes-Picot agreement, assigning what would become Syria and Lebanon to French control and Mesopotamia and Palestine to the British. The atmosphere of anti-colonialism that Woodrow Wilson and others brought to the peace negotiations, though, rendered outright annexation of this territory impossible. As Mark Sykes (the British diplomat who had helped construct the 1916 Sykes-Picot agreement) put it, "Imperialism, annexation, military triumph, prestige, White man's burdens, have been expunged from the popular political vocabulary, consequently Protectorates, spheres of interest or influence, annexations, bases etc., have to be consigned to the Diplomatic lumber-room." [104] As a reluctant compromise, the Allies agreed on a new system: a set of "mandate" territories, in which European control would be (theoretically) temporally limited and overseen by the Permanent Mandates Commission of the League of Nations. The postwar treaties thus created a number of new states across the Levant, declaring Syria, Lebanon, Transjordan, Iraq, and Palestine mandates under British or French authority. Technically, these new mandate states were supposed to be moving toward eventual sovereignty under European supervision and guidance; in practice, they were largely governed as additions to the British and French colonial empires. [105] The League's formulation for the Middle Eastern mandates borrowed concepts of ethnicity, religion, and nationality's relevance to citizenship from three main sources: nineteenth-century European diplomatic agreements on empire, Zionist visions of Jewish nationhood, and the just-concluded minorities treaties.

The late nineteenth-century diplomatic agreements that had divided up Africa for European colonial consumption directly and clearly informed the documents that outlined the mandate system, with their valorization of European civilization, emphasis on technocratic forms of development, and legitimization of violence as a response to native resistance. [106] The Berlin Act of 1885, with its declaration of intent "to regulate the conditions most favourable to the development of trade and civilization," was now given new expression in Article 22 of the League's Covenant, which famously declared that in areas "inhabited by peoples not yet able to stand by themselves under the strenuous conditions of the modern world, there should be applied the principle that the well-being and development of such peoples form a sacred trust of civilization." [107] The division of these peoples into "A," "B," and "C" mandates—according to the League's assessment of their level of readiness for independence—likewise drew on nineteenth-century concepts of global racial hierarchies and made the case in advance that the violent imposition of a neocolonial authority could be justified by reference to an international civilizing mission.[108]

But there were other influences at work as well. The official League of Nations mandate for Palestine incorporated the full text of the Balfour Declaration, declaring that "recognition has thereby been given to the historical connection of the Jewish people with Palestine and to the grounds for reconstituting their national home in that country" and enshrining the earlier British commitment to European Jewish immigration into Palestine in international law. Further, it made provisions for the international Zionist movement to operate as the "public body" representing the interests of the Jewish population in Palestine and established the mandate government's right to create a nationality law, "framed so as to facilitate the acquisition of Palestinian citizenship by Jews who take up their permanent residence in Palestine."[109]

The legal documents underpinning the Middle Eastern mandate system also made use of language taken from the recently concluded minorities treaties, guaranteeing freedom of religious worship and "the right of each community to maintain its own schools for the education of its own members in its own language" (qualified somewhat by the government's right to maintain "such supervision over religious or eleemosynary bodies of all faiths in Palestine as may be required for the maintenance of public order and good government").[110] The mandate assigning Syria and Lebanon to French rule made similar assumptions about ethnicity, nationhood, and citizenship, guaranteeing "respect for the personal status of the various peoples and for their religious interests," promising "the right of each community to maintain its own schools for the instruction and education of its own members in its own language" and guaranteeing that mandate authorities would "refrain from all interference . . . in the management of religious communities and sacred shrines belonging to the various religions, the immunity of which has been expressly guaranteed."[111] Nearly identical wording appeared in the mandate for Mesopotamia: "The right of each community to maintain its own schools for the education of its own members in its own language (while conforming to such educational requirements of a general nature as the Administration may impose) shall not be denied or impaired."[112] All this was overlaid on the principle of "preserving existing rights" for religious communities, particularly with regard to Palestine's "Holy Places" and Mesopotamia's "sacred shrines"—the British imperial principle of the status quo previously developed in India and Egypt.[113] The mandates for Palestine,

Syria, Lebanon, and Mesopotamia thus drew simultaneously on Zionist eth-nonationalist political claims, new visions of minority rights, and long-standing liberal imperial concepts of empire and civilization to legitimize European mandatory rule over the Eastern Mediterranean. They also made plain the League's broad acceptance of ethnic nationalism and (particularly in the case of Palestine) large-scale population movement as viable state-building strategies.[114]

Like the minorities treaties, the mandate agreements had a bureaucratic machinery within the League of Nations that served as the main venue for the many internal disagreements about the nature of the mandate system and the League's role. The Permanent Mandates Commission (PMC), made up of nine appointed members from various member states deemed to be "experts" in colonial administration, was charged with the task of reviewing and discussing the reports to come out of the mandates and advising the League Council on any follow-up actions.[115] There was also a section of the League Secretariat devoted to supporting and documenting the PMC's work. The League Council had final responsibility for any actions related to the mandates, though its powers to change the course of governance in any particular mandate territory was mainly limited to exerting public pressure.[116] Despite their evident limitations, the mechanisms for engaging with both the mandatory authorities and the PMC—formal petitions, correspondence, and annual reporting—were far from meaningless to local populations who consistently studied, analyzed, and made use of them to engage in vigorous advocacy for their own interests and political desiderata within the mandate system.[117] Despite most League officials' essentially colonial interests and deep-seated resistance to acknowledging the views of Middle Eastern colonized populations, this system of petitions and reports meant eventually that the League's archives came almost inadvertently to record a discourse of great vibrancy and scope from a wide range of local actors across the mandate territories.[118]

. . .

The theory and practice of ethnonational separatism arose out of a particular confluence of geographically disparate but philosophically linked political developments in the late nineteenth and early twentieth centuries. Three key precedents—British and French colonial policy, Zionist political ideology, and the multilateral practices of ethnic cleansing that characterized late

Ottoman-Balkan-Caucasian encounters—came together following the war into a shared geographical and political space, namely, the mandate territories of the Arab Middle East, once part of the Ottoman sphere and now temporarily claimed by the British and French empires under the auspices of the new League of Nations. In the postwar era, the treaties coming out of Paris, Sèvres, and Lausanne collectively created a formal legal regime that supported the theory and practice of ethnonational separatism via League enforcement of minority protection in eastern Europe and supervision of neocolonial mandate governments across the Middle East.

And the League had a final role that would further set the stage for the promotion of ideologies of ethnic separation: guardian of the huge numbers of refugees whom the war had left homeless and stateless. The refugee regime that emerged in Syria and Iraq for displaced Armenians and Assyrians after the First World War quickly became a major raison d'être of the League and the British and French mandate authorities alike. Over the next decade, refugee spaces would offer novel venues for the League and its partners to forge particular visions of ethnicity and nationhood as well as new iterations of international authority across the newly colonized Middle East.

TWO

The Refugee Regime

The First World War left much of the Middle East in shambles. The destruction resulting from the campaigns across Syria, Lebanon, Iraq, and Palestine caused major food and water shortages across the region, exacerbated by the mass appropriation of resources for military purposes; and natural disasters like a major locust infestation in Palestine compounded the suffering.[1] Between 1914 and 1918, the Ottoman Arab provinces endured greater population losses than any European country involved in the war except Russia; one estimate suggests that as many as 600,000 people—roughly 18 percent of the population—died in greater Syria between 1915 and 1918.[2] Even these losses paled in comparison to the destruction within Anatolia itself, where a pre-1912 population of approximately 17.5 million people was diminished by 3 million Muslims and 300,000 Greeks, as well as the enormous numbers of Armenians (variously estimated between 600,000 and 1.5 million) who perished in the genocide of 1915–16,[3] along with perhaps 200,000–275,000 Assyrians killed as part of the same set of operations.[4]

After the war, some of the survivors of this violence found themselves at the center of a new international refugee regime. In 1918 British officials set up a camp for Assyrians and Armenians at Ba'quba, just north of Baghdad, that functioned not only as a humanitarian relief project but also as a public exhibit for new forms of national and international political authority. The camp at Ba'quba established its refugees as more or less permanently dependent on international entities for their maintenance. Camp administrators took on state-like roles, determining the layout of the physical space, running local bureaucracies, distributing goods and services, and—not least— ensuring the separation of the refugees from the surrounding Arab and Kurdish communities. Emphasizing these refugee communities as sites of international rather than Iraqi state authority, camp officials also engaged in intensive campaigns of refugee nationalization, declaring Baʿquba a space for the "preservation" of ethnonational identities until such time as the refugees could be removed and resettled in a newly constituted independent Assyrian or Armenian nation.

As the territorial claims of the new Turkish republic became clearer and the European powers retreated from the idea of creating Armenian and Assyrian homelands, the mandate authorities and the League moved away from defining these populations as potentially independent nations-in-waiting and recast them as permanent ethnonational enclaves within their host countries. This decision involved making non-Arab refugees legal residents (and sometimes citizens) of the mandate states, while also attempting to maintain them as identifiably separate communities who might be useful to struggling European colonial governments. Assyrian refugees at Baʿquba were resettled in discrete but divided blocs of territory around Mosul and became key elements in a plan to establish and legitimize British political and military authority in northern Iraq as a necessity for protecting Assyrian "minorities" from a potentially hostile majority population; the camp's Armenian residents were separately sent to Transcaucasia. In the 1920s French mandatory authorities took a similar approach (minus the formal label of "minority," a term specific to nonrefugee groups in the Syrian context)[5] to the tens of thousands of Armenian refugees scattered around greater Syria. Their gradual resettlement of Armenians in distinct refugee encampments on the outskirts of cities like Aleppo and Beirut served the practical purpose of bolstering French colonial authority in challenging areas while demonstrating a notional sympathy to Armenian national identity for an international audience.

In the absence of any practical movement toward sovereign nationhood for Iraq, Syria, Lebanon, or Palestine, British and French authorities could present their maintenance of refugee groups in physically distinct and carefully nationalized spaces as visible evidence of the mandate powers' abstract commitment to the preservation of small nations. And even as the idea of Armenian or Assyrian sovereign statehood faded, British and French officials (now with League assistance) continued this policy of maintaining separate refugee enclaves in the hope that they would provide bulwarks of colonial control in difficult territory—a plan often undermined by resistance from both the refugees themselves and the populations among whom they were settled.

THE INTERNATIONAL CONTEXT: MISSIONARIES,
DIASPORAS, AND THE RHETORIC OF AID

During the war itself, Assyrians and Armenians became the subject of massive aid campaigns in Britain, France, and the United States, mainly spearheaded by missionary and church groups. In 1915 and 1916, when Armenians and Assyrians were being massacred in the eastern reaches of the Ottoman Empire, relief organizations like the American group Near East Relief began to cast their refugee work in specifically national terms. They called for donations not only to relieve the suffering of those Armenian and Assyrian populations dispossessed and persecuted in the war, but also to save their existence as civilized Christian "nations" facing the wrath of a benighted, barbaric Muslim rage.[6] On the premise that donors were preventing the disappearance of ancient nations, these institutions appealed for international aid, casting the idea of a postwar Assyrian and Armenian assimilation into the new states of Syria and Iraq as a kind of national and racial annihilation.

Many of the relief agencies running camps in Syria and Anatolia came out of a nineteenth-century pro-Armenian missionary tradition. Some, like the British organization Friends of Armenia, had long advocated for the creation of an autonomous Armenian homeland. The British Armenia Committee, established in 1913, lobbied for the improvement of Armenian conditions and promoted Armenian national goals; many of its personnel became involved in the Lord Mayor's Fund, which took on a dual role as a public advocate for Armenian interests in Britain and a major administrator for relief efforts in Transcaucasia. These British groups worked alongside the bigger and longer-established Near East Relief, a mission-derived American organization that became the most significant refugee relief organization for Armenians and Assyrians in the Ottoman Empire during the war. In 1919 the new American Relief Administration, headed by Herbert Hoover, began sending food supplies to supplement Near East Relief's work in Transcaucasia.

Groups like these operated on a set of assumptions developed in the context of the nineteenth-century associations between various Ottoman Christian groups and the European states and organizations claiming to act as their protectors and now furthered by Armenian activists anxious to make the most of these ties. Armenian nationalist leaders had long disseminated narratives to French audiences about the historical connections between France and the medieval kingdom of Little Armenia. "Cilicia, so full of French memories," wrote the bishop of the diocese at Adana to the French

Foreign Ministry in 1898, "so dear to our hearts.... It was our Armenian knights who accompanied Godefroy de Bouillon and the Duke of Lorraine from Tarsus all the way to Jerusalem."[7] Some also made ethnographic and linguistic claims about the ancient civilization of the Armenians, juxtaposing a narrative of an ancient Christian nationhood with an aggressive arriviste Muslim Turkish presence, as argued in an Armenian petition to the French Foreign Ministry in 1920: "Even today the Armenians are the most important and numerous Christian group [and] constitute a crushing numerical superiority in Cilicia. This is in contrast to the heterogenous and disparate Muslim elements, including the Turks—all of them backward.... The majority [of the Muslims] are alien intruders—emigrants artificially implanted in the country in the course of the last fifty years with the deliberate purpose of de-Armenizing Cilicia."[8] Portraying Armenians as part of a beleaguered Christian nation with long-standing ties to France and the West represented a central aspect of such organizations' fund-raising, lobbying, and eventual support to refugees.

The construction of Assyrian identity as national rather than religious, communal, or ethnic similarly owed much to earlier Western missionary interventions. Like other indigenous Christian communities in the Middle East, the Assyrians had through the nineteenth century been objects of interest for British and American Protestant missions. Unlike most of these other Christian communities, the Assyrians also interested archaeologists. The rising European missionary presence in the Hakkari region coincided with a number of archaeological excavations of the ancient ruins of Nineveh and Babylon, and especially with the discovery of the Nimrud palace of Ashurnasirpal II in 1848. Missionaries drew on these recent discoveries of pre-Islamic Assyrian greatness to promote the idea of this branch of Eastern Christians as direct descendants of this ancient empire. In fact, it was only now that Western missionaries began to popularize the word "Assyrian," previously only one of a number of possible designations for these Christians and not the most prominent, as a mode of identifying the present-day community with the ancient empires. Local assistants to the excavations, like the Assyrian archaeologist Hormuzd Rassam, may have originally suggested this idea. Certainly it buttressed community ambitions for local autonomy, as well as romantic missionary imaginings of an untouched "original" Christian community.[9]

The recategorization of Assyrian identity from communal and ethnic to national was thus already well under way even before the First World War.

The centralization of Ottoman authority in the final years of the empire, as the Ottoman state tried to take firmer hold of its borderlands, furthered this process as Assyrian leaders sought to defend their long-standing autonomy in Hakkari and resisted closer surveillance and incorporation into the Ottoman sphere.[10] In this context, many Assyrian leaders saw their association with Western missionaries and archaeologists as potentially beneficial and began to adopt a mission-derived language of national independence for their own purposes.[11] The missionary presence also created new venues for the dissemination of this new national identity, as mission schools became important educational institutions for Assyrians and the printing press allowed for the publication and distribution of both religious and secular material in modern Syriac.[12] As the war approached and the Ottoman government broadly began to view its Christian subjects as potential threats to the state, the Assyrian relationship with the beleaguered Ottoman administration began to erupt into violence. The increasingly hostile encounters between Assyrian Christians and a Sunni Turkish-dominated Ottoman government gave both Assyrians and their supporters in the West further reason to describe the community as a religiously persecuted "nation."

Processes of Armenian and Assyrian nationalization, then, predated the war and were often located in missionary organizations that functioned as protohumanitarian outfits. The idea that Armenian and Assyrian communities were essentially inassimilable in any Muslim state was already well established in European and American circles well before 1914, and had also taken hold to some degree among Armenian and Assyrian diasporas in Europe, the United States, and Latin America.[13] And, of course, the Ottoman state's genocidal violence against Armenians and Assyrians during the war furthered their portrayal as "Christian nations" long and brutally besieged by hostile Muslim Turks.

BA'QUBA AND THE MECHANICS OF REFUGEE NATIONALIZATION

In the first Armenian/Assyrian refugee camp in Iraq, set up in the village of Ba'quba just north of Baghdad in 1918, these long-standing ideas were explicitly rendered into a new physical and spatial reality. Set up to house Armenians and Assyrians who had engaged in a military campaign against the Ottomans in the final stages of the war, Ba'quba became a physical manifestation of British ethnographic categorization and Allied commitment to the principles of national sovereignty.

At Urmia in the spring of 1918, a group of Assyrians originally from the Hakkari region joined with a small and mostly local Armenian force to engage in battle against the Ottomans (and, sporadically, local Kurdish tribes as well). That June, a British force sent from the Persian town of Hamadan entered Urmia and informed the holdouts of the British military advance to Sain Qala. The remaining Assyrians and Armenians evacuated Urmia for Hamadan under British protection, where the British, despite some resistance, formally incorporated the Armenian soldiers into the British army. Anticipating the declaration of British control over what would become Iraq, British officials marched these Assyrian and Armenian communities several hundred miles to the village of Baʿquba, where a camp was under construction to serve as a temporary solution to the refugees' homelessness. This epic journey, during which nearly a third of the refugees perished through disease and attacks, is still marked in Assyrian historical memory as *Raqa raqa,* or "the Flight." [14]

This was at a juncture when the British hold on Mesopotamia and the nature of its future governance was still very uncertain. There was considerable resistance to the imposition of British rule across Iraq, and already several anticolonial societies encompassing both Sunni and Shiʿi leaders had sprung up in the cities to organize an anti-British campaign. Though founders of the nascent League of Nations were in discussions with the British over the precise nature of its rule over Iraq, it had no formal mechanisms yet in place to provide oversight or suggest policy.[15] In fact, the nature of British rule in Iraq would not really solidify until after a widespread revolt in 1920 forced the reformulation of the mandate for Mesopotamia into the Kingdom of Iraq, via the 1922 Anglo-Iraqi Treaty, and initiated a partial devolution of power into Iraqi hands.[16] The Baʿquba camp was therefore very much under local British control, in cooperation with a refugee Assyrian military leadership with whom the British had established a semicollaborative relationship.

The inhabitants of Baʿquba camp included 24,579 Assyrian refugees, nearly all originally from Hakkari, along with 14,612 Armenians from Van, Mosul, and Urmia. The British officials in charge, making decisions about the camp's administration in the absence of much contact or input from London, viewed it as having three central purposes: first, to house refugee populations on a temporary basis with a view toward repatriation; second, to promote, record, and preserve what they understood as the "national" cultures of the Armenians

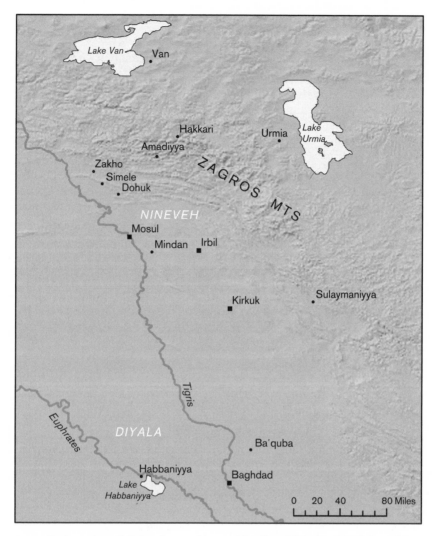

MAP 2. Border regions of Turkey, Iran, and Iraq and location of Baʻquba and Mindan refugee camps. Map by Sachi Arakawa.

and Assyrians; and third, to create an orderly modern space distinct from its geographical location and therefore essentially mobile. Although the Baʻquba camp itself did not last long, it served as an important model; all three of these premises would become well-established principles for dealing with refugees and the place of camps in the new international order.

Initially, the camp at Baʻquba was viewed as a temporary solution until mass Assyrian repatriation and resettlement could be arranged. The refugees themselves were passionately in favor of an eventual repatriation to Hakkari and Urmia, as demonstrated by any number of lobbying efforts and a failed attempt by the Assyrian leader Agha Petros to take a group back into Hakkari in 1920. Dr. J. M. Yonan and Pera Mirza, both members of the Assyrian National Committee based in Urmia during the war, appealed to the British Legation in Tehran for assistance in resettling the Assyrians back into Urmia on the basis of their military assistance to the British and the refusal of the Persian government to offer assistance. "These are the conditions and these are the sacrifices," they wrote, "and we therefore pray the Allies and most especially Great Britain 1. To return our people to Urumia 2. To grant our people protection without which it would be impossible to reside in Urumia. We would especially beg that protection be granted and guaranteed to the members of the Central National Committee who had been very active in the arrangements of National affairs and therefore have incurred the special enemity [sic] of Turks and Kurds and Persians who are pro Turkish." [17] Another Assyrian statement of political goals, sent from a committee to the British headquarters in Baghdad with a view toward having it read at the peace talks, requested "re-establishment in own country under British pro-tection," clarifying that this meant the region of "Kurdistan up to line of Jezireh-Seri-Bash-Kala and Persian territory between Lake Urmi and Turkish frontier," and "Government recognition of Patriarch Marshimmun as head of nation," accompanied by an assurance that "if granted these things hope to live peaceably with Kurds under British protection." [18]

Such demands indicated not a national determination to acquire Assyrian nation-state sovereignty but rather a desire to return to the relatively autono-mous political position the Assyrians had enjoyed in the late Ottoman period, in the same geographical space.[19] Even the redoubtable Surma Khamman (sister of the late patriarch and enthusiastic advocate for Assyrian affairs in London), despite her practiced promotion of Assyrian national identity to sympathetic British officialdom, proposed that membership in an independent Kurdistan might represent a viable future for the Assyrians: "Should prefer British protection and mandate for Hakkiari district, but recognize this impossible. If Kurdistan independent could live there in Hakkiari in old homes with Kurds, supposing armament provided for self-protection. Much prefer this alternative [to repatriation to Persia or Turkish territory]." [20] Such expressions of willingness to negotiate with Kurdish regional interests stood alongside at least one Assyrian document's inclusion of Yezidis and Shikaks (a Kurdish tribe based around Urmia) as part of a broad and flexible understanding of Assyrian political identity.[21] British advocates for Assyrian nationhood, though, constructed this enthusiasm for return as an expression of ethnonational commitment and began to prepare for mass refugee resettlement as part of the creation of an independent Assyria and Armenia—this despite the fact that the idea of autonomous Assyrian and Armenian states had already been rejected as a governing principle of a postwar order at the talks. As a London official minuted in 1919, "The new Mesopotamia will give the Assyrians their real desiderata (i) security and (ii) union in a single state (though this state will of course not be a national Assyrian state, but Arab-Kurdish-Syriac)."[22]

The long trek from Hamadan claimed many lives, and those who did survive the journey were often in poor health upon their arrival. Initially, conditions at the camp were chaotic and unsanitary; one British army officer working there reported a stream of destitute arrivals and more than eighty deaths daily.[23] But as time went on and it became clear that the camp was at least a semipermanent institution, in the absence of any viable possibility of immediate repatriation, the British officers in charge began to organize its population to reflect and prepare for a future in which both Armenians and Assyrians would enjoy national sovereignty. Because of the long history of missionary and other European interests in Ottoman Christian populations, the discussions in Paris were more sympathetic (although in the end perhaps not essentially more committed) to the national claims of Christian "minority" communities with ties to Europe than they were to non-Christian communities, like the Kurds, who lacked this history of contact and collaboration with European interests.[24] Refugee statelessness therefore emerged as a concept that applied to Assyrians and Armenians but not to Turkish or Kurdish displaced populations, and camps like Ba'quba were understood not as aspects of a general humanitarianism but as a solution designated specifically for "national" (Christian) populations in a condition of temporary limbo while their states were being created. Thus British and French officials taking over their new mandated territories in Iraq and Syria pursued tactics of sedentarization and local resettlement for displaced Kurdish, Yezidi, and Arab populations in the borderlands,[25] but organized the camp at Ba'quba around the fiction of future sovereign Assyrian and Armenian nation-states.

A memorandum on the camp reported an initial process of separating refugees by ethnicity into defined national spaces: "For the first month or so the people were all mixed up, Armenians and Assyrians together. But as they became more settled, a census was held, and the people arranged throughout the sections according to their tribal divisions and affiliations."[26] The British camp administrators also set up committees to deal with "questions of national customs and religious duties,"[27] which they considered central to the preservation of Armenian and Assyrian national character until the communities could be reconstituted in a "homeland." To that end, daily life in the camp included instruction in Armenian and Syriac for the children, classes in traditional Armenian lace making and sewing for the women, and the careful recording of Armenian and Assyrian customs.

The conception of the camp as a space for the preservation of the "race" soon became a central stated principle for the British officers in charge. H. H. Austin, the camp commandant, recorded that this idea had to be conveyed and enforced to the refugees themselves:

> The proportion of deaths among newly-born infants at one time became so high, particularly with the Assyrians, that I pointed out to [the Assyrian Patriarch] Mar Shimun there seemed, in the opinion of my medical officers, to be good reason for believing that mothers were in the habit of purposely overlying their babies shortly after birth . . . I begged him to appeal to mothers to do everything in their power and to take full advantage of the facilities afforded by our maternity wards, to rear up their infants. The nation was already so reduced in numbers by their sufferings during the war that it was simply *race suicide* if this high death rate amongst babies was allowed to continue. In response to my request the Patriarch issued a proclamation to all mothers, and expectant ones, exhorting them for the sake of the future welfare of the nation to give every care to newly-born children.[28]

Such language indicated that British and American administrators were engaged in constructing particular kinds of narratives about the camps as national spaces and the refugees as the survivors of an attempted holocaust, and needed the assistance of Assyrian and Armenian collaborators to broadcast these messages to the refugees themselves. As Dudley Northcote, one of the British officials in charge of the Armenian sections of the camp, noted in a letter home, "If you are an ordinary regimental officer in a British regiment, it is astonishing how little opportunity you have of getting to know anything about the natives of Messpot, because of course all your work is with your own men, but now it is part of my job to *study* 1300 Armenian men, women and children" (emphasis added).[29] He added in a different context how utterly dependent he was on his "headman," who had spent some of his early years in the United States and could speak English "after a fashion."[30]

FIGURE 1. Royal Air Force aerial photograph of "Baqubah Refugee Camp, Diyala," 1919. AIR 1/2384/226/18/2 A-C. Courtesy of The National Archives, Kew.

Under British authority the camp became a disciplined and self-contained space in which access to Arab Iraq was restricted and government and social organization was entirely internal. The military officers in charge of its administration imagined it as a carefully organized, mapped-out institution: "The whole camp which covers roughly an area of one square mile has been divided into three areas: 'A,' 'B,' and 'C' respectively. Each of these areas are subdivided into sections, varying from 11 to 13 in number in each area. Over each area there was a British officer, and each section had a British officer looking after it assisted by 3 or 4 British soldiers." [31]

Another observer praised the way the "tribal census" had clarified the ethnic territory of the camp: "As a result of the 'General Post,' the Armenians were all located in 'A' area; whilst 'B,' and 'C' were occupied by Assyrians, who were arranged throughout the sections in accordance with their tribal divisions and affiliations. The supply, and other questions of administration and discipline were greatly simplified in consequence." [32] The Assyrian and Armenian children in the orphanage section of the camp were kept mainly separate: "The large cook-house and bathing-sheds were common to both Armenian and Assyrian children; but they worked at lessons and played apart—each nationality having its own school tents, and giant-strides, horizontal and parallel bars, swings, see-saws, etc."[33]

Camp schools likewise revolved around this idea of maintaining collective racial and ethnic memory. Levon Shahoian, who was eleven years old at the time of his sojourn in Baʿquba, recalled the schooling as little more than a process of recollection: "For days at end our sole curriculum was repeating our own names and family names. We had to stand up and repeat our, as well as our father's and mother's name, the names of our siblings, and the city or village from where we had been exiled."[34] Armenian nationalist history and language, along with English lessons taught by a group of American missionaries, constituted the remainder of the curriculum.

This national separation between Armenians and Assyrians was essentially a fiction of the camps. Across the Hakkari, Diyarbekir, and Van regions, Armenians and Assyrians often lived closely interspersed, spoke one another's languages, and shared sets of religious practices. This cultural closeness had been further advanced by a sense of shared persecution in the final years of Ottoman rule, which had targeted both Armenian and Assyrian communities as threats to the state. Lucille Aroosian, who had emigrated to the United States as a child following her family's destruction in the genocide, remembered the Armenian-Assyrian relationship as a close one: "The Assyrians are Christian, and in Diarbekir they lived side by side with use, suffering dearly at the hands of the Turks."[35]

Employment at Baʿquba was entirely controlled by the British military, which put the men in the camps to work distributing supplies and building roads, drains, and other infrastructure. Some of these jobs were outside the camp, but they were assigned and paid through the British army and did not involve significant contact with the Kurdish and Arab populations in the surrounding area.[36] Such contact as did occur was often hostile, with sentries firing on Arabs approaching the camp in an attempt to "prevent Arab thieves getting into one part or another of the camp at night, and stealing animals and private property of the refugees and others."[37] During the initial stages of the camp's setup small groups of Assyrians constructed external outposts for themselves and their livestock, but as tensions rose with local Arab and Kurdish populations they were ordered to return to the camps, "where they were less likely to be molested at night by Arab thieves."[38] Not surprisingly, there was considerable resentment on the part of local Arab and Kurdish populations over the British, Assyrian, and Armenian appropriation of property and aggressive defense of the camp. The refugees sometimes took their animals into land belonging to Arab farmers, damaging crops and causing anger and reprisals in the form of livestock theft and threats of violence. Austin reported on a series of such encounters that resulted in British arrests of some of the Arabs involved:

> There is little doubt that some of the [Assyrian] men and boys out with different flocks did not exercise proper control over the movement of their sheep and goats whist grazing in the vicinity of [Arab cultivators'] crops . . . relations now became very strained between the Assyrian herdsmen and Arabs, who, as reprisals, endeavoured at night to steal sheep and goats from these isolated encampments of Tiari. . . . [The Assyrians] were held responsible for the safety of their own animals by night; and right well these burly ruffians, armed with stout staves, guarded their property. Several would-be Arab sheep-stealers were captured, and pretty roughly handled in the process before being made over to the camp authorities, and thence despatched to the Political officer at Baqubah town—for incarceration in the local jail.[39]

In such encounters the refugees clearly had the backing of the colonial state machinery, increasing local Arab resentment. But they themselves were also operating under strict limits. Refugee movement was carefully controlled, with constant surveillance of the camp itself. Much of the employment available to the refugees involved participation in the running and servicing of the premises; each tent had a headman and workmen, who were paid to maintain order and cleanliness in their "section," and received inspections from the British officer assigned as overseer nearly every day.[40] (One Assyrian camp inhabitant remembered, "If a man happened to die in a tent, the headman was imprisoned and the tent's rations were reduced for a long time.")[41] The refugees' limited excursions outside the camp were likewise carefully monitored; they were usually accompanied by members of the Assyrian levy battalion established for the purpose of camp "security." Men were not allowed to look for work outside the camp, "as it was feared that they might drift off and leave their families on the hands of the Government"; any who went absent were arrested and their families expelled from the camp.[42]

The ideas of repatriation, resettlement, and separation thus dominated the physical setup of the Ba'quba camp as well as its daily administration and the relationship of Armenian and Assyrian refugees with the surrounding areas. Through 1919, officials like Dudley Northcote declared that the repatriation of the refugees had been delayed only because of the difficulties of crossing hostile Kurdish-held territory on the way to Hakkari, Urmia, or Yerevan. As the terms of the peace accord became clearer in 1920, the situation of the refugees became muddier; many of the British administrators running the camp were unwilling to drop the idea of repatriation, even as its impossibility became abundantly evident. F. Cunliffe-Owen, director of repatriation in the Baʿquba camp, told the British government as much in 1920: "My conclusions are therefore:— Either (i) Continue the present mode of living with hopes of and efforts for repatriation. In this case the community cannot be self-supporting. . . . Or (ii) Accept the idea that repatriation is not within the range of practical politics as yet and settle the community in zones which must be found and where the people would have to resume their customary avocations. This could of course entail an initial outlay and would be largely experimental in strange surroundings. I myself recommend the first course."[43] Such conversations were also governed by increasing concern in London about the costs of the camps and the French High Commission's refusal to provide financial assistance.

The refugees themselves broadly favored some form of return to their old district of Hakkari, and often opposed British attempts to solidify their status as refugees and colonial collaborators in Iraq. The Assyrian leader Agha Petros, who had already been expelled from Hamadan because of his unwillingness to assist with Assyrian military recruitment into the British-run forces, proposed a large-scale repatriation of the refugees to the lower hill district on the Turkish-Iranian frontier in March 1920. The contrary British decision to "proceed with the repatriation of the Assyrians by a process of gradual infiltration" instead led Agha Petros to spearhead a campaign of non-cooperation with the British authorities and begin to explore the possibilities of a collaboration with the French mandatory government emerging in Syria. Following an unsuccessful attempt to take four thousand followers across the border and set up some form of settlement in Syria—and in the absence of any French support as the French army was preparing to evacuate from Cilicia— Agha Petros found himself deported to France, leaving the Assyrian leadership to the patriarch and his generally more pro-British faction.[44]

In the summer of 1920, the previously somewhat disparate and ad hoc Iraqi resistance to the British military occupation began to organize itself into a broader and more nationalist revolution that some participants argued had the "main purpose" of establishing a sovereign Iraqi state.[45] At the very least, it aimed at repelling the British occupation; as the newly formed newspaper *al-Istiqlal* in Najaf declared, it would "respond to the occupiers' deception, worry them, reveal their barbaric offenses."[46] Beginning in late June, tribal leaders throughout the middle Euphrates region collaborated with each other to attack British positions and spread the revolt further afield.

Responding to the rebellion, British authorities began to make use of Baʿquba as a militarized bastion of colonial control, arming refugee men as irregular auxiliaries to serve as punishment columns against Arab and Kurdish anti-colonial forces.[47] The violence reached Diyala in early August, when local forces cut off the railway lines to Baghdad. British officers there feared an attack on the town and requested military backup, but were instead ordered to evacuate. The Baʿquba refugee camp had to be hurriedly shuttered and the inhabitants removed as quickly as possible; and on August 12, the town suffered mass looting as the rebels moved in.

Once again, the fate of the refugees depended on their ethnicity. Initially, they were all moved north to temporary encampments around Mosul, where they were divided into Armenian and Assyrian quarters with separate administrations. As some Armenians hopefully awaited resettlement in an independent Armenian state as proposed in the Treaty of Sèvres, the British government and the League of Nations were simultaneously considering alternatives. One proposal had Armenian refugees placed on an agricultural colony in Kirkuk; others suggested similar rural settlement plans in Syria. Neither of these ideas proved acceptable to the refugees themselves, who categorically refused to cooperate, and the British decided simply to evacuate all the camp's inhabitants with a small sum of money to find other accommodation.[48] When this policy was implemented in the fall of 1921, most of Baʿquba's Armenian residents were transported to Transcaucasia, as the closest possible option to repatriation in the now-defunct Armenian nation-state. The Assyrian refugees were mainly moved to another camp at Mindan, outside Mosul, while the British and the League attempted to come up with an appropriate repatriation plan for them.[49]

Though the revolt had been put down, the colonial victory had come at an enormous cost in terms of both lives and money. The British administration therefore decided to rethink its approach to its new mandatory charge. Inspired by earlier models of informal empire, it put together a nominally independent monarchical government to be headed by the Hashemite scion and wartime Allied partner Faysal, who was searching for a new political opportunity following his recent expulsion from Syria at the hands of the French military. Though it was clear to everyone involved that the new Hashemite monarchy would remain under some degree of British control, all of the parties involved had incentives to maintain a visible distance between the new government and the British colonial presence. The Iraqi government under Faysal thus faced the difficult situation of trying to project an impression of independence from British interests while constructing some form of national identity that could make a viable project of governing the new jerry-rigged state of Iraq.

To this end, Faysal and his government began setting up a new Iraqi army as one of their first acts. It was headed by Ja'far al-'Askari, a veteran of the Hashemite forces in the Arab revolt and a former Ottoman officer. Al-'Askari recruited the first officer corps mainly from Sunni urbanites who had been his associates in the Ottoman forces—including his brother-in-law Nuri al-Said, who would become a major Iraqi partner for the British during the interwar era.[50] Facing the difficult task of constructing a viable government for their fragile new state, Faysal, Ja'far al-'Askari, and Nuri al-Said made an early decision to commit to a form of Iraqi national symbolism that privileged Arabs and Sunnis, with non-Muslim communities often falling under suspicion for their historical associations with European actors. Indicating the Iraqi government's inchoate notions of Iraqi national identity as specifically Muslim and Arab, al-'Askari expressed a common feeling toward Iraq's non-Muslim elements when he later wrote, "Other groups, such as Jews and Christians, generally enjoy good social and economic status in Iraqi society, one reason no doubt being that they receive backing and material support from religious and missionary establishments abroad. The government should nonetheless take certain measure to unify their education with the rest of the population in the Kingdom, and try to instill patriotic feelings in them."[51] Such an approach to Iraqi nationalism left little room for Assyrians within the emerging Iraqi state and fueled both the British and the Iraqi government's redefinition of the Assyrian refugee community as more or less permanent colonial allies within an emerging Arab Iraq.

To this end, when the formation of the new and predominantly Arab army under a theoretically independent Iraqi government left gaps in the British colonial forces known as the Levies, British officers began to recruit Assyrian villagers in the impoverished camps around Mosul to fill the spaces. The Levies acted primarily as colonial troops, crushing Kurdish and Arab rebellion and protecting the border with Turkey. They worked particularly closely with the Royal Air Force, providing ground forces to support and assist the British air power that had replaced earlier large garrisons of Indian and British ground troops. As the Assyrian historian of the Levies Solomon (Sawa) Solomon reports, this was primarily an economic decision: "The British responsibility in Iraqi could be fulfilled more economically by the use of air power rather than by the large garrisons of Indian and British troops which were stationed there. This doctrine was accepted by the British government by October 1922, but the R.A.F. aircraft needed ground troops for protection, so the two Assyrian battalions were transferred from British army control to R.A.F. control." [52] Colonial officials echoed this assessment; as one official noted cynically, "The British Treasury was also able to economise very considerably by the employment of Assyrians rather than British or Indian troops." [53]

This development further alienated the Assyrian community from its Arab and Kurdish neighbors. [54] In 1923, nearly a hundred and fifty notables from Mosul sent a petition to the British and Iraqi governments suggesting the mass ejection of Assyrian communities from Mosul. [55] For the Assyrians themselves, almost wholly dependent on the British as refugees in new territory and with little stake in the emerging Arab Iraqi state, the Levies represented an opportunity not only to access colonial salaries (virtually the only employment available for many young Assyrian men) but also to access force and weaponry to advocate for their own autonomy. Even so, many of the refugee men recruited at the Mindan camp were reluctant to serve; the initial fifty who joined the Levies after months of urging tried to resign shortly thereafter, and were forcibly separated into two groups and removed from the camp area to other Assyrian settlements at Nabi Yunis and Aqra. [56]

In 1923 and 1924, the Levies engaged in active military campaigns against both Turkish incursions and Kurdish uprisings, sometimes simultaneously. A 1923 encounter with Turkish forces at the town of Rowanduz involved attempts both to expel Turkish forces and to put down the claims of the Kurdish leader Sheikh Mahmud of Sulaymaniyya, who was "communicating with the Turkish, and spreading anti British propaganda." [57] In March 1923 both battalions of the Levies evicted the Kurdish position at Spilik Dagh following RAF air strikes and then expelled the Turks from Rowanduz, which they were charged with clearing and holding while British troops marched on Sulaymaniyya to deal with Sheikh Mahmud. [58] Clashes between Kurdish forces and the Levies continued in Kirkuk through 1924, by which time it was clear that the Levies had become a centrally important ally to the British military machine in northern Iraq.

FROM "NATION" TO "MINORITY"

Britain had made attempts to ensure the inclusion of the Mosul region in a British-controlled Mesopotamia almost from the beginning of the war. The de Bunsen report, written in 1915, detailed the strategic requirements of the imperial state: "We cannot maintain permanently in Mesopotamia a force of such size as could successfully cope with an invasion from the north. We require, therefore, a frontier where an enemy's advance can be delayed until the arrival of reinforcements . . . such a frontier can only be found along the range of hills to the north of the Mosul vilayet." [59] But in the years following the war it was not at all clear that Britain would succeed in claiming this territory, as the new Turkish state pressed its claims against the exhausted and financially strapped Allied powers. Resettling Assyrian refugees in the area thus had the strategic purpose of creating a new ethnographic claim to Mosul, as well as placing a barrier between the rest of Iraq and Turkish forces. As Percy Cox noted, it would be a boon to British interests to have Iraq's northern border "garrisoned by a race of sturdy mountaineers whose vital interests were involved in resisting attacks from the north." [60]

In 1924 the British succeeded in having the question of the Turkish-Iraqi border and the fate of the Mosul region turned over to the League of Nations, which appointed a boundary commission to settle the dispute. They made use of the Assyrian question as a central rationale for British control over Mosul: "The British authorities also informed the Commission that the future treatment of the Assyrians would depend entirely on the decision taken with regard to the frontier. If the territory occupied by the Assyrians is not assigned to 'Iraq they cannot be granted any local autonomy, because in that case they would not be settled into homogenous communities. If the frontier were drawn towards the south, thus incorporating in 'Iraq only a small part of the former Assyrian territory, it would be impossible to find land for the Assyrians in 'Iraq." [61] Further, the British made extensive and effective use of the new League framing of "minority" rights to make the case for its retention of the area. In arguing against the idea that the fate of Mosul should be determined by a plebiscite, they appealed directly to the language of minority rights and explicitly cited European precedents under League supervision:

It is unnecessary to dwell at any length on the evil consequences that flow from a frontier settlement by plebiscite. They are a matter, not of theory, but of actual experience. The minority inevitably find themselves in an unhappy position when the verdict goes against them. They are exposed to reprisals and persecution. . . . It is a matter of common knowledge that all this has happened, and is happening at the present moment, in European States whose frontiers have been determined by the League of Nations by means of a plebiscite. If the danger exists in Europe, and experience has proved that it does exist, it will be far greater in a remote region such as the Irak frontier, where the restraints of general public opinion are necessarily less operative.[62]

Promises that the mandate would provide some sort of special status and protection for ethnic and religious minorities within Iraq helped to sway the commission's opinion in favor of British claims. Following on a long tradition of European interest in Eastern Christian communities, the commission's members were particularly struck with the claims they encountered from Assyrian refugees: "In the north what interested them most was the disgusting way, as they called it, in which the Christians were bought and sold by the Kurds, and had been ill-treated during the Turkish regime. There is no doubt that the Assyrians and the other Christians seen by the commissioner left a very great impression upon their minds."[63] In addressing the Turkish foreign minister Tewfik Rushdy's objections and claims directly, British colonial secretary Leo Amery further emphasized the "minorities" question: "I laid special stress on the necessity for ensuring a satisfactory settlement of the Assyrian problem [and] added that I accepted the Commission's recommendations for special measures to ensure the protection of minorities on the assumption that the Turkish Government would similarly accept them in Turkish territory.... The Turkish representative made a very brief and ineffective reply to my statement of the preceding day, in which the only point worth noting was a refusal to consent to the discussion of the question of the protection of minorities."[64] He later added that "surely it is no small thing that we have created in that country a system of government progressive, and yet essentially Oriental, a system of government which is national, and yet tolerant of minorities and which appreciates the help and support we have rendered."[65] Reports to the commission coming from local officials on site in northern Iraq repeatedly emphasized Turkish attacks on Christians.

When the commission published its report, it found (as the British appear to have expected) that Mosul should be attached to Iraq and that Turkey should give up its claims to the region—which it did, reluctantly, in 1926. So once the border had been determined and Mosul's inclusion in Iraq confirmed, Assyrians had been redefined as a minority in need of particular special protections that legitimized and justified both British and League claims of authority over Mosul's territory. The commission noted this in its final report, which declared that "Assyrians should be guaranteed the re-establishment of the ancient privileges which they possessed in practice, if not officially, before the war ... the Sovereign State ought to grant these Assyrians a certain local autonomy, recognized their right to appoint their own officials, and contenting itself with a tribute from them, paid through the agency of the Patriarch." [66] This central concern was also referenced in the actual decision, which called on the British to "act, as far as possible, in accordance with the other suggestions of the Commission of Enquiry as regards measures likely to ensure pacification and to afford equal protection to all the elements of the population." [67]

The Assyrians themselves resisted both the categorization as a "minority" among an Iraqi Arab majority and the permanent incorporation of the Mosul area into the new state of Iraq—which was also opposed by much of the Kurdish and Arab populations of the region, as even the commission recognized.[68] The Assyrian refugee leadership once again proposed their original solution: repatriation to their old homes in the Hakkari region and the reestablishment of Assyrian villages in Turkish territory. Several Assyrian attempts to cross into Turkey met with violence, and by 1928 the Turkish government had formally informed the Iraqi state that any Assyrians discovered entering Turkey would be subject to arrest and punishment.[69]

Instead, the Iraqi government and the British together implemented the so-called Z Plan, which transferred Assyrian refugees to agricultural settlements scattered among Kurdish villages around Mosul with the explicit goal of using them as buffers between the Iraqi government and potentially hostile Kurdish communities.[70] The British had already distributed money for resettlement, with "each Assyrian, man, woman, or child, receiving £9 from the British government." [71] In 1927 a British Levies officer, one Captain Fowraker, was appointed "Settlement Officer" for the Assyrian population and moved most of the former camp dwellers into villages, encouraging them to find work in the towns and settle into their new spaces. Relatively few of the former refugees were able to find employment; British commentators blamed this on the Assyrians' unwillingness to learn Arabic, and noted that "in fact after all the settlements, some of which appeared to be quite successful, many of the Assyrians still persisted in considering themselves to be refugees [and] ... had many grievances." [72]

The Iraqi government carried out much of the actual transport and paid part of the costs of the agricultural settlement plan through tax relief and financing of agricultural projects, infrastructure, and housing.[73] The Iraqi Ministry of the Interior even supported an Assyrian levy company presence in some resettlement areas "to afford settlers the necessary sense of security"—a plan that aroused nervousness among local Kurdish leaders.[74] With a view to the postindependence landscape, the Iraqi and British officials carrying out the Z Plan were careful not to place the Assyrian villages in a bloc for fear of creating a de facto self-governing Assyrian enclave, instead scattering the new settlers among Kurdish villages to break up the population. At least one observer in the 1930s believed that if the Assyrians had been settled together they would have had the military capability to achieve an autonomous region at the expense of the Iraqi state.[75] While the earlier camps had emphasized collective maintenance, the new policy of assimilation meant that these new, mainly agricultural settlements were deliberately and sometimes forcibly integrated into local Kurdish populations, separating some villages from others—a source of grievance for some Assyrian leaders, who protested that their settlements should be in a "compact body" and not under the ownership of Kurdish landholders.[76]

In protest against the resettlements and against the abandonment of any plan for local autonomy, refugee Assyrian villagers engaged in periodic hostilities against local Kurds and Arabs, as well as participating in other forms of resistance to the government such as refusing to register for the census (for which "ringleaders" were fined and imprisoned), refusing to pay taxes, and failing to register weapons as was required in Iraqi law.[77] As the 1920s wore on, and especially as the British began to investigate the possibility of abandoning the mandate and permanently devolving power onto Faysal and his Iraqi bureaucracy, this Assyrian resistance was increasingly directed at the Iraqi government. The Assyrian patriarch Mar Shimun, engaging in a petition campaign from Cyprus where he and his family had been deported, continued to protest to Iraqi representatives that there was enough "empty land" in the region for all the Assyrians to be settled together: "It has *not* been proved to the satisfaction of impartial observers that lands combining the requisite conditions for settlement of the Assyrians in a *homogenous group* do not exist in Iraq . . . there are more than sufficient deserted land, the property of the Iraq Govt, to the north of Dohuk in Amadia and the northern hills, upon which the latter class of persons could be permanently settled."[78]

Some longer-standing Assyrian communities, anxious to preserve their relationship with the soon-to-be independent Iraqi state, vigorously opposed this antigovernment refugee position. In 1931, a writer styling himself as "Chaldean" in the pages of the Baghdad newspaper *al-Istiqlal* accused refugee Assyrians of creating political difficulties for local Christian communities by serving the interests of the British, who were providing the settlers with "all that is calculated to disturb public peace and security, in the same way as he did in the case of the Zionists who have become his obedient soldiers."[79] Bishop Mar Yuwalaha, the main ecclesiastical leader of the villages in the Barwar region of Dohuk, wrote to the League to protest the patriarch's hostile attitude, publicly declaring his community's "entire contentment with their present circumstances and their loyalty to the Iraqi government" and attempting to dissociate himself from the anti-Iraqi stance of the newer arrivals.[80]

He was right to be worried. By the early 1930s, refugee Assyrian resistance to incorporation into the Iraqi state had led to a situation of open hostility between the Iraqi government and the newly settled refugees in the north of the country. Addressing a meeting of more than a hundred Assyrian community leaders in Mosul in 1933, Khalil Azmi Bey, the *mutassarif* of the Mosul *liwa,* deployed increasingly threatening language:

> The Assyrians ought to obey the rule of the country, and the government will not tolerate, in their capacity as an independent State, to see any one in the country ignoring the laws and order, under which all the subjects are bound. But the patience extended by the Government towards the Assyrians, and the kind treatment they met with are specially due to the humane and kind attitude of a kind government towards the refugees in her lands. But I do not mean that these shall continue for ever, for those who cannot be loyal subjects try to do worse, and do not deserve their privilege.[81]

This worsening antagonism between the Assyrian settlers and the Iraqi state would represent the backdrop to the 1933 massacre and the subsequent British and League commitment to removing the Assyrians (including some nonrefugee communities) from Iraq altogether.

ARMENIAN REFUGEE CAMPS IN LEBANON AND SYRIA

The discussion of eventually "repatriating" Armenian refugees in Syria to a sovereign state was, if anything, even more transparently a rhetorical justification for the imposition of League and French colonial oversight, since it largely emerged after an attempt to construct an Armenian state had already collapsed. At the end of the war, it briefly appeared that there would be French and British support for an Armenian "National Home" in the southeastern Anatolian region of Cilicia, where the French had about forty thousand forces stationed by May 1920. In hopes of joining the new nation, thousands of Armenians who had spent the last years of the war in Syria arrived in Cilicia under the impression that they would be building their new Armenian state under French protection.[82] In truth, the French military was utterly unable to maintain its occupation of the region, in which local populations (of whom Armenians represented a distinct numerical minority) were overwhelmingly hostile and Turkish military incursions were attempting to regain as much territory as possible.[83] In August 1920, the Treaty of Sèvres divided the remains of the Ottoman Empire into several pieces, including a designated Armenian nation; but the Allied powers' military exhaustion, financial incapacity, and lack of political will to extend the war by enforcing the punitive division of Anatolia opened the way for the Turkish nationalist leader Mustafa Kemal to reassemble the pieces and overrun the weak Armenian Republic. When the French agreed to a treaty with Turkey the following year that signed Cilicia over to Turkish control in return for French economic privileges in the new Turkish state, tens of thousands more Armenians fled back into Syria, Lebanon, and Palestine. In 1922 Turkish and Soviet leaders formalized the Treaty of Kars, dividing the proposed territory of Armenia between the two powers and establishing the remains of the state as the Armenian Soviet Socialist Republic, to be incorporated into the new U.S.S.R.

Facing this new wave of people, the French government set up formal camps in Aleppo and Beirut where the majority of Armenian refugees were concentrated, as well as in Damascus, Alexandretta, and Latakia. By the mid-1920s there were more than 100,000 Armenian refugees across Syria and Lebanon. Some were far from destitute—the more than 28,000 Armenians extracted from Cilicia by sea brought with them some 25,000 cubic meters of luggage—and settled quite quickly into new Armenian urban enclaves springing up around the cities.[84] Others languished longer in the camps, which were often crowded and unsanitary; one source cites an infant mortality rate of 70 percent for some of these shantytowns.[85] The national Armenian identity that French authorities and various humanitarian and diaspora organizations were so intent on preserving was belied by the multiplicity of languages, religious and cultural practices, class backgrounds, and interest in assimilation among the refugees themselves.

The refugees were highly conscious that the camps were designed to maintain Armenian separation from the surrounding Arab populations, both physically and culturally, and they sometimes protested their enforced segregation. Even as the French mandate authorities encouraged Armenian churches, community organizations, and refugee assistance organizations to develop Armenian educational institutions that would insist on a separate linguistic and cultural identity, many Armenian refugees began to learn Arabic in hopes of moving out of the camps and joining the ranks of the much better off Lebanese and Syrian Armenians with a well-established presence in the trades.[86] Bayard Dodge, who became president of the American University of Beirut in 1923, remembered this as a central issue in his work with Near East Relief in the first years after the war: "In Lebanon, some of the teachers thought that the most intelligent pupils [in the camp orphanages] should be trained to become literary leaders of the new Armenia. Many of their friends encouraged this idea, but with the help of the exceedingly wise Catholicos, religious leader of the Armenian community, and several of the leading businessmen, we insisted on teaching the orphans Arabic and trades."[87]

By this point, the League of Nations too was developing a more specific approach to the Armenian refugee question in Syria and Lebanon. It was in some ways late to the question of refugee relief in the Middle East. The beginnings of a League-sponsored refugee regime did not come until 1921, some years after private relief organizations as well as various Allied governments had engaged in the creation of refugee camps across the former Arab provinces of the Ottoman Empire. Its first formal iteration was the League's appointment of a "General Commissioner for the Russian Refugees" at the suggestion of a group of humanitarian agencies including the International Red Cross. The slot was filled by the redoubtable Fridtjof Nansen, a Norwegian diplomat and former Arctic explorer, who was charged with the task of either finding ways to repatriate refugees to Russia or find employment for them in their new homes. When a new Soviet decree stripped the refugees of their citizenship the following year, Nansen turned his attention to the possibilities of formal legal asylum elsewhere. This development followed on the heels of the collapse of the short-lived Republic of Armenia, which rendered the idea of imminent "repatriation" impossible for Armenian refugees holed up in camps in Syria, Lebanon, Palestine, and Iraq.

In 1922 Nansen, now the League's high commissioner for refugees, created a new document called the Nansen Passport, which allowed holders to travel within the states that agreed to recognize it. Fifty-four states signed agreements to recognize Russian Nansen Passport holders and thirty-eight agreed to honor it for Armenian holders.[88] Such documents provided a certain degree of mobility for their holders in search of employment, without guaranteeing any sort of permanent settlement or path to citizenship. At its core, the Nansen Passport system represented an attempt to deal with the loss of the possibility of repatriation for Russian and Armenian refugees; and in 1928 eligibility for the Nansen Passport would be expanded to include "any person of Assyrian or Assyro-Chaldean origin."[89]

Nansen and his associates, though, were already beginning to distinguish cases like Russian refugees, for whom emigration, asylum, and eventual assimilation into a new home country were considered desirable outcomes, from distinct "nations" like the Armenians and Assyrians, for whom some sort of eventual sovereign space was envisioned. As historian Keith Watenpaugh has noted with regard to the Armenian case, "Critical to this particular form of Humanitarianism was the underlying resolve not just to ease the suffering of individual Armenians but also to prevent the further erosion of the Armenian nation,"[90] unlike Russian (and other) refugees who were not categorized as national minorities but as stateless individuals. During the course of an investigation of nonaffiliated refugees seeking League assistance, a member of the Council tersely noted, "The mere fact that certain classes of persons are without the protection of any national Government is not sufficient to make them refugees."[91]

The League's refugee office, then, continued to maintain the fiction that these Syrian and Lebanese refugee settlements were temporary until such time as Armenia could be reconstituted as a sovereign nation. But even as the League disseminated rhetoric about the eventual construction of an independent Armenia, it also began to help the French High Commission dissolve the French- and American-run camps in Aleppo and Beirut and promote permanent resettlement schemes for Armenian refugees. In 1924 Nansen and the League Council made the decision to turn much of the work of refugee settlement over to the International Labour Organisation headed by the former French minister of munitions Albert Thomas, who was broadly sympathetic to the concerns of the French mandatory governments in Syria and Lebanon.[92] French and League authorities thus came to agree on a broad approach of settling the refugees in self-reliant but segregated Armenian enclaves on an essentially permanent basis (though Nansen himself remained committed to the idea of at least some degree of Armenian refugee "repatriation" to Soviet Yerevan).[93] As the Assembly put it in 1925, "Until an Armenian National Home can be established, every possible facility should be given to the refugees to establish themselves in productive employment in other countries so as to maintain and safeguard their national existence."[94]

The French High Commission's promotion of Armenian ethnic nationalism, expressed particularly in the making of Armenian enclaves in the new Armenian quarters of Beirut and Aleppo, had a clearly self-preserving rationale. The idea of creating distinct Armenian communities around Syrian and Lebanese urban areas arose both from a consciousness of anti-imperial Arab and Syrian nationalist feeling and from the fear that dire conditions in the camps might give rise to Communist sympathies among the refugees.[95] (This French fear was not unfounded; it derived not only from opposition to the Soviet Union but also from Armenian Communist commitment to Arab nationalist causes and active participation in anti-French political activism.) Armenian resettlement policies sought to further fragment the ethnoreligious landscape in postwar Syria, while providing a fiction of cross-communal political participation as required by the League. As high commissioner for Syria Henri Ponsot noted, the French goal now was not to imagine an autonomous homeland for the Armenians but to make them a permanent (albeit separate) feature of the Syrian state: "One fears that as soon as they have a little savings, they will wish to go elsewhere. This must be avoided. . . . [and] This task is underway."[96] Of course it could not be avoided altogether, and many Armenians did go elsewhere, sometimes to become vocal international advocates for the idea of an Armenian homeland from their new vantage points as immigrants in places like Marseille and Boston.[97]

Beginning from about 1925, then, the French mandate government—in collaboration with the League—began to develop resettlement plans for the Armenians in the camps that envisioned the development of "temporary" but long-term Armenian enclaves around Aleppo and Beirut, rather than repatriation to Soviet Armenia or somewhere else. Anxious about the numbers of Armenians congregating in Aleppo and Alexandretta, the French mandate government also moved some of them to camps in the interior "in order to relieve congestion in the arrival points and to spread them according to the economic absorptive capacity of the country"[98]—the same phrase that was used to describe modes of determining how many European Zionist settlers Palestine could support, and which appeared frequently in League assessments of state viability. In the Jazira, the French mandate government set up all-Armenian villages at Tell Brak, Tell Abiad, Tella Beri, and Tell Aswad, where they often endured very primitive conditions.[99]

Like the Assyrians in Ba'quba and Mosul, Armenians in these settlements remained almost wholly dependent on French and international assistance— not only for funding for the camps themselves, but also for employment and political opportunity. The French High Commission, anxious to establish Armenian loyalty to the mandate, privileged the refugees for civil service and government jobs and unilaterally bestowed citizenship and voting rights on them in 1924. This type of political and economic assistance served a dual purpose for the French mandate government: it moved Armenians out of camps where they were financial burdens on the state, and it built a relationship of dependency with the Armenian community that the French hoped would be useful in consolidating their grip on a highly resistant Syrian Arab population. In the districts of Aleppo and Beirut, which according to League estimates housed as many as 55,000 and 40,000 Armenian refugees respectively by the mid-1920s, French authorities spent considerable money on developing the camps into permanent settlements and encouraging mass settlement in specific neighborhoods on the outskirts of the cities. These camps-turned-settlements quickly became small, self-contained towns, with schools, businesses, and medical facilities springing up to serve the refugee population. Despite some international (British and American) criticism of the conditions of these settlements, French officials declared it was neither possible nor desirable to break up the refugee community and settle Armenians on an individual basis in the cities, on the grounds of the centrality of national bonds. "However desirable such schemes may appear at first sight to their authors," one wrote, "they would meet with insuperable obstacles. All Armenians who have not yet attained a certain degree of economic independence wish to be members of groups consisting of their own countrymen, as they derive a sense of security from the existence of groups of this kind." [100]

This strategy of maintaining physical divisions between the Armenian and Arab populations became especially useful with the outbreak of a general anti-French revolt in 1925. The French army recruited heavily in Armenian camps and settlements, relying on Armenian troops (along with Circassians and Kurds, also situated in opposition to Arab and Syrian nationalism in official French thinking) to help put down anti-French resistance in the Ghutah and Damascus and deal with outbursts of violence in the Jazira. Armenian recruits played a significant role in helping the French eventually regain control over the country, including helping French forces clear rebels from some quarters in Damascus and its environs. [101] Though this colonial coercion was not always successful—the Armenian Communist leader

Artine Madoyan, for instance, helped smuggle arms to the Jebel Druze and Atrash's forces from Beirut during the revolt, in direct opposition to the many Armenians assisting the French—the mandate government's recruitment of Armenians damaged both French and Armenian positions among Syrian nationalists.[102] Syrian Arab nationalist publications railed against the Armenian presence in the country and labeled French financial and political support for Armenian refugees a tactical move in a bid for extended imperial power. One report on military violence against civilians in the Ghutah reported that "the presence, in these irregular [French colonial] formations, of Christians who, to add to native resentment, are Armenians, refugees dependent on Arab hospitality, has aroused dangerous passions among the Moslems." [103] Resentment against Armenian-French collaboration was strong enough to inspire several violent attacks on refugee settlements during the revolt, including one instance in which an Armenian camp outside the Damascus neighborhood of Bab Tuma was set on fire.[104]

By the end of the 1920s, the French in Syria had moved away from thinking of Armenian refugees as members of a stateless nation and refigured them as geographically distinct ethnonational blocs helping to support French rule in a largely hostile Syrian Arab state. By this point the concept of Armenian "repatriation" was quietly being put to rest in Geneva as well; instead, the League offered funding to help the French move refugees into newly built or rebuilt Armenian quarters on the outskirts of the cities, where they existed in a separate social, economic, and political sphere from their Arab neighbors. Camp-like accommodations that had originally featured tents and jerry-rigged shacks were rebuilt as stone-built homes to create permanent, established Armenian urban enclaves.[105] The Nansen International Office for Refugees, established in 1930, assisted this process further by providing legal help to Armenians in Beirut to claim deeds to land and property, in order to make their claims to these spaces legal and permanent. Armenian "Compatriotic Unions" sprang up in both Aleppo and Beirut, sometimes helping to recreate specific Armenian village geographies in these new Armenian quarters. By the early 1930s this movement of Armenians out of the camps and into permanent Armenian quarters on the outskirts of Lebanese and Syrian cities had become an established fact of the urban landscape across the French mandates.[106]

As for Assyrians in Iraq, early rhetoric about maintaining Armenians in Syrian and Lebanese camps until they could be resettled in a "homeland"—in this case even more clearly a rationale for mandate control, given that the

Armenian national project had already collapsed—gave way by the mid-1920s to resettling refugees as national blocs that could prove helpful to colonial governments struggling to maintain their authority in resistant areas. French resettlement of Armenians in ethnically differentiated urban neighborhoods in Aleppo and Beirut or rural settlements in the Jazira echoed British practices of resettlement for Assyrian refugees in northern Iraq. The League, the British, and the French were all coming to understand these "national" refugee communities as potentially useful to colonial governments—an idea that was also beginning to play out, in somewhat different circumstances, for Zionist settlers across the border in Palestine.

· · ·

The officials running the refugee camp that emerged at Baʿquba in 1918 deliberately configured its governance and physical space to nationalize its Armenian and Assyrian residents. They sought to emphasize ethnic nationalism as the fundamental basis for refugee identity, maintaining the camp as a mobile ministate where Armenians and Assyrians would "preserve" their national identities until they could be repatriated to a national homeland. Baʿquba served as a concrete demonstration of the international commitment to Assyrian and Armenian sovereign nationhood, even as negotiations were underway for the large-scale absorption of Ottoman territory into the British and French empires.

As the idea of creating Assyrian and Armenian homelands became less useful to the British, the French, and the League, this narrative morphed into a reconstitution of these refugee populations as geographically discrete communities who required protection from a majoritarian state and whose interests were naturally aligned with the mandates. As Baʿquba's Armenian residents were deported from Iraq, the British army moved refugee Assyrians to the Mosul region and resettled them in discrete ethnic blocs. Now British mandate authorities made use of the refugee population in a different way, refuting Turkish claims to Mosul and its surrounds by declaring that the "minority" Assyrian Christians required external protection from a potentially hostile Iraqi Arab majority. A similar situation arose in Aleppo and Beirut, where Armenian refugees came under the control of a French state intent on maintaining them as a geographically distinct ethnonational subcategory in the French High Commissions of Lebanon and Syria. As in Iraq, the idea of building permanent, segregated Armenian settlements in Syria and Lebanon demonstrated the hope that unassimilated non-Arab communities could help ensure French control over difficult colonial spaces—an idea in which the League now actively concurred, despite frequent opposition from both refugees themselves and the communities among whom they were settled. Now, as the mandate system began to face even greater local resistance, the disengagement of these refugee communities from their settings and the presumed mobility of their segregated ethnic enclaves began to tempt colonial governments and the League to engage in further ethnic engineering through what they would euphemistically term "transfer."

THREE

The Transfer Solution

By the mid-1920s, the original rationale for maintaining Armenians and Assyrians in distinct and unassimilated refugee settlements—to demonstrate a notional commitment to the principles of minority nationalism and self-determination—had largely fallen away. As mandate governments found themselves struggling to maintain control over large populations broadly and deeply opposed to British and French rule across the mandate territories, and especially as mass Jewish immigration from Europe started to change the demographic picture in Palestine, they began to consider more ambitious schemes of ethnic engineering via population "transfer."

The Zionist discourse of mass resettlement of the Jews in other parts of the globe, most notably but not only Palestine, offered a useful model for working out the practicalities of this kind of ethnic engineering. Prewar negotiations between the British government and Zionist territorialists over Jewish settlement in Africa, in particular, had provided an early venue for articulating how ethnically based relocation could be presented to the international community as a mode of minority national empowerment while in practice serving to advance the imperial interests of its sponsors. Late Ottoman practices of expulsion and resettlement provided a further important foretaste and model of internationally sanctioned minority "exchange" in the Balkans. The immediate postwar years saw the Allied powers and then the League negotiate and organize financial and practical support for population swaps among Bulgaria, Greece, and Turkey that recalled and reflected the mass Ottoman-Balkan displacements of the previous two decades.

These precursors helped to shape two localized minority transfer projects in British- and French-occupied Iraq and Syria in the 1920s and 1930s. In

Syria, facing enormous resistance to the imposition of mandate rule (developing by 1925 into a mass revolt), French colonial authorities began to pursue a policy of internal resettlement that placed Armenian communities collectively not only in sensitive urban areas but also in rural borderlands as a buffer against Syrian Arab nationalism. By the beginning of the 1930s similar Iraqi resistance had led the British to conclude that an independent Iraq, kept close to Britain by restrictive treaty arrangements, would be a cheaper and simpler mode of maintaining access to the country's resources—a decision that left the Assyrian refugee community whom the British had introduced and then co-opted into colonial military service vulnerable to Iraqi Arab and Kurdish anger. When Assyrians became victims of a brutal Iraqi army massacre following the formal British withdrawal from Iraq in 1932, British officials and the League began to discuss a more radical ethnic "transfer" following closely on the logistical and philosophical approaches of Zionist territorialism: moving the community en masse to some far-flung territory like Brazil or British Guiana, on the grounds that there were no longer any remaining options for successful Assyrian integration into an Arab and Muslim majority Iraq. More modest versions of this proposal suggested following on the Armenian model and resettling Assyrian refugees in border areas in Syria, with French assistance.

Such proposals sparked vigorous and often agonized conversations within the affected communities, both refugee and host, who engaged forcefully and consistently with the League bureaucracy to advocate for their own interests. The Permanent Mandates Commission alone fielded more than three thousand formal petitions in its brief lifetime, about 80 percent of which concerned the Middle Eastern mandate states.[1] The correspondence, petitions, and appeals that colonized populations in mandate territories sent to the League constituted a centrally important attempt to articulate objections to colonial rule that would carry political and legal authority in the emerging international system.[2] In their voluminous correspondence with the mandate governments and the League, local Arab, Assyrian, and Armenian leaders made use of the League's own formulations and bureaucratic mechanisms to vocally reject neocolonial proposals for shaping the state via migration and "resettlement" and offer alternative visions for their own political futures.[3]

At the same time that the League was debating the specifics of Assyrian transfer to Latin America with various Assyrian communities, the Iraqi government, and a still-extant British colonial apparatus, Jewish territorialism was having a last moment in the sun. The Freeland League's proposals for mass European Jewish resettlement in Australia, Canada, or Suriname (among others) attracted international attention as the Nazi threat to Jews in central and eastern Europe became clearer, even receiving a mention in Michael Hansson's speech accepting the Nobel Peace Prize on behalf of the Nansen International Office for Refugees in 1938. The League had developed a discourse (albeit a somewhat incoherent one) of transfer and resettlement that viewed large-scale ethnic engineering across the Eastern Mediterranean as a positive step toward the creation of viable sovereign states there—a rhetoric designed in part to mask its practical support for British and French imperial designs in the Middle East.[4]

THE TERRITORIALIST MODEL

The concept of transfer or resettlement as a solution to the "problem" minorities presented had a powerful model in the Zionist movement. Calling for mass resettlement of Jews worldwide, Zionism provided an example of a voluntary mass movement of a clearly defined and persecuted minority into an altogether new location, not as individual refugees but as a collective national entity in search of a new geographic base. The early working out of the Zionist vision—and particularly the "territorialist" proposals for settlement in East Africa as an immediate solution to the problem of anti-Semitic persecution—established some of the concerns and parameters the British and the League would later consider for the resettlement of other groups categorized as minorities in eastern Europe and the Middle East.

The territorialist movement advocated resettling Jews as a bloc somewhere other than (or as well as) Palestine. Leon Pinsker's *Autoemancipation,* often considered a foundational text for Zionism, also laid the groundwork for a territorial approach, declaring that Palestine did not represent the only possible homeland for Jewish nationalism: "We need nothing but a large piece of land . . . which shall remain our property, from which no foreign master can expel us."[5] Later in his life, he argued against Palestine as an impractical solution and promoted the idea of Jewish national settlement in Argentina. Theodor Herzl also considered Argentina a viable possibility for mass Jewish settlement: "Shall we choose Palestine or Argentine? We shall take what is given us, and what is selected by Jewish public opinion . . . Argentine is one of the most fertile countries in the world, extends over a vast area, has a sparse population and a mild climate."[6] Similarly, Maurice de Hirsch's Jewish

Colonization Association advocating mass Jewish resettlement in Argentina and elsewhere attracted considerable support in the last years of the nineteenth century.

The idea of resettling European Jews somewhere other than Palestine caught the attention of the British government at an early stage. In 1903, the British colonial secretary Joseph Chamberlain traveled to the British protectorate in East Africa and began to concoct plans for European settlement there, largely with the goal of providing a market for an underperforming railway the British had spent a great deal of money building. After discussions with Leopold Greenberg, a Zionist journalist and editor of the London-based *Jewish Chronicle*, Chamberlain declared his interest in creating an autonomous Zionist space in the region to house as many as a million European Jewish settlers. That same year, after extensive negotiations and conversations with Chamberlain, Greenberg collaborated with other leading British Zionists to put together a proposal for a "Jewish colonization scheme" in Uganda and Kenya, requesting British assistance with the construction of an autonomous Jewish homeland to be carved out of British colonial holdings in East Africa.

The Zionist proposals for settlement in Uganda were detailed and thorough. Greenberg and his allies proposed a two-stage plan: a first stage in which the British would turn over administration to the Jewish Colonial Trust for the administration of mass emigration and settlement, and a second stage involving the promulgation of a formal constitution for the territory and the development of national institutions including courts, legislative bodies, police forces, tax agencies, and a national flag. The settlement, to be called "New Palestine," would be allowed to expand territorially if necessary, on the basis of numbers of settlers. It would also have the right to expel inhabitants deemed a threat to the creation of an autonomous settler nation—the only part of the proposal addressing the question of the relationship between settlers and indigenous communities.[7] The British government agreed to consider the idea and eventually offered a modestly worded commitment:

> Lord Lansdowne will be prepared to entertain favourably proposals for the establishment of a Jewish Colony or settlement, on conditions which will enable the members to observe their National customs. For this purpose he would be prepared to discuss ... the details of a scheme comprising as its main features: the grant of a considerable area of land, the appointment of a Jewish Official as chief of local administration, and permission to the Colony

to have a free hand in regard to municipal legislation and as to the management of religious and purely domestic matters, such Local Autonomy being conditional upon the right of His Majesty's Government to exercise a general control.[8]

Despite the term "Uganda Scheme" by which the proposal became known, much of the proposed territory for settlement had been transferred to the East Africa Protectorate and would become Kenya in 1920.

The primary considerations of these early explorations were geographic, noting potential for agricultural work, the abundance and accessibility of natural resources, and—crucially—the relative seclusion of the territory. As Charles Eliot, the British commissioner for East Africa, noted in 1903, "It is a grassy plain, well watered and possessing a temperate climate. In August I myself found it disagreeably cold but this objection would doubtless not be felt by Jews from Eastern Europe. . . . The position is sufficiently isolated to protect Jews from any hostile demonstrations of other races."[9] Israel Zangwill, later founder of the Jewish Territorial Organization (ITO) and the primary theorist and advocate for the East Africa settlement plan, reported in a speech before the Sixth Zionist Congress the thought process by which Chamberlain had come to the idea of Jewish settlement in East Africa: "For passing through a beautiful unoccupied region of British East Africa, a region in appearance like our own Surrey hills, healthy in climate, temperate by its elevation, and though so near to the equator, eminently a white man's country, Mr. Chamberlain had said to himself, 'Here is the very land for Dr. Herzl.'"[10] And indeed, the population of the region was actually down from normal levels due to nearly simultaneous epidemics of rinderpest, bovine pleuropneumonia, and smallpox, though it would recover shortly.[11]

When Theodor Herzl put the proposal to the Sixth Zionist Congress the reaction was mixed, but the proposal went to a vote that supported sending a commission to the region to investigate conditions and report back to the congress the following year. The commission's initial exploration was delayed due to lack of funds and internal confusion, as well as by Herzl's sudden death at the age of forty-four. When it finally set out in December 1904, funded by a last-minute contribution from a sympathetic British Christian Zionist, it included three commissioners: St Hill Gibbons, a travel writer and Boer War veteran; Alfred Kaiser, a surveyor who worked for the Northwest Cameroons Company and who had converted to Islam during an assignment in the Arabian peninsula; and the Russian Zionist Nahum Wilbusch, the only Jewish member and an engineer by training. After landing at Mombasa, they took the underused Uganda railway to Nairobi and Nakuru and then made the four-day journey to the Guas Ngishu plateau that Chamberlain had imagined as a site for Jewish colonization. The commission's eventual report, published in both English and German in 1905, did not come to a unified conclusion about the territory's potential. However, it did indicate a set of shared assumptions about the criteria for a Jewish settlement: agricultural viability and emptiness. As Wilbusch, who was by and large unsympathetic to the plan, noted in his part of the report, "The chief and most characteristic feature of the territory in question is the total absence of any population . . . there is no population whatever, and the native question is solved, and there now arises the labour question"—by which he meant that European Jewish settlers "could never perform the work done by negroes under the burning equatorial sun." [12] (Zangwill reacted incredulously to this comment, noting, "There are no people—but this is exactly what we want. . . . I suppose if he graveled through Palestine, he would report joyously: 'Saw half a million Arabs.'")[13] This focus on climate, agriculture, and local populations would recur in later commissions on transfer coming from both the British and the League.

Zangwill viewed the proposal as a creation rather than a recreation of a Jewish nation-state and actively sought to align his cause with the rhetorical and political formulations of British imperial thought. In this he was following Herzl, who had drawn heavily on European imperial models for his own vision of Jewish national settlement under some sort of external imperial protection. Historian Mark Levene has argued persuasively that Herzl was influenced by the unfolding of the European scramble for Africa, noting that he reached out to King Leopold of Belgium to explore the possibility of Jewish settlement in the Congo under Belgian authority and contacted Cecil Rhodes to propose a Jewish colony in Palestine on the model of "the British chartered company for South Africa." [14] Herzl compared his own role in developing the Jewish state to the explorations of Stanley and Livingstone, even going so far as to imagine Jewish colonists landing in Palestine wearing "a distinctive cap à la Stanley," [15] and consistently sought to ground his Zionist settlement concept in an economically hardheaded project for capital expansion.[16] While Herzl's interest in territorial solutions was in the end rejected by the majority of the Zionist Organization's members, the idea of organizing the movement as a colonial charter company that would eventually yield profits to its shareholders survived Herzl's death.[17]

Like Herzl, Zangwill and other territorialist thinkers sought to further what they saw as a mutually beneficial relationship between the Zionists and the British empire by casting Jewish colonial settlement in imperial and civilizational terms. Noting that Jewish settlement in Africa could double the white population of the British colonies, Zangwill compared its potential effects to what he saw as the positive effects of mass white settlement in South Africa. "With all Judea helping us," he noted rhapsodically, "... we could create a colony that would be a source of strength, not only to Israel but to the British Empire, a colony second to none in loyalty to the British flag, a colony that would co-operate in extending civilization from Cairo to the Cape, and which, even when Palestine was resettled by our people, would remain one of the brightest gems in the British Imperial Crown." [18] The Anglo-Jewish diplomat Lucien Wolf, generally opposed to Zionism on the grounds that it threatened Jewish assimilation in Europe, supported the ITO's proposals as well, envisioning a Jewish colony within the British empire that would eventually have "white dominion" status.[19] Similar language came from Eliezer Ben-Yehuda (famous as the reviver of Hebrew as a modern language), who advocated for the East Africa plan in a series of articles published in Palestine: "A great government, one of the greatest in the world, has opened the gates of Africa to us and, like Cyrus, has called on us to go found a free Jewish state there, where we can live as free men and do what is good and right under the paramount protection of the great, free English nation." [20] Such commentary tied the Zionist settlement project in with three already-established British imperial strategies: settler colonialism as a form of territorial control, the use of "protectorates" over ethnoreligious minorities to legitimize imperial intervention, and a discourse of racial superiority.

Zangwill faced considerable opposition to this plan from both within and without the Zionist movement. Although Herzl himself remained interested in the East Africa idea as well as in the possibility of Jewish settlement in Argentina, his sudden death in 1904 turned the movement over to Russian Zionists who opposed the territorialist approach on ideological grounds. Menachem Ussishkin, the Russian Zionist leader who led the charge against the territorialists at the Seventh Zionist Congress, feared that any alternative Jewish settlement would weaken the Zionists' case for Palestine internationally and impede or prevent the emergence of a Jewish state there. He therefore presented the findings of the commission, which was internally divided on the question of whether the East Africa area had promise as a Jewish colony, as proof that the proposed territory was not suitable for white settlement.[21] When the Seventh Zionist Congress decided to drop the proposal, Zangwill and a number of his territorialist colleagues resigned from the

Zionist Organization and founded their own Jewish Territorial Organization (ITO) in August 1905.

The ITO operated as an independent organization until it disbanded in 1925, when most of its members rejoined the mainstream Zionist movement. Territorialism itself would return as a political force in the 1930s, though it would never again be so central to the international discussion of the fate of Europe's Jews. However, it clearly made a mark on British perceptions of the strategic possibilities of Zionist colonization, and recast minority transfer as both a solution to the "Jewish question" and a potential boon to a sponsoring imperial state. Zangwill's and Herzl's impassioned presentation of the benefits of British-sponsored Jewish mass resettlement built the groundwork for British imperial support for the Balfour Declaration more than a decade later. It also formulated some precise ways in which a British imperial agenda could benefit from defining ethnoreligious minorities as *national* entities requiring imperial protection—a model that resonated with already-extant colonial practices.

Zangwill became increasingly embittered as his ideas were voted down and rejected by the Zionist establishment, which viewed the construction of a state in Palestine as a goal whose importance far outstripped providing an immediate solution for Jews suffering under persecution in Galicia and Russia. However, the principles of territorialism, which aligned a specific conception of autonomous, isolationist political rights for national minorities with the needs and territorial ambitions of the British imperial state, had now formed the basis for the British relationship with Zionism and created a template for "minority" removal and resettlement as a useful tool of imperial control.[22]

TRANSFER AND RESETTLEMENT IN THE FIRST YEARS OF THE LEAGUE: SETTLER COLONIALISM AND POPULATION EXCHANGE

At the same time, other iterations of demographic engineering were emerging in former Ottoman lands from the Balkans to the Levant. Techniques of ethnic cleansing and mass deportation, which had already done a great deal to homogenize both the breakaway Balkan states and the Ottoman imperial center, were now being adopted by the emerging Republic of Turkey as Mustafa Kemal sought to expel Allied (mainly Greek) forces from Anatolia and establish an ethnically specific nation-state.[23] The hostilities of the Greek-Turkish war and the mass displacements of the previous two decades formed the backdrop for British, French, and League negotiations with Turkish, Greek, and Balkan actors to create a new regional order in the ex-Ottoman territories. On the basis of the practices of the recent Ottoman-Balkan past as well as European political principles of ethnic nationalism, the Allies and then the League actively pursued population transfer in Bulgaria, Greece, Turkey, and Palestine, exploring practices of ethnic engineering as a way to create stable, homogenous nation-states out of the ruins of the old multiethnic empires. First in the voluntary population transfer between Bulgaria and Greece in 1919, and then in the more extensive compulsory population exchange between Greece and Turkey in 1923, they helped formalize and finalize the ethnic cleansing that had taken place before, during, and after the war—in effect giving a stamp of international authority to the messy local processes by which the Ottoman Empire and its former Balkan territories had come to their present state of separation. At the same time, they also actively committed to supporting and promoting voluntary but large-scale European Jewish resettlement in Palestine.

These mass ethnic transfers in the Balkans had immediate precursors: two treaties proposing exchange of Muslim and Christian populations between Bulgaria and the Ottoman Empire in 1913 and between Greece and some Ottoman territories in 1914. The Ottoman-Bulgarian agreement of 1913 proposed an "authorized reciprocal exchange" of (Christian) Bulgarians and Muslims within fifteen kilometers of the whole shared border, specifying that the exchange was to involve "whole villages."[24] This was mainly an ex post facto formalization of migrations and removals that had already occurred throughout the border zone. Similarly, the 1914 agreement between the Ottomans and the Greek government reflected the on-the-ground reality of the expulsion of Greeks from the Aegean coast that had begun earlier the same year; the Ottoman and Greek agreement that an exchange would be carried out only "on ascertaining [a] spontaneous desire to emigrate" was a hollow recasting of an ongoing violent campaign.[25] In any event, the outbreak of the war rendered the agreements moot; both were signed, but neither was actually carried out.

The idea reappeared after the war. In 1919, nearly 350,000 Bulgarian and Greek citizens were offered the option of compensated relocation for the purpose of creating more homogenous postwar states; approximately half of them accepted the offer and were eventually moved under League supervision in 1924–25. The solution of exchange met with more enthusiasm on the Greek side than in Bulgaria, whose government signed on only after guarantees of the exchange's voluntary nature and maintained the hope that most of the relevant minority communities would not actually leave.[26] The Greek government, on the other hand, hoped that mass emigration from Bulgaria into Greece could be turned toward the colonization of their newly acquired territories in Macedonia and Thrace, helping to shift the demographics of the regions toward a more substantial ethnic Greek majority.[27] The Allies, in reworking the mass refugee crisis of the Balkan wars and the unimplemented earlier Greek-Bulgarian agreements into a formal policy supported by international law, presented mass exchange—with its goal of "unmixing" populations—as a legitimate, internationally sanctioned form of state building.

From the perspective of the League, looking back on the exchange a decade later, the scheme emerged as a successful example of state engineering. As the Mixed Commission tasked with evaluating the success of the exchange put it in 1929, it had created "emigrants on the way to becom[ing] peaceful citizens, instead of refugees addicted to *Comitadjilik* [revolution]."[28] The only barrier to the scheme's total success, according to the League, was its failure to convince all minorities to relocate to their ethnic homeland. The approximately 10,000 Greeks and 82,000 Bulgarians who ultimately declined the League's offer continued to represent a problem in the eyes of both the League, committed as it was to the principle of ethnic nationalism, and the Greek state, intent on creating a homogenous ethnic space. (For Bulgaria, which hoped to retain a significant ethnically Bulgarian population in Greek territories, the remaining minorities constituted less of an issue.)[29]

The reluctance of a substantial portion of these "minority" communities to relocate to their recently designated homeland played a role in the League's decision four years later to abandon the principle of voluntary individual migration in favor of mass deportation. The Greek-Turkish population exchange of 1923, agreed between the new revolutionary Turkish government of Mustafa Kemal and Eleftherios Venizelos's Greek administration, forcibly denationalized approximately 1.2 million Anatolian "Greeks" and 350,000 Muslim "Turks" under the aegis of the League of Nations, with Fridtjof Nansen supervising the proceedings. It took as its justification the same fundamental argument that had been deployed for the Bulgaria-Greece exchange: the making of ethnically homogenous nation-states with a view toward long-term political stability.

Initially, Nansen described the exchange as an "emigration of the *racial minorities* in Turkey and Greece," interpreting the complicated landscape of linguistic, religious, and national identifications in Anatolia and Greece as primarily encompassing racial distinctions.[30] But as the three players—Greece, Turkey, and the League—began hammering out the details, they made the collective decision to define the relevant populations by religion. This became a point of contention as the Commission took up the task of judging which populations and individuals falling into the category "Turkish nationals of the Greek Orthodox religion" would be allowed to claim exemption from the exchange, a question it did not directly address until 1927. The Turkish government lobbied for a purely communal definition that would include every adherent of the Greek Orthodox church regardless of ethnicity—that is, any residual Arab, Albanian, Bulgarian, or Russian Christians affiliated with the Greek Orthodox church would be sent to Greece. The members of the Commission universally rejected this argument, despite the very broad parallel application of the expulsion orders to all Muslims in Greece, on the basis that "all Moslems in Greece of whatever origin (with the exception of Albanians) had a Turkish national consciousness, whereas the same was not true of all followers of the Orthodox religion in Turkey."[31] After consulting the *Encyclopedia Britannica* on the various autocephalous churches of Eastern Orthodoxy, the Commission decided to exclude certain communities that seemed insufficiently Hellenic to qualify for the exchange—for instance, an Arab Greek Orthodox refugee community in Mersin whom the Turkish government wanted to include in the exchange and expel to Greece.[32] For the League, then, religion served as shorthand for ethnonational and even "racial" identity; it was not an irreducible category of its own.

Like the exchanges planned before the war, this proposed homogenization partly reflected already-extant realities on the ground. The Greco-Turkish military encounter that began in 1919 involved mass destruction of property and ethnically conscious brutalities against civilians on both sides.[33] As Turkish nationalist forces advanced to the coast in 1922, burning towns and engaging in reprisals against local populations (culminating in the torching of Smyrna in September), Greek Orthodox communities fled in overwhelming numbers. As in the earlier Balkan wars, the violence itself became the most important factor in redrawing ethnic boundaries; the postwar agreements legitimized, justified, and finalized the process of homogenization. The exchange thus unfolded in two phases. Of the approximately 1.2 million

Christian refugees who acquired Greek nationality in the exchange, all but about 200,000 had already fled by 1923. The remaining exchangees—mainly from central Anatolia rather than the coastal areas—came to Greece as part of a more officially organized exodus over the next three years, at the same time that about 350,000 Muslims expelled from Greece were resettled in the new Republic of Turkey.[34]

The 1923 exchange came out of the confluence of two different but overlapping ideologies and practices of ethnic nationalism: a well-established though uneven pattern of Ottoman and Balkan ethnonational violence and ethnic homogenization, and the postwar international commitment to ethnic nationalism as the foundation of state stability. The League's formal acceptance, legitimization, and continuation of the ethnic cleansing perpetrated by the Turkish army during the war rested partly on its own ideological commitments and partly on a sense of the irreversibility of the recent past. Nansen expressed the combination of these criteria precisely in a statement to the Commission in 1922, saying that the "Great Powers" supported the exchange because "to unmix the populations of the Near East will tend to secure the true pacification of the Near East and because they believe an exchange of populations is the quickest and most efficacious way of dealing with the grave economic results which must result from the great movement of populations which has already occurred."[35] Later generations of politicians in the League often viewed the outcome as a success, as did many later analysts. As recently as 1998, a lecture at the Norwegian Academy of Arts and Letters lionized Nansen as having managed to "excise" a "festering minority question.... The mind boggles at the concept today of a Greek minority in Turkey, and a Turkish one in Greece. How many lives would have been lost on that account?"[36]

The solution of population transfer (and the use of medicalized language to describe the problem of ethnic conflict, which would reappear later in Palestine) arose from the same basic political assumptions that also led the Permanent Mandates Commission to promote the idea of Jewish settler colonialism in Palestine: that mass ethnic migration was an already established trend, that ethnonational homogenization could help stabilize a highly volatile state system in eastern Europe and the Middle East, and that "minorities" would thrive best when transformed into "majorities." While the principles of population transfer for the Balkans were being hammered out, the new Permanent Mandates Commission (PMC)—charged with overseeing the newly created mandates of Palestine, Iraq, Lebanon, and Syria—committed itself broadly to the cause of Zionist resettlement in Palestine.

Unlike other instances of settler colonialism arising under the League's purview, including South Africa and Tanganyika, the League almost without reservation viewed European Jewish claims as trumping Palestinian Arab desires for self-determination from the beginning.[37] In the first years of the mandate, members of the Commission, particularly the Swiss lawyer William Rappard, established personal friendships with Zionist leaders like Chaim Weizmann and expressed sympathy for the Zionist cause. The League repeatedly requested that the British government make reports on the encouragement of Jewish immigration into Palestine, and consistently and repeatedly expressed support for proimmigration British policy—declaring, for instance, that "the Permanent Mandates Commission is of opinion that the policy of the mandatory Power with regard to the land has been wise, and hopes that it will continue more and more to encourage the close settlement of Jews on the land."[38] When challenged by Palestinian Arab leaders, who submitted hundreds of petitions of complaint against Zionist immigration, or by British colonial officials in Palestine, who began to recognize the impossibility of the situation only a few years into their tenure, Rappard and his colleagues on the PMC replied that they were not in a position to challenge the terms of the mandate, which explicitly required British encouragement of Jewish immigration and made no mention of Arab political or national aspirations. As the Commission put it in 1923 in response to petitions protesting the workings of the Palestine and Syria mandates, "It is clear that this demand lies outside our competence."[39]

Historian Susan Pedersen, in her study of attitudes toward settler colonialism at the League, has suggested that the PMC's difference in attitude toward Zionism and other forms of settler colonialism can be attributed to the fact that the settlers were not British nationals and thus could be understood not as part of an imperial project but as "an effort to constitute a new nation within an already colonized space."[40] But beyond this, the PMC viewed Zionist colonization—unlike other settler experiments in the mandates—as part of the League's more general remaking of Europe and the Middle East as a collection of ethnically defined nation-states. The League's assumption that Europe's Jewish minority would have a more secure future in a nationally defined and politically autonomous territory than as a minority population in multiethnic and multireligious states derived in part from earlier conversations surrounding Zionism, territorialism, and the value of resettlement to both minority nationalisms and their imperial protectors. As the Zionist Organization put it in a memorandum addressed to the PMC in 1924, "If the

Jews seek to rebuild their national home in Palestine, it is in order that they may liberate themselves from conditions which at once menace their security and undermine their self-respect."[41] The PMC largely supported this vision and imagined that eventually Jewish immigration to Palestine would result in a Jewish-majority state through which a coherent Jewish national identity could be expressed. One Commission member traced the arc of League visions for Palestine: "There would, in the end, be a Jewish majority capable of administering a Jewish State. . . . The attainment of that end would require government by force, which would have to last until, by gradual evolution, a [Jewish-majority] Palestinian nation had come into being."[42]

Both Ottoman precedent and Zionist ideology, then, lent backing to British, French, and League policies that advocated for various iterations of exchange and resettlement as modes of settling postwar issues of ethnicity and nationhood on terms advantageous to the European imperial powers. Now Nansen and other League officials began to apply these principles of ethnic separation to the Christian "national minorities" coming out of the old Ottoman Empire, whose long history of participation in British and French imperial politics and recent history as targets of the Ottoman state led both British and French colonial officials to hope that they would play an essentially collaborative role in the League-sponsored extension of European empire into the Eastern Mediterranean.

ARMENIAN RESETTLEMENT

The League began to consider a variety of transfer and resettlement plans for displaced Armenians immediately after the peace conference, which made provisions for an Armenian state to be carved out of a fragmented Anatolia. The Armenian population of Syria and Lebanon, which already included more than sixty thousand refugees in camps in Aleppo, Beirut, Alexandretta, and other smaller encampments, exploded again in the aftermath of the French withdrawal from Cilicia and its handover to the emerging Turkish Republic.[43] In December 1921, 16,500 refugees were moved from Mersin to Syria by sea, and 12,000 more entered Aleppo and Alexandretta overland. The following year, all the Armenian children who had been in French orphanages in Adana were transported to Lebanon. In the summer of 1922, an additional 27,000 Anatolia Christian refugees (of whom two-thirds were Armenian, one-third Greek, and about a thousand Assyrian) fled Turkish-controlled territory following further Turkish-Greek military encounters, arriving mainly in Aleppo.[44] During 1922 and 1923, the Turkish government introduced a series of "Abandoned Properties" laws confiscating the land and property of non-Muslims who had fled during the war. The enforcement of these laws, together with tactics of forced urbanization, boycotts, punitive taxation, and various forms of violence against the remaining Armenian (and other non-Muslim) populations in Turkish territory, pushed yet another wave of Armenian refugees into Syria.[45]

League officials were divided on the question of what should happen to what it viewed as a global community of Armenian refugees, estimated at between 300,000 and 400,000 people.[46] The League Council remained interested in the idea of mass "repatriation" to the Caucasus, which would allow the League to maintain its commitment to the concept of Armenian nationhood. But by the mid-1920s Fridtjof Nansen and other officials, including advisors from the Armenian Lord Mayor's Fund and Near East Relief, were also considering a permanent solution for Armenian refugees that would resettle some of them in Soviet Armenia and integrate most of the rest into their various host countries as permanent, legally protected ethnonational minorities. In a report from 1925, Nansen's reporting committee (which included Nansen himself, a French representative from the Ministry of Agriculture, an English representative who was a former official in the Egyptian colonial administration, an Italian from the Commission for Emigration, and a Norwegian representative serving as secretary) placed Armenian refugees in a hierarchy of need based on location, deeming those still in camps in Greece and Turkey to be in the most dire need of resettlement. Those refugees in Syria, on the other hand, could be assisted with local resettlement for permanent incorporation into the Syrian landscape: "The establishment of a maximum of 10,000 [out of a total of about 100,000] on the land would liquidate substantially the acute portion of the Armenian refugee problem in Syria . . . a revolving fund of 1,000,000 French francs would constitute an important step towards the realisation of this proposal."[47] Syria, then, was to be a space for the permanent incorporation of Armenians as a distinctive national community (with League funding), while their nationhood played out in the context of resettlement in "the Republic of Armenia, which must be regarded as the only existing and possible national home for the scattered Armenian people."[48]

The refugee section's two-part plan—to transfer the worst-off refugees to a national homeland in the Soviet Union and permanently settle a separate

Armenian national community in Syria—reflected a familiarity with the language of Zionist resettlement in Palestine and elsewhere. In lobbying the League to approve a loan for this resettlement scheme, Nansen drew on already-extant themes and arguments:

> Our task was to discover some means which would permit of the settlement of "a substantial number of Armenian refugees in the Caucasus or elsewhere." The first problem which we had to consider, therefore, was to find a place where such an establishment might be carried through, where there were possibilities of economic development which would permit an imported population to support itself by its own work.
>
> We examined all the possibilities and we came to the conclusion, unanimously and without any doubt that we were right, that the only place where a large body—I emphasise a *large* body—of the destitute Armenian refugees now in Europe can be settled is in the Armenian Republic of Erivan....
>
> There is this other important fact, namely, that the Armenian refugees themselves wish to go to Armenia and to go nowhere else. They wish to go and make a national home.[49]

Like the territorialist commission twenty years earlier, Nansen's committee focused on providing detailed reports of the geographical and climatic nature of the territory, arguing for the installation of an extensive irrigation system to increase the numbers of refugees the territory could absorb. The commission's report, and Nansen's impassioned speech, made no reference to the Soviet context in which the Armenian republic was operating, except in an oblique assurance "that the Republic of Armenia is a real Armenia, that its population is 95 per cent Armenians, that its Government and its Government departments are exclusively Armenian in personnel, and that the only official language used or tolerated is Armenian.... There is, in fact, in this little Republic a national home for the Armenians at last."[50]

This rosy view of mass Armenian resettlement as a fulfillment of a long-delayed national imagining belied the realities on the ground, the attitudes of actual refugee communities with no particular attachment to the idea of a "return" to Soviet territory, and the Soviet attitude toward the immigrants. Unsurprisingly, the actual desire of many refugees was to return to their original homes and towns in Turkey, an impossibility in the postwar environment.[51] Historian Peter Gatrell cites one Armenian priest attempting to transport a thousand refugees from Tehran to the new Soviet republic as reporting that his charges "'long to return and rejoin their families and work in peace as agriculturalists,' rather than continue to suffer 'moral and physical torment.'" [52] The casting of resettlement in Yerevan as a "return," as Nansen did in his speeches to the League, made little sense to Armenian refugees with no connection to the Soviet Union or, in most cases, the physical territory under discussion. Further, the still-shaky new Soviet government was by no means eager to accept enormous numbers of destitute Armenian refugees, whom it considered both a burden on the state and a potential ideological threat. Fearing international repercussions if they refused the refugees entrance, the Soviet authorities instead constructed elaborate entrance requirements, quizzing applicants on their political affiliations, their Russian-language capabilities, and their families in Russia and abroad.[53]

At the same time, then, the League also began to expend funds for the permanent settlement of Armenian refugees in Syria and Lebanon where, the French representative on the Armenian commission argued, "the results of private initiative, acting in close co-operation with the Government, have been most satisfactory."[54] This collaboration resulted in a further incarnation of the idea of collective "resettlement" for the Armenians: the transfer of some urban refugees to rural, agricultural sites in the Syrian Jazira along the Syrian-Turkish border, the Ghab valley to the west of Hama (soon to become a proposed site of Assyrian refugee resettlement as well), and the sanjak of Alexandretta, as a central part of what the same official called a "final and permanent solution of the Armenian problem."[55] The French mandatory authorities made the claim that this policy was intended to address the needs of refugees who were originally rural populations and could not adjust economically to the urban settings into which they had originally been thrust; one resettlement site on Jabal Musa in the sanjak of Alexandretta, for instance, was reserved specifically for refugees from the Anatolian highlands.[56] But more centrally, these transfers sought to create Armenian buffer zones in various areas where French control remained tenuous—particularly, but not exclusively, in the border areas between the new Syrian mandate state and the Turkish Republic, whose government complained incessantly about the Armenian colonization of the area and Armenian and Kurdish threats to Turkey. Such agricultural resettlement of refugees also served as a way of directing development money away from potentially nationalist Arab Syrians and toward Armenians whose privileges within the mandate state depended on their cooperation. Focusing on Armenian "development" carried the added benefit that extra backing could be solicited for this purpose from the multiplicity of pro-Armenian lobbying groups in Europe and the United

States.[57] This French approach explicitly tagged Armenian refugees as a non-Syrian national population to be used for purposes of internal settler colonialism, with League support and—in some cases—funding.

This rural refugee resettlement aroused further suspicion and unease among Syrian nationalists, some of whom saw parallels between mass Armenian settlement in Syria and mass Jewish settlement in Palestine. Many state officials feared that this kind of land allocation to non-Syrians had the eventual goal of shrinking Syria's territorial footprint. By the 1930s, following the multiple plans to resettle and relocate Armenian refugee communities around Syria in ways that could reinforce state control and buttress French authority, press coverage began targeting Armenians as a nonnative element signifying colonial intervention and reactionary antinationalism. Such commentary often argued that Armenian communities being moved into and around the Jazira represented a threat to the political cohesion and territorial integrity of the Syrian Arab state, parallel to the threat posed by Zionists in Palestine. A 1931 headline in *al-Yawm,* a newspaper based in Damascus, made this comparison clear, asking, "The Armenian national home: Is it a fantasy or a reality?" going on to name a series of spaces in the Jazira that could potentially be compromised by French-supported Armenian claims but that Syrian Arab nationalists wanted included in still-developing concepts of the motherland.[58] Repeated references appeared in the press during the early 1930s about Armenian, Assyrian, and Kurdish claims to a "national home," subtly linking these with Zionism as threats to Arab Syrian and Arab Palestinian nationalisms. Similar language cropped up in Lebanon, where Arab leaders were accusing the Armenian refugee community as early as 1925 of trying to establish a "national home" within Lebanese borders.[59]

Armenians themselves were initially divided on the question of separatism versus assimilation in Syria. As the process of refugee settlement moved forward, Armenian interests fragmented into several political forces: a pro-French bloc led by the clerical leadership and the Dashnak Party, a Hunchak bloc advocating for improved relations with the moderate Syrian Arab nationalists of the National Bloc, and an active Armenian communist branch long committed to a more radical anticolonial Arab nationalism. Gradually, though, the community began to move away from its role as an ally of the colonial state and toward integration within a Syrian nationalist framework. By the late 1930s, as French mandate rule began to falter, Armenians were playing a significant role in the Syrian nationalist movement; four Armenian candidates won office in the 1936 elections that brought the National Bloc to power, and two years later the formerly pro-French Dashnak Party switched its position to favor Arab nationalist movements in both Lebanon and Syria.[60] The French handover of Alexandretta to Turkey in 1939 created yet another Armenian refugee outflow into Syria and further weakened support for the mandate government among Armenians, many of whom now viewed their political future as lying firmly within Syrian Arab nationalism.

ASSYRIAN TRANSFER

The enforcement of resettlement and transfer as a "solution" for ethnic minorities developed in still more dramatic ways for the Assyrian communities of northern Iraq, gathered in refugee camps following their British-driven removal from the Persian and Turkish borderlands in the last stages of the war. As we have seen, as hopes for a return to Hakkari faded and the border with Turkey was finally settled, the British began to plan for a permanent resettlement of the Assyrians as a semiautonomous community dependent on external support in the mandate state of Iraq, plans that echoed the French use of Armenian resettlement in Syria. By the end of the 1920s, the process of settling Assyrian refugees as British collaborators within the Iraqi state—particularly in the north of the country—appeared to be essentially complete.

But the British decision to withdraw and promote a truncated version of Iraqi independence changed the situation. By the mid-1920s, officials in both London and Baghdad were already discussing the possibilities for a withdrawal that would reduce operating costs in Iraq—long a contentious issue within the metropole[61]—while maintaining British influence over a theoretically independent Hashemite government. Despite considerable internal dissent over the desirability of withdrawal, in 1929 the British government formally informed Faysal, the Baghdad administration, and the Permanent Mandates Commission that it was willing to begin the process of drawing up an Iraqi independence treaty and would support Iraq's entrance into the League of Nations in 1932. The League's rather weak protests that Iraq's readiness for independence was in doubt, citing particularly Baghdad's lack of protections for Iraq's "minorities" (Kurds and more particularly Assyrians), failed to stem British determination to shed the mandate. Negotiations immediately began within the Commission and among the British, the Iraqis, and the League to determine the precise nature and limits of Iraqi sovereignty.[62]

In Iraq itself, the debate around terminating the mandate—initially a British proposal about which the League was quite skeptical—helped to fuel a stream of newspaper articles, pamphlets, and public speeches affirming Iraq's identity as Arab and sometimes explicitly demonizing Assyrians, Armenians, and even Arabic-speaking Jews. In 1931, the Kirkuk correspondent for the Iraqi newspaper *al-Istiqlal* accused Armenian refugees in northern Iraq of taking away jobs and business from local Arab artisans and acquiring citizenship by less than legal means, suggesting that the government should "warn these and their likes to sell their properties within 3 months, and confine the right of [land] ownership to the genuine sons of the people."[63] In April of the same year, Christian communities protested an article accusing them of disloyalty and blasphemy by one Haj Na'man al-Adhari, the principal of a *waqf* school outside Baghdad.[64] An Assyrian lawyer in Mosul wrote to the Assyrian activist Hormuzd Rassam to report deteriorating relations between Muslims and Christians in the city, recounting a story that a local priest had been told by a local notable that the Christians would "soon be punished for [their] ingratitude, as we have formed a secret society to stop your game by bloodshed, since nothing else will stop it."[65] Some publications even began to explicitly link the Assyrians with the Zionists, as in another contribution to *al-Istiqlal* accusing the "foreign usurper" of working for "the grant of land in the northern districts to Assyrian vagabonds, whom he has introduced into this country from Persia, Russia and Turkey. We now find these offering competition to Iraqis, it being [the foreigner's] object of *making of Iraq a second Palestine*."[66]

Like Armenians in Syria, many Assyrians were seeking possible modes of assimilation into the postcolonial state, and Assyrian reactions to this sort of hostile and exclusionary language often pleaded for a more pluralistic understanding of Iraqi identity. In the spring of 1931, following this spate of public antagonism, the Chaldean Patriarch for Babylon Yusef Emmanuel took the occasion of an Easter speech in Mosul to advocate for a different vision of the "fatherland":

> I have been hearing of late of venomous and vicious utterances having for aim the tearing to pieces of the fatherland and of harmful propaganda made in the name of the minority and that of the majority and also in the name of the various racial elements and creeds. These are matters which grieve us exceedingly. Our fathers and grandfathers lived for numerous centuries in perfect peace and amity with our Muslim and other brethren, all being copartners in this dear fatherland in times of both happiness and misfortune. We have all

come out of this sacred soil to which we are all bound to return. . . . The advocates of evil attempt to fish in the muddy waters of this distasteful propaganda which had proved disastrous to this country and its inhabitants and which I entreat you to combat with all your might.[67]

Such sources suggest that antirefugee invective, initially targeting Assyrian and Armenian newcomers to Iraq, had now begun to include long-established indigenous Christian groups as well and affect their relationship with the state. It also suggests that some of these "minority" voices, far from advocating for removal and the construction of separate ethnic homelands, remained committed to the idea of integration into a multifarious postcolonial nation. But a more exclusionary concept of Iraqi identity was clearly gaining ground. By the 1940s, this was beginning to extend to Arabic-speaking Iraqi Jews as well, with a number of press articles labeling them threats to the state for their potential attachments to both Zionism and communism and even suggesting their forced expulsion to Palestine.[68] The fact that such racist diatribes represented only a small percentage of the nationalist political views expressed in the Iraqi press did not erase the nervousness some non-Muslim and non-Arab communities—particularly Assyrians who had come to the country as refugees and remained dependent on British economic support—felt as the end of the mandate approached.

The prospect of Iraqi sovereignty and a concomitant British withdrawal panicked many segments of the Assyrian refugee population, especially those whose livelihoods and political claims were tied to the Levies. The Assyrian patriarch Mar Shimun emerged in the late 1920s as the main lobbyist for some guarantee of permanent British protection for an autonomous Assyrian community as Iraq moved toward independence. Mar Shimun had long-established British connections. Born in 1908 in Qudchanis in southern Turkey, he had ascended to the position of patriarch at the age of twelve after his uncle was killed in Turkish attacks on the Assyrians in 1920, but spent the first years of his rule abroad in England studying at St Augustine College in Canterbury and then Cambridge. His father, David, had been an important figure in persuading the initially reluctant Assyrian refugee community to participate in the Levies, and was eventually appointed the Levies' chief liaison officer. Despite some local Assyrian opposition, Mar Shimun returned to Iraq in 1927 and began lobbying the British, the Iraqi government, and the League for the creation of some sort of Assyrian enclave in the north. In 1931, he submitted a petition to the League of Nations outlining the community's requirements for an independent state—one submission among masses of correspondence from both Assyrians and Kurds protesting Iraq's proposed independence and demanding some form of local or regional autonomy or sponsorship for mass Assyrian emigration out of Iraq.[69]

Whatever its rhetorical flourishes about minority rights, the PMC had neither the will nor the power to resist strong British determination to dismantle the mandate. In November 1931, its members gave what J. E. Hall of the Colonial Office termed "a very grudging 'pass' degree"[70] to the plan for Iraqi independence, conditional mainly on the maintenance of most-favored-nation status for League members for ten years and promises to honor already-extant foreign contracts, and, secondarily, on some rather abstract promises about protecting the rights and security of Iraq's minorities, drawing on the language of the Polish treaties.[71]

In disbelief at the termination of the mandate, the Levies "submitted their resignations in a body, and for a time were in a state bordering on mutiny," as one British observer had it.[72] Mar Shimun, sent by the British High Commissioner to persuade the Levies to return to their posts, took on the self-appointed role of representing the Assyrian community directly to the League of Nations on a visit to Geneva. His mission to convince the League to settle the Assyrians en masse in their own autonomous enclave failed utterly. Upon his return to Iraq he entered into equally unsuccessful negotiations with Hikmat Sulayman's government, which ordered his detention following his refusal to give up his claims to political authority over northern Iraq's Assyrians. Forbidden to leave for the Assyrian encampments around Mosul, he languished in Baghdad for some time living at the Y.M.C.A.

In the meanwhile, a group of Assyrian leaders meeting at Amadiyya drew up a document they called the Assyrian National Pact, which (again) called for an Assyrian return to their former homes in the Hakkari region. Failing an agreement with Turkey, they requested a semiautonomous Assyrian "millet" under the leadership of the patriarch, to be located in Amadiyya, Dohuk, and Zakho, along with compensation for lost property, the establishment of Assyrian schools and a hospital, and—crucially—communally based representation in the Iraqi House of Deputies.[73] These requests fell far short of demands for national independence. Rather, they reflected an interest among Assyrian refugees to recover some of the local autonomy they had enjoyed under the Ottomans, even making use of Ottoman language of "millet"-related authority and rights. The desire to reach some form of accommodation with the Iraqi government was evidently strong enough that two Assyrian advocates for emigration—Yako Ismael and Malik Loko—felt compelled to travel around the Amadiyya and Sapna areas "to persuade Assyrians to not accept Iraqi nationality and any new settlement."[74] While Mar Shimun and his allies pleaded with Britain and the League for assistance, other Assyrian leaders like the *qaimaqam* of Dohuk Mekki Beg al-Sherbiti tried to persuade their communities of the viability of working with the new Iraqi government on a new set of resettlement plans.[75]

In this fluid and uncertain situation, divided Assyrian communities debated what to do next while anti-Assyrian invective took hold in Iraqi Arab political discourse. In the Iraqi parliament, representatives publicly denigrated Assyrians as traitors to the nation, invective that reached a large audience through its publication in the Baghdad newspaper *al-Istiqlal*. In the summer of 1933, small groups of villagers and Levies soldiers began to attempt to cross the border into Syria, where the French mandate government vacillated over the question of whether or not to allow Assyrian resettlement there. In late July, one such group clashed with some Iraqi army units on their way back into the country. Rumors that Assyrians had mutilated the bodies of some of the Iraqi soldiers killed in the encounter aroused anger among Iraqis, who began to call for punishment—some, like the Ikha al-Watani Party in Mosul, going so far as to demand the purging of all "foreign elements" from Iraq.[76] The army, assisted by members of Iraq's newly formed civil service and led by the Kurdish general Bakr Sidqi (later the engineer of a successful military coup against Prime Minister Yasin al-Hashimi and briefly the primary authority figure over Iraq before his assassination in 1937) moved into Assyrian villages and began arresting, torturing, and executing unarmed Assyrian men.

As lootings followed the violence, rural residents began to leave their homes and gather in Simele, the largest Assyrian village in the region. On August 11, Iraqi army units arrived in Simele and opened fire on a gathering around the police station. They proceeded to conduct a systematic massacre in the village, killing three hundred men and raping some of the women. This violence spread to other Assyrian areas, where the army continued to murder men, burn villages, and threaten women and children. One report described the massacre as a deliberate effort at annihilation: "Every Assyrian they shot out of hand. Clearly by now the Army had decided that the Assyrians, as far as possible, were to be exterminated."[77] The numbers of Assyrians killed in the massacre is uncertain; the British estimated it at around six hundred, but Assyrian sources cite as many as three thousand casualties. Bakr Sidqi and the army units responsible for the massacre returned to Mosul to a hero's welcome. Triumphalist parades were held in Baghdad, Mosul, and Kirkuk despite official Iraqi denials of government-sanctioned army involvement. As historian (and bitter critic of Iraqi nationalism) Elie Kedourie recorded, "The massacre having taken place, the king decided to return to Baghdad, where his last public act was to stand at a balcony of his palace and acknowledge the acclaim of the delirious crowd celebrating Bakr Sidqi's victory."[78]

Reports of the violence quickly reached Europe and the United States, receiving extensive press coverage and attracting attention from international humanitarian groups like the Save the Children Fund.[79] The public outcry in the West marked the beginning of an international campaign to protest the evident failure of the League, despite its extensive "minority treaties," to protect a Christian community within one of its member states. (This campaign included the Polish lawyer Raphael Lemkin, who denounced the Iraqi army's crimes at a meeting in Madrid in 1933 and kept copious notes on the Assyrian massacres that he would eventually use to construct his legal concept of genocide.)[80] The publicity represented an opportunity for Mar Shimun, whose argument for Assyrian nationhood was buoyed by the wave of international outrage. In 1933, facing deportation, Mar Shimun left Iraq. From Cyprus, still a British crown colony, he launched a campaign for Assyrian independence that encompassed much of the substantial Assyrian diaspora in London, Paris, and the United States, drawing on the tropes of minority nationhood and potential racial extinction that had long circulated in Europe and America.[81]

In Iraq itself, most Assyrian communities were still primarily lobbying for settlement within Iraq in the absence of any real possibility of return to Turkey. Even some of Mar Shimun's supporters focused on the idea of permanent settlement within the country. "Since our arrival in Iraq some 15 years ago, we have loyally served the British and the Iraqi governments. . . . We thought that in consequence of our silence," Assyrian villagers in Dohuk wrote to the British representative in the camps, "we would be compensated by giving us a home in Iraq in return for all our services."[82] But from the diaspora, different themes emerged. In October, following the massacre and his own deportation, Mar Shimun appealed to the League as to the impossibility of remaining under Iraqi rule: "Facts have shown that it is not possible for Assyrians to live under ordinary Iraqi administration and equally impossible for Iraqis to receive them . . . failing some effective protection, the Assyrians will either be destroyed, or the more vigorous will scatter over the earth while the weaker are reduced to the status of serfs of Iraqi landlords."[83] His campaign, referring to the "Assyrian National Movement," clearly presented an Assyrian case for national statehood or, at least, some degree of national political autonomy. Mar Shimun's writings also effectively deployed the language of the League itself surrounding the protection of minorities: "The [Iraqi] Government Officials in Mosul did their utmost to force the Assyrians to submit to their policy which ignored the sacred minorities guarantees given to the League of Nations. . . . The League of Nations betrayed us 1. by giving our old lands and homes to Turkey, 2. by handing us over to an Arab Government."[84]

It could not be denied that the political atmosphere in Iraq was broadly hostile to any idea of incorporating the Assyrians into an Iraqi state and was increasingly supportive of violence against Assyrian communities. As one scholar of Hashemite Iraq has sardonically noted, "The 1930s were typified by national, nationalist, and ultranationalist discourses"[85]—and these were not discourses that admitted either any form of administrative decentralization or the entrance of non-Arab, non-Muslim British protégées into the governing structures of the new Iraqi nation. By 1936, Bakr Sidqi and Hikmat Sulayman were lobbying for support under the motto "Iraq for the Iraqis."[86] Sati ʿal-Husri, one of the period's major spokesmen for a narrower definition of nationalism, worked in educational policy in Iraq during the 1920s and 1930s and articulated an interpretation of the roots of nationalism that clearly excluded Assyrians: "A common language and a common history is the basis of nation formation and nationalism . . . neither religion nor the state nor a shared economic life are the basic elements of a nation, and nor is common territory."[87] An Egyptian critic of al-Husri rightly noted the ethnonational elements inherent in such a philosophy, defining "Husrism" as "the feeling that to labour for the sake of Arabism requires the adoption of an inimical stance towards non-Arab elements whether those elements are found within the Arab environment or outside it."[88] Political societies like the right-wing pan-Arab Muthanna club took an aggressive approach to their promotion of Arab national and political identity; and Jaʿfar al-ʿAskari, one of the main architects of the Iraqi army and two-time prime minister under Faysal, expressed a common feeling toward Iraq's non-Muslim elements when he described them as benefiting unfairly from "material support from religious and missionary establishments abroad."[89] By the time of the massacre, this brand of exclusionary nationalism was well established, and was particularly judgmental toward Assyrians whom many Arab Iraqis viewed as British stooges—hence the street slogan praising the king following the massacre, "Ghazi shook London and made it cry."[90]

The massacre created a major public relations problem for both the British government and the League of Nations. They were too committed to the continued operation of the new Iraqi government to allow the Assyrian debacle to impinge on Iraq's theoretically independent status or its national government, which had allowed for continued British access to Iraqi oil reserves; there would be no British or League inquiry into the massacre, on the grounds that such an investigation could not be forced on a sovereign nation.[91] Nevertheless, the League of Nations had long declared itself an international protector of minorities, and had just made the new state of Iraq sign on to the League's already-extant minority protections regime.[92] The British and the League had now to find a way to extract themselves and the Iraqi government from what had become an international scandal without threatening Iraq's new nominal independence.

They decided that a solution lay in some form of Assyrian "resettlement" on the territorialist model. In 1933, the Minorities Section formed a "Committee for the Settlement of the Assyrians of Iraq," who began their work by writing to a number of foreign governments proposing a mass resettlement of Assyrians within their borders. The committee justified this approach with the argument that Assyrians were already a displaced people: "The Assyrians," declared one member, "could not return to their country of origin and were largely an alien element in the country of their present residence."[93] Their other main argument for resettlement (and condition for location) concerned the refugees' religious affiliation: "The difficulty was not only to find suitable land for the Assyrians, but also to reconcile a Christian community with populations of different race and religion" (i.e., Muslim Arab Iraqis).[94] As in the earlier Greek-Turkish exchange, religion emerged as a primary marker of national difference—an idea influenced by colonial interpretations of communal identity, the League's commitment to Zionism, and the perceived practices of the defunct Ottoman state, which had now become an established principle in European colonial dealings with non-Muslim "minorities" across the Middle East.

The idea of resettlement was immediately taken up in Europe as a cause célèbre. The Save the Children Fund published a brochure in 1935 promoting the idea of resettlement, declaring, "There is not the shadow of a doubt that the majority of the Assyrians are desirous of leaving Iraq and are willing to go anywhere where they can have a modicum of security."[95] In the same year, Leo Amery wrote to the London *Times* echoing these sentiments: "By every ordinary canon of gratitude and honour we are under a direct moral obligation to help this interesting and unhappy little Christian people in the misfortunes that have befallen them."[96] The Iraqi government itself was willing to facilitate mass Assyrian resettlement on the condition that it would not represent a cost to the government, telling the settlement committee that "since a large number of the Assyrians are in a position themselves to defray the cost of transport, settlement, etc., it will be preferable to adopt a system of compulsory contribution by the emigrant towards the cost of settlement."[97] Among the Assyrian refugee communities themselves, even after the massacre, the idea of resettlement was met with resistance. One survey conducted by the Iraqi government determined that only about 2,045 Assyrians could be found who were willing to emigrate, leaving "17,500 persons whose intentions with regard to settlement outside Iraq have to be ascertained"—almost certainly a low estimate.[98]

Greece, Ecuador, Canada, Australia, and South Africa, among others, rejected the League's initial overtures. Brazil responded with potential interest, and negotiations continued with the colonial governments of British Guiana and French West Africa for settlement in Timbuktu. The League also pursued talks with the French mandate government to settle some Assyrians in Syria, either in the Ghab or the Khabur valley, where there was already a small Assyrian settler community. The League sent commissions to both these places, charged with the task of finding suitable spaces, with a focus on opportunities for agricultural work. One member of the League's resettlement committee described the process thus: "Whenever land has been offered for the settlement of the Assyrians, the Committee has asked for as detailed information as possible, more particularly on the following points: exact situation of the land and value from the point of view of output, facilities for development and improvement, kinds of crops, possibilities of stock-breeding, means of communication and markets, possibilities of labour other than stock-breeding and cultivation, liberty granted from the point of view of religion and education. The Committee has always attached particular importance to climatic and health conditions"[99]—precisely the same concerns of the territorialist commission sent to East Africa more than three decades earlier.

The two most seriously considered proposals were for settlement in British Guiana or Brazil. In Brazil, a private company called the Parana Plantation Limited—an enormous coffee, tobacco, and cotton plantation with headquarters in London that had been involved in some League settlement proposals for European Jews—was trying to attract support for the extension of the Rio Grande railway to connect its property with Curitiba and

Paranaguá. To this end, the company wanted to attract overseas settlers, particularly German and Russian refugees; as the chairman told a board meeting in 1933, they were trying to make known "the favourable conditions for overseas settlement obtaining on the Land Company's property. We are hopeful that ere long some of the bread thrown upon these waters may return to us."[100] They had made overtures to the League before the massacre of 1933 made Assyrian resettlement a pressing concern. In June 1933, the company put forth a proposal offering to settle any refugees on its territory for a set price of 400,000 milreis per *alqueire* (2.42 hectares), with rates of 20 to 30 percent interest applying to outstanding debts after one year. The company advertised the climate as "moderate and suitable for northern Europeans" and declaring the "existing colonists" to be "happy and prosperous."[101] When the League began investigating the possibilities of Assyrian resettlement, the plantation's owners declared themselves willing to sell the League land for the project—partly as a money-making endeavor in itself, partly anticipating that the Assyrians could constitute a source of cheap plantation labor, and perhaps also in the hope that large-scale settlement would strengthen the company's case for the railway expansion.

Only a few months after the massacre, the idea of mass Assyrian resettlement in Brazil had gained steam in Geneva. The Brazilian representative to the League, Bandeira de Mello, told a Brazilian newspaper that the League had put forward the idea of emigration to Brazil before, "as a means of a solution of the problem of the unemployed, principally with regard to the Russian and Armenian refugees who had rejected the Soviet regime. Now the question is being brought up again as a means of solving the conflicts of race and religions at present occurring in the Near East." He further noted that Brazil had a history of accepting refugee communities, most recently from Germany, Poland, and the Volga.[102] With mild encouragement from the Brazilian government, the League appointed Brigadier General J. Gilbert Browne, a longtime advocate for Assyrian nationalism and the author of a book on the Levies, to head a commission to examine the territory's suitability for Assyrian settlement. Two other members joined him: T. F. Johnson, secretary general of the Nansen office, and Charles Redard, counselor of the Swiss Legation.

They were already facing opposition within Brazil, with a spate of newspaper articles decrying the idea of mass Assyrian immigration—part of a more general anti-immigrant campaign originally targeting Japanese migrants but now extending to other communities as well. (The commission reported indignantly that it appeared to be "a movement against the arrival in the country of any more people of Asiatic race," adding that many of the articles "were extremely ill-informed, and some of the illustrations which appeared were not of the Assyrians at all." [103]) Following some days of interviews with Brazilian government representatives and stakeholders in the plantation, the members went on to examine the territory itself and were generally impressed, declaring that "the Company's lands were suitable in all respects for Assyrian settlement," [104] and noting with pleasure "the degree of prosperity which can be reached by a new settler, especially one coming to the country with little or nothing at all." [105] They recommended mass Assyrian settlement in two sections south of Londrina, with the Assyrians who were political allies of Mar Shimun placed in one section, and his opponents in the other, "separated by the eighteen kilometres of forest." [106]

Encouraged by the report, the Nansen office began to work with the Paraná company to produce a detailed plan for settling twenty thousand Assyrians there in the space of nine or ten months, declaring that the territory was "specially suitable for mass colonisation and would offer favourable conditions, not only climactic, but also economic, administrative, etc." [107] They were especially concerned to maintain some form of minority rights for the settlers, trying to hammer out precisely what Assyrian rights would be with regard to "full liberty to follow their religion and to manage their religious affairs," as well as to maintain and teach their language and run private Assyrian schools—shades of the minorities rights treaties imposed on eastern Europe.[108] But even as they were working out the details, public opposition to the plan was intensifying, with hundreds of editorials in papers all around Brazil protesting the mass introduction of an alien element who might end up depending on the state for their support.[109] In the summer of 1934, the pressure of this public campaign led the Brazilian government to pass a law severely restricting immigration, ending the negotiations for mass Assyrian resettlement in Paraná.

Undeterred by this failure, the British and the League turned their attention to British Guiana almost immediately. The settlement commission's members were enthusiastic, producing an early report that focused on buoyant descriptions of British Guiana's available land and its agricultural and marketing potential; the only mention of existing populations was a brief note that "apart from the Indians, for whom, as already indicated, well-defined reservations exist, the population consists of only a few settlers and ranchers." [110] As in Brazil, the settlement proposal depended on a relationship

— Errou o caminho, seu Assirio. A casa da mãi Joanna é do outro lado.

FIGURE 2. Political cartoon published in *Jornal do Brasil,* February 1, 1934. "You've got the wrong street, Mr. Assyrian. Mai Joanna's house is on the other side."

with a private, British-owned corporation—in this case, the Rupunini Development Company, which the committee noted was the largest agricultural landholder in the area with a total of 1,500 square miles under either government permits or long-term leases. "The Government of British Guiana," the committee reported, " . . . have taken the necessary steps to secure an option under which if the League of Nations decide to proceed with the scheme, the entire assets of the company could be purchased for the sum of 168,000 dollars at any time prior to the 20th March, 1935." [111] A map was included which showed "Indian Reservations" on several borders of the suggested area for Assyrian settlement. The fantasy of resettlement simultaneously solving a "minority" problem and expanding existing colonial markets in a theoretically uninhabited space, even while aspects of the reports acknowledged a local indigenous population, all reflected the assumptions of earlier "territorialist" plans for settling European Jews in East Africa.

In September 1934, a two-man commission made up of Browne and one Dr. Guido Renzo Giglioli, an Italian agricultural expert who had written a

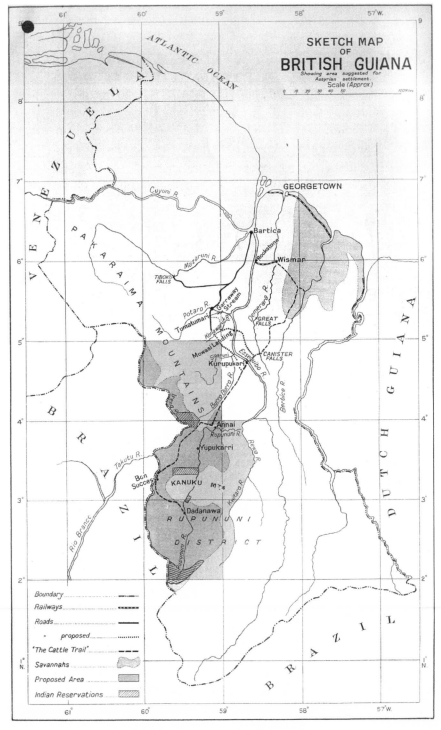

FIGURE 3. Sketch map of settlement proposal for Assyrians in British Guiana, 1934. LNA R3945 4/20316/13763. Courtesy of United Nations Archives at Geneva.

pamphlet detailing agricultural and economic conditions in British Guiana, departed on their mission. The men spent several months traveling through the area, sometimes separately, and the reports of their work recalled earlier tropes of imperial exploration: "Between November 3rd and January 18th the mission travelled about 2,000 miles, of which about 1,000 were accomplished in the saddle or on foot. Of the remainder some 700 were covered in small boats on rivers difficult and laborious to navigate owing to rapids and fallen trees." [112] Such language emphasized both the personal bravery of the explorers and the untouched nature of the land they were considering for settlement and development. Browne and Giglioli ultimately decided that the scheme was impractical, largely because they could not imagine a successful cattle-raising development in the territory as the League had envisioned. "Generally speaking," the committee reported, "the mission concluded that the immediate possibilities of settlement were very limited, and that the eventual prospects depended upon the improvement of agricultural conditions, of market conditions and above all of the cattle situation. . . . [The area was] even then unlikely ever to be capable of maintaining in prosperity more than a fraction of those for whom it is the Committee's task to try to find a home." [113]

While these events were unfolding, negotiations were also going on over a more modest plan to resettle at least part of the Assyrian refugee community in Syria. The idea of moving Assyrians into French-controlled Syrian territory originated partly with the refugees themselves. Before the massacre, in July 1933, a group of Assyrian tribal leaders had written to the minister of the interior in Baghdad to explain their intentions in crossing the border: "The Iraq Govt Policy was explained to us both regarding settlement & Patriarch. Mutasarrif openly said 'those unsatisfied with this policy are free to emigrate from Iraq,' accordingly we have come to the frontier and we request the Iraq Govt not to block the road to those who want to join us. We got [sic] no intention to fight unless forced." [114] Unlike the idea of resettlement in Brazil, which was driven primarily by diaspora leaders and League and British enthusiasm, this scheme had some local support among the Assyrians themselves, to the point that some had begun to attempt crossing into Syrian territory in advance of a formal agreement.

The French government, fearful of the chaos that expulsions might bring and seeing an opportunity to use the Assyrians to establish a greater degree of state control in difficult rural areas, agreed in principle to accept a limited number of Assyrian refugees into Syrian territory following the massacre.

The League itself was so enthusiastic about this plan that some officials proposed making a commercial film about the resettlement proceedings, declaring that it would be an ideal vehicle for promoting the League's unique capabilities for simultaneously solving a problem of ethnic conflict and developing underused territory (a familiar territorialist trope):

> All the main elements of the League are involved, for the subject is at once political, economic and humanitarian. Political, in that the film would show the settlement by the League of a thorny local problem which has been disturbing the Near East for a considerable time; economic, in that the film would show what the League can do to help the development of uninhabited land; and humanitarian, in that the film would show how well an international organisation can handle a problem akin to the refugee problem when all national efforts have failed.[115]

They went on to add that "another advantage is that a film on the Assyrians is highly unlikely to arouse any strong political feeling."[116]

Initially, settlement proposals focused on the Ghab, a flat plain west of Hama whose agricultural productivity was hampered by its swampiness but which French and League officials believed could be made cultivatable through a program of systematic drainage and irrigation. One French member of the League subcommittee investigating the possibilities listed the major projects as "essential works (the construction of the Acharna barrage, the dredging of the Orontes, the tunnel of Karkor etc.) which are necessary not only for the reclamation of the land allocated to the Assyrians but also for the reclamation of the remainder of the Ghab Plain in due course."[117] By 1936, this proposal had aroused significant opposition among Syrian Arab nationalists who opposed the use of state funds to accommodate non-Syrian, non-Arab refugees in the region, as well as local landowners who were demanding higher prices for the land to be appropriated for the project than had been originally budgeted.[118] The costs of the drainage and dam-building plans also proved to be beyond the budget of the French mandate government, already under significant financial and political pressure from rising nationalist unrest across Syria. The eventual estimate of total costs for the irrigation engineering projects, including compensation for landholders whose land would be flooded, came to about 86 million francs in League estimates (of which the financial subcommittee admitted they could not find 13½ million) and more than 122 million francs in some of the French estimates.[119] Further, the original French plan to clear land for the Assyrians by forcing foreclosures on indebted properties in the Ghab became untenable as nationalist feeling rose in 1936. The French ambassador Alexis Leger wrote to the League of the multiple difficulties the scheme was raising:

> The increasingly uncompromising attitude of the majority elements in the Levant is a fact. . . . Already landowners are showing little disposition to offer the Trustee Board acceptable terms and this at a time when the current political evolution deprives the mandatory authority of part of the means previously at its disposal to create a conciliatory state of mind. Furthermore the Assyrian immigration is arousing a Press campaign of considerable liveliness, and it is to be apprehended that this matter, by drawing attention to the question of minorities, may have harmful effects on the fate of members of the indigenous minorities.[120]

As the London *Times* reported more simply, Syrian Arabs were "not at all anxious that men of their country and religion should lose land for the benefit of a batch of Christian aliens."[121]

The next proposal, then, moved away from the Ghab in favor of a much more remote and sparsely populated area in the Khabur valley, in the northeastern reaches of Syria. This was where a small number of Assyrians (about five hundred) who had crossed the border illegally in 1933 following the massacre had been allowed to stay, with their families eventually joining them as part of a brokered agreement between the French High Commission and the Iraqi government. These were joined in 1935 by about 340 more settlers who had been residents in the Mosul refugee camp set up just after the massacre; another thousand "taken from among the poorest members of the Mosul community" were transferred shortly thereafter under Iraqi government supervision.[122]

The French administration had less purchase but also met with less resistance in this region, where land acquisition plans rested mainly on the appropriation of territory from local Bedouins. With funds from both the French and (reluctantly) the Iraqi government, Assyrian villages were built and maintained with some limited assistance for food and agricultural supplies. The proposal to expand these settlements clearly demonstrated the limits of French knowledge of the area; a French foreign ministry memo on the resettlement idea cited five possible locations, of which only one was "sufficiently well known for the projection concerning to be considered a certainty as of now."[123]

FIGURE 4. Assyrian refugees preparing to leave Mosul refugee camp for Syria, 1937. LNA R3941 4/23407/11757. Courtesy of United Nations Archives at Geneva.

Even in this relatively remote locale the plan met with resistance from Syrian nationalists, and several members of the League committee proposed trying to put in place the legal "option" to buy land that had been proposed in British Guiana as insurance against the same resistance from uncooperative Arab landowners that they had faced in the Ghab.[124] Resistance was also rising from the Iraqi government, which had grudgingly contributed funds for the scheme but now declared that the Iraqi administration would oppose "any further transfer of Assyrians from Iraq to the Khabur unless as part of new scheme to remove the Assyrians permanently far away from Iraq." [125] The uncertain future of the French mandate state after the French government's refusal to ratify the 1936 treaty of independence with Syria preempted further negotiations, though the approximately nine thousand Assyrians who had been settled in the Khabur at various times between 1935 and 1937 remained—against the will of the transferred refugees themselves, who repeatedly demanded repatriation to Iraq and were refused. "When it was explained to them that the Government of 'Iraq would not permit them to recross the Tigris," one observer reported, "they finally settled down to make the best of a bad bargain." [126]

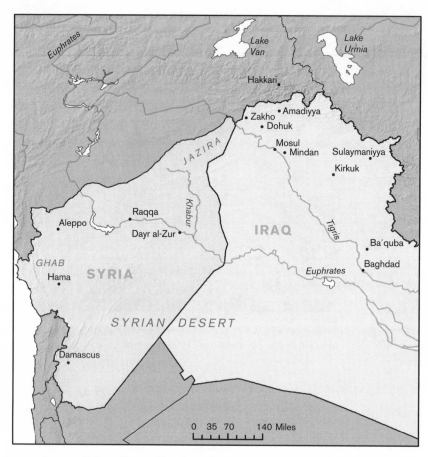

MAP 3. Interwar Syria and Iraq and locations of various sites of proposed or realized Armenian and Assyrian settlement in the Jazira, Ghab, and Khabur regions. Map by Sachi Arakawa.

THE REVIVAL OF TERRITORIALISM

In the late 1930s, at the same time that the British, the Iraqi government, and the League were debating the possibilities for mass Assyrian resettlement, a constellation of factors combined to revive interest in territorialism. The increasingly violent persecution of Jews in central Europe—encompassing the Nuremberg laws and leading up to the Kristallnacht attacks on Jews across Germany in November 1938—alongside the broad refusal of the Western democracies to admit large numbers of Jewish refugees, and the outbreak of a major anti-British and anti-Zionist revolt in Palestine, were collectively leading to a European Jewish refugee crisis of epic proportions.

In this context, a conference of the various territorialist associations held at the Russell Hotel in London in the summer of 1935 resulted in the foundation of the Frayland Lige (Freeland League), a successor to the ITO that would press for mass Jewish resettlement outside Palestine in precisely the same terms being deployed by proponents of Assyrian resettlement. Like the Assyrian plans, the Frayland Lige called for Jewish resettlement into an internally and culturally autonomous canton rather than the sovereign nation-state Zangwill and Herzl had originally envisioned.

The leading figure of the new territorialist movement, a Latvian-born lawyer named Isaac Steinberg, framed its goals and approaches in much the same ways that Zangwill had. Like Zangwill, he focused on the benefits—indeed, the necessity—of choosing an uninhabited space, and represented Jewish settlement of empty imperial territory as beneficial both to the Jews and to the British empire. He thought that Australia, which he conceived of as having vast swathes of uninhabited territory, represented the most promising site, and spent some years during and after the Second World War negotiating with the Australian government for permission to settle European Jews in the western territory of Kimberley, where they could retain a Jewish cultural identity while also becoming essentially Australian: "It is impossible for a man's body and imagination to remain unchanged in a land of kangaroos, crocodiles and cockatoos, of bottle-trees, man-high grass and fiery sun." [127]

Australia was an especially popular proposed destination for Europe's Jews in the many transfer schemes the League received in the late 1930s. One group based in Geneva wrote to the Australian delegate at the 1938 Evian Conference (convened by Franklin Roosevelt to consider the increasingly desperate plight of European Jews) that Swiss experts had considered "the western parts of North America, Canada, Africa (Rhodesia, Kenya-land, Uganda), South Africa, and Australia. . . . there will be no dearth of many fertile, healthy and extensive areas." [128] They went on to detail the benefits for the sponsoring powers, suggesting not only that resettlement was a way to reduce the population of undesirable minorities and refugees in the metropole but that it would also mean "a reduction in the competition of the indigenous population on the home market" and that "in all probability the colonists would remain in economic contact with the Promoter States . . . thereby influencing favourably the export trade of those countries." [129] Another territorialist writing from Warsaw proposed a scheme in which an international body should be created "to provide great quantities of land in different countries" for Jewish refugees. [130] Another proposal from London emphasized the appeal of Australia in classic imperial terms: "Australia is about the size of the United States of America, which has about 130 millions of inhabitants, whilst the number of inhabitants of Australia is only 10 and ½ millions, with the tendency to become even less populated, considering, that the natives of that country are physically so much exhausted, that they will probably become extinct in a couple of decades . . . [Jewish] installation in Australia should be patronised and facilitated by Great Britain." [131] Territorialist proposals even came from Jews in Palestine, including one from Tel Aviv with the warning that "it is of the greatest import for the regeneration of the Jewish race that the climate of the countries of immigration should not be tropical in view of the fact that intellectual properties are bound to degenerate under the conditions of a tropical climate." [132]

Such petitions, coming in to the League from all corners of the globe, attested to the continued power of the territorialist framework and the idea of mass minority resettlement. Michael Hansson, president of the League's Nansen Office on Refugees, encapsulated the League's approach to the concept of Jewish resettlement in his Nobel Peace Prize acceptance speech in 1938: "For some of the Jewish leaders the idea of a return to Palestine remains a sacred one, but many others have come to the conclusion that it would be better for them to try to settle elsewhere. They are therefore seeking a country which they can look upon as their home and which can, after a time, receive a mass immigration of Jews from Europe; whether this be in America, Africa, or Australia does not really matter as long as they can be together on their own, for they wish to avoid creating new Jewish problems." [133] Even Franklin Roosevelt was interested in this idea, asking the geographer Isaiah Bowman to propose some locations where Jews might be resettled as a response to Kristallnacht: "What I am looking for is the possibility of uninhabited or sparsely inhabited good agricultural land to which Jewish colonies might be sent." A few years later, Roosevelt's wartime "Migration Project" proposed mass Arab transfers from Palestine to Iraq and the construction of a Jewish state in Palestine as two linked components of a "New Deal for the Middle East." [134]

Through the 1940s, the Frayland Lige continued to put forth proposals for mass Jewish settlement elsewhere, including New Zealand, Canada, and Suriname, arguing for relocation as a logical response to the horrors of the Holocaust and the political and logistical problems posed by the postwar "displaced persons" camps. But in the aftermath of the 1948 war and the emergence of the Israeli state, Steinberg and his colleagues used their platform to issue criticisms of Israel, which they saw as betraying Jewish morals in its turn to militancy and aggression. The Israeli army's massacre of civilians in the West Bank town of Qibya in 1953 was an occasion for judgment of the harshest kind: "The fact that Jews—be they soldiers or citizens at large— could in cold calculation murder dozens of innocent men, women, and children in the Arab village of Qibya, is in itself a hair-raising crime. But far worse is the indifferent or satisfied reaction to this event on the part of the Jewish population in Israel and almost everywhere else in the world. It has been made 'kosher' by all possible strategic, political, sentimental arguments—and the moral issue has been completely ignored." [135] Despite these protests, Steinberg's Lige had lost the attention of the international community, which had no stomach to imagine other Jewish "solutions" in the aftermath of the Holocaust. When he died in New York in 1957, the Lige shut down.

This minor-league revival of the territorialist idea, at the same moment that resettlement had become a cause célèbre for the Assyrians and at the end of a longer period of Armenian resettlement across the Arab Middle East, indicated the longevity of the idea at the international level. Although Steinberg did not succeed in attracting the same level of international attention as the earlier generation of territorialists, his work indicated the continued vibrancy of two narratives: the idea that removal constituted the only solution to an increasingly dire situation for European Jews, now clearly demarcated as a "minority," and that there was, somewhere within the British empire, some empty space in which this minority could be recategorized as a nation, if not a state. The dialing down of territorialism's political ambitions from statehood to cultural enclave nevertheless indicated a hard truth about the movement: that it depended entirely on an imperial framework. As Britain's empire went into decline, so did the idea of preserving some kind of Jewish (or other "national minority") colonial space within it.

· · ·

The transfer solution, in its essence, rested on the assumption that empires (or, in the case of the League of Nations, international defenders of imperial rule) had both the capacity and the incentive to dole out territory for settler colonial purposes. This represented an entirely plausible idea at the beginning of the twentieth century, when settler colonialism represented a standard imperial strategy, the racial hierarchies of empire served to legitimize and promote settler colonial ideologies and practices, and the legal concept of "terra nullius" encouraged imperialists to think in terms of strategic approaches to unclaimed territory.[136] (Fridtjof Nansen's own previous career as an explorer of uninhabited, unincorporated Arctic lands may have influenced his views on this point.) The late nineteenth- and early twentieth-century history of large-scale voluntary migration, including mass emigration by "minorities" like European Jews, also contributed substantially to the plausibility of transfer as a mode of remaking geopolitical realities. But by the late 1930s, with challenges to empire mounting, it became less and less likely that the European empires—and by extension the League—would be able to locate "empty" imperial spaces that could be used for the resettlement of national minorities. The opposition the League faced to its resettlement plans for the Assyrians—in Brazil, and also in colonized spaces like Australia, South Africa, and especially Syria—reflected the increasing impotence of the British and French empires in the face of rising nationalisms, anticolonial activism, and internal challenges. The League's internal disarray and its increasingly evident structural limitations further contributed to the devolution of earlier grand schemes for resettlement and transfer into a hodgepodge of smaller-scale, piecemeal solutions by the late 1930s.

The concept of transfer was built on a proposed collaboration between "minority" settlers and colonial governments. In Armenian, Assyrian, and Jewish territorialist visions, settler colonies could benefit minority nationalists—providing them with political autonomy, economic protection, and international recognition—while at the same time extending the reach of imperial power and providing new labor, military recruits, and captive markets for the host state and the protecting empire. But as the viability of settler colonialism faded (and, not incidentally, as the Nazi use of transfer ideology to reengineer populations in a German-controlled central Europe was tainting the idea of resettlement),[137] its advocates began to give up on the idea in favor of another solution to the problems of minority nationalism: partition.

FOUR

The Partition Solution

By the 1930s, with the rise of ethnonational hostilities and the decline of the imperial framework that had briefly made transfer seem viable, local activists and mandate officials alike in Palestine, Iraq, and Syria began to look for other modes of structuring the state by ethnicity. In Palestine in particular, as Jewish immigration driven by European persecution skyrocketed along with Arab dispossession, Palestinian Arab resistance and Zionist reprisal led to an increasingly impassioned public debate about how to resolve the seemingly impossible situation that the mandate had created.

The British had occupied Palestine at the end of 1917 and almost immediately set up an interim government, the "Occupied Enemy Territory Administration," to administer the country. In 1920, the negotiations at San Remo formally assigned the mandates for Palestine and Mesopotamia to Britain, and Syria and Lebanon to France. The British acted quickly to set up a more permanent colonial bureaucracy; their first high commissioner for Palestine, the Jewish Liberal politician Herbert Samuel, arrived in Jerusalem the same year. The mandate agreement, binding the British not only to govern Palestine but also to encourage mass European Jewish immigration with a view toward building a "Jewish National Home," was finalized in July 1922; in September an addendum carved out Transjordan as a separate principality, to be administered by the Hashemite scion Abdullah. Both agreements came into formal effect following the ratification of the Treaty of Lausanne in 1923, by which time the British mandate government had already been operating in Palestine for three years.

In 1914, on the eve of the First World War, Palestine had a population of about 722,000 people: approximately 582,000 Muslim Arabs, 80,000 Christians, and 60,000 Jews, about 8 percent of the population.[1] Following the

Balfour Declaration of 1917, European Jewish immigration to Palestine rapidly became a significant demographic phenomenon. In 1922, British census information suggested that the Jewish population had risen to more than 83,000, about 11 percent of the population; by 1931, it was 175,000, about 17 percent; by 1945, in the wake of the Nazi crimes against the Jews in central and eastern Europe, it had reached more than 550,000, 31 percent of the total. This astounding and rapid demographic transformation had especially dramatic effects on the social, political, and economic landscape of Palestine because of the practices of the British mandate administration. Under mandate rule, the Yishuv (the European Jewish settler community) enjoyed a number of collective rights and privileges not extended to the Arabs: a recognized internal representative government, explicitly nationalist schools and language policies, a flag, and the development of military capabilities. The stated commitment of Labor Zionism—the most important political faction in the Yishuv after 1920—not to employ Arabs in any capacity on Jewish-held settlements and land (though often not successfully enacted) further divided the communities.[2]

These factors combined to create mass unemployment and dispossession among the rural Arab peasantry in the 1920s and 1930s, resulting in large-scale rural migration to slums ringing all the major urban centers of Palestine. Arab protest against Zionist immigration and land purchase began almost as soon as the mandate was in place and intensified through its first decade. In 1929, demonstrations and protests at the Western Wall turned violent, killing 133 Jews and 116 Arabs.[3] Demonstrations broke out again in 1933 despite brutal British police suppression; and in 1936 an Arab general strike turned into a three-year rebellion in which the British lost control of much of the country.[4]

This revolt triggered the first formal proposal for the partition of Palestine. In 1937, a Royal Commission sent out from London to investigate the "unrest" proposed to divide Palestine into three separate territories: a continued British mandate over Jerusalem and its surrounds, an independent Jewish state, and an Arab state to be attached in some unspecified way to Transjordan. In debating the British partition proposal, the Permanent Mandates Commission began to redefine Zionists in Palestine as a "minority" who would inevitably face oppression in an independent, majority-Arab Palestinian state. This novel application of the minority label to a European settler colonial community allowed advocates to defend partition as a mode of protecting minority rights and the principle of national self-determination—the same rationales used to promote the idea of transfer. And here again, as in earlier objections to transfer, local communities sought an effective method of opposing proposals of partition by making active use of the formal legal language and channels provided by the League of Nations itself.

PRECURSORS TO PARTITION: SYRIA AND IRAQ

Colonial governments from 1919 onward had repeatedly experimented with redrawing Middle Eastern borders. In both Syria and Iraq, the early French and British mandate governments discussed redividing territory as a way to ease the burdens of imperial governance. In Syria, this took the form of carving out Lebanon as a separate state to be dominated (under supervision) by the Maronite community, a long-standing recipient of French patronage, and dividing up the remainder of the Syrian state into ethnically inflected "statelets." In Iraq, the British considered the possibility of carving out the northern part of the state to constitute a separate Kurdish or Kurdish/Assyrian nation, before abandoning the idea in favor of a unified Iraq under an imported monarch. Unlike in Palestine, these envisioned or enacted partitions did not involve population transfer or the creation of homogenous ethnic enclaves—largely because of the advocacy and activity of the indigenous "minority" communities involved, who mainly imagined their political future as a new version of Ottoman-style local autonomy rather than an absolute form of national self-determination. Neither the Maronites, nor the Kurds, nor the Assyrians (with a few exceptions, mostly coming from the diaspora) advocated strongly for independent Western-style nation-statehood in the immediate aftermath of the war. Rather, they thought of themselves as communal units that had enjoyed significant autonomy under the Ottomans, which they did not now wish to lose to Sunni Arab-dominated urban centers.

The idea of dividing Syria into two separate mandates arose both from imperial concerns about governance and from the longer history of French Catholic involvement in the Mount Lebanon region.[5] The well-established Jesuit presence in Lebanon advocated strongly for some form of autonomy for Lebanon's Maronites, as did the Maronite patriarch Elias Butrus Hoyek (Hawayik) and some of the leading Maronite clergy.[6] To increase the purchase, both political and economic, of what would have been a tiny Christian enclave centered on Mount Lebanon, the French added some predominantly Muslim coastal regions (including Beirut) to the Lebanese mandate state, thus creating a new national formulation with a slight but not overwhelming

Christian majority. The Maronites would dominate the new state of Lebanon, but at about 30 percent of the population their numerical strength was not so great that they could maintain their position without French assistance.[7]

The French had discussed the separation of Lebanon from Syria for years, and hoped to rely on Syrian and Lebanese diaspora support for its accomplishment. During the war, the French military recruited a Syrian unit of the Légion d'Orient from the very broad Syrian-Lebanese diaspora in France, Latin America, and the United States, with the purpose of creating what historian Simon Jackson calls "a global auxiliary political constituency, nominally willing to back French plans for the postwar Eastern Mediterranean."[8] The French Foreign Ministry likewise tried to create a base of support for its postwar Syrian plans by creating global communications networks to lobby for French interests among the Syrian diaspora. George Samné, a Melkite journalist originally from Damascus but now based in France, and Shukri Ghanim, a Maronite from Beirut, accepted French funds to run a recruitment organization called the Comité central syrien, charged with presenting both military service with the French army and a potential postwar French colonial government as modes of liberating Syria from oppressive Ottoman Muslim rule.[9] Though many diaspora groups, even those accepting French money, supported the emergence of some form of Greater Syria, there were also a few diasporic Lebanist groups working for the detachment of Lebanon as an independent Christian state. Yusef Sawda, the head of the Alexandria branch of the separatist Alliance libanaise, laid out a Lebanese nationalist case for independence in his 1919 book *Fi Sabil Lubnan,* which defined Lebanese national identity as Phoenician rather than Arab.[10]

Nevertheless, the postwar delimitation of Lebanon and Syria met with resistance from nearly every party involved except a small group of Maronite elites. Syrian nationalists, mainly educated urban elite Sunnis who had just come through the brutal and humiliating French military demolition of Faysal's constitutional monarchy set up in Damascus, resented the loss of Beirut and the coast as well as the agriculturally important Biqa valley. The residents of Mount Lebanon were divided, with Druze and Muslim notables generally opposed to detachment from Syria and Christians speaking on both sides of the issue.[11] Even some leading Maronites were uncertain about the wisdom of Lebanon's creation, particularly the inclusion of so much Muslim-dominated territory. George Samné, who not long before had collaborated with the French in recruiting sympathetic Maronites from the diaspora, argued against the expansion of the Christian state, calling it the "squaring of a circle"; the Maronite politician and later architect of the National Pact Emile Eddé privately told French officials he would support the removal of Tripoli and Akkar from Lebanon and their reassignment to Syria.[12]

The question of the postwar disposition of greater Syria mobilized activists throughout the substantial Syrian diaspora. The New Syrian National League, based in New York, sent the prominent writer Abraham Rihbany to Paris in 1919 armed with petitions signed by thousands of Syrians in the United States advocating for Syrian independence under American leadership.[13] In Cairo, the editors of two prominent Syrian journals led the charge for a "Syrian Union" party demanding a decentralized greater Syrian federation including Palestine and Lebanon.[14] Similar language came from Khalil Saʿadih's anticolonial Syrian nationalist party based in Buenos Aires, which explicitly rejected the sectarian logic of dividing Lebanon from Syria: "We are no longer Muslim, Christian, Druze, or Jew. . . . We are now Syrians, Lebanese, and Palestinians, without factions, religions, or sects."[15]

France's decision to sponsor a delegation headed by the Lebanese-Egyptian activist Daud ʿAmmun and his Hizb al-Ittihad al-Lubnani (Party of Lebanese Unity), based in Cairo, reflected a careful search for diaspora actors willing to lend legitimacy to an essentially imperial agenda. There were also some local leaders interested in working toward some form of Lebanese autonomy, especially among the Maronite elites of Mount Lebanon; the Maronite patriarch Elias Hoyek, in particular, developed a vision for a postwar Lebanon that drew on a tendentious vision of a "historical" Lebanon separate from Syria. But such visions were provisional, subject to negotiation, and heavily influenced by the political agendas of diasporas; as historian Carol Hakim points out, it was not until some months after the end of the war that the patriarch and his administrative council "first staked a claim for the independence of a clearly delimited Greater Lebanon, whose contours clearly bore the mark of the programs formulated by the emigrants abroad."[16] And even within this group there was no firm commitment to working out a program of independence in conjunction with France. In 1920, seven members of the Lebanese Administrative Council tried to bypass the French authorities and reach a separate independence agreement with Faysal's Syrian Arab government based in Damascus—an effort for which they were arrested, charged with treason, and sentenced to years of exile by a French military court.[17] The division of Syria and Lebanon into two separate states was thus accomplished for French colonial purposes, without a significant devolution of power onto any of the local political actors in either part of the now divided region.

Discussions of dividing Iraq by ethnicity to produce a separate Kurdish or Kurdish/Assyrian enclave in the north were similarly dominated by British imperial concerns. In the immediate aftermath of the war, the British were interested in the possibility of supporting some form of Kurdish tribal governance in northern Mesopotamia as a kind of client substate, to the extent that they appointed the Kurdish leader Sheikh Barzinji governor of Lower Kurdistan in December 1918 and expressed the hope that low-paid Kurdish military units could eventually take over from the British units stationed there the task of defending Mesopotamia.[18] But facing a multiplicity of local Kurdish rebellions against the imposition of British rule in the first years after the war, alongside a small elite movement touting a broader form of Kurdish nationalism, the British abandoned their plan to rely on Kurds as colonial collaborators and focused instead on remaking Iraq as a client monarchy headed by the imported Hashemite king Faysal.[19] Many Kurds and Assyrians, even those who had been brought to Iraq as refugees dependent on the British army, expressed a willingness to live under Turkish rule given a certain degree of local autonomy—a position that continually surprised the British as they sought to exert control over the Mosul region.[20]

This Kurdish and Assyrian emphasis on local control over "national" self-determination, and their reluctance to work with the British and acquiesce to European colonial rule, quickly led British officials to decide that the Hashemite monarchy and a cohort of Sunni administrators drawn from the old Ottoman ranks would make easier partners (though, of course, the British continued to depend on Assyrian military assistance). Further, the imperial determination to ensure control over the oil fields in the north by tying Mosul to the central government of Iraq meant that by 1925 the British had essentially committed to an imperial policy of maintaining Iraq as a single client state. As in Lebanon, these decisions were taking place against a backdrop of colonial consolidation of power.

Neither of these territorial divisions constituted partition in the modern sense: that is, although they proposed to divide up territory in new ways, they did not plan to devolve real political authority onto local populations newly defined as national.[21] As such, they resembled earlier imperial divisions of territory from above for administrative purposes more than the later partitions of the twentieth century: Korea, Vietnam, India, Germany. As sociologist Robert Schaeffer has put it, "The simultaneous devolution and division of power is what distinguishes partition in these countries from the division of other countries in previous times."[22]

In both Syria and Iraq, power remained with the colonial authority. While the (abrogated)[23] mandate for Mesopotamia made nods to the way ethnic identity might inform or relate to citizenship, it allotted political control so firmly to the mandate authorities as to allow for little discussion of self-governing ethnic nationalisms within the subject body. The text of the mandate included two references to the possibility of ethnonational autonomy, both limited: first, "the right of each community to maintain its own schools for the education of its own members in its own language" (reflecting the language of the minorities treaties for eastern Europe); and second, the possibility of allowing the mandate government to established "a system of local autonomy for predominantly Kurdish areas as [the high commissioner] may consider suitable."[24] The extremely limited nature of Iraqi sovereignty, made especially clear in the promise to "secure the co-operation of the Mesopotamian Government, so far as social, religious, and other conditions may permit," rendered the matter of ethnic differentiation the purview of the mandatory state. The same language appeared in the mandate for Syria and Lebanon, which noted laconically, "The Mandatory shall, as far as circumstances permit, encourage local autonomy." This document, too, gave particular and limited notice to communal identities within the state, allowing for the right to communal schools and language instruction as well as management of "religious communities and sacred shrines belonging to the various religions, the immunity of which has been expressly guaranteed."[25] It was the mandate authority, not local representatives, who could dictate the rights and limits of local communal or ethnic autonomy.

In Palestine, by contrast, the possibility of eventually devolving power onto the Zionists was written into the mandate. It provided a clear framework of ethnonational sovereignty for the nonindigenous population and tied citizenship rights to ethnic affiliation. Acknowledging and incorporating the Balfour Declaration, the League declared that "the Mandatory shall be responsible for placing the country under such political administrative and economic conditions as will secure the establishment of the Jewish national home, as laid down in the preamble, *and the development of self-governing institutions,* and also for safeguarding the civil and religious rights of all the inhabitants of Palestine, irrespective of race and religion."[26] The mandate laid out the nature of these self-governing institutions for the Jewish settler community: "An appropriate Jewish agency shall be recognised as a public body for the purpose of advising and co-operating with the Administration of Palestine.... The Zionist organisation, so long as its organisation and constitution are in the opinion of the Mandatory appropriate, shall be recognised as such agency." [27] It made specific provision for working with the proposed Jewish agency to develop public infrastructure and resources. Finally, unlike the other mandates, this document specifically proposed a "nationality law ... framed so as to facilitate the acquisition of Palestinian citizenship by Jews." [28]

The founding documents of the Palestine mandate thus legally enshrined the principle that Jewish (if not Arab) ethnonational identity was fundamental to subjects' relationship with the state and could form the basis for eventual political sovereignty. Though Palestinian Arab communities repeatedly demanded precisely the same kind of national recognition from the beginning of the mandate, they did not enjoy the same defined relationship with state authority in the mandate's foundational texts. Instead, their rights were noted as being "civil and religious"—the same words that had appeared in the Balfour Declaration—and no specific representation, citizenship, or immigration rights were mooted for them. This legal differentiation between the Jewish settler community, defined as national, and the indigenous Arab community, defined as civil or religious, structured the mandate from the beginning.

THE PEEL COMMISSION AND THE NARRATIVE OF IRRECONCILABILITY

In the spring of 1936, an Arab general strike brought Palestine to a standstill. Anti-Zionist and anti-British riots brought out huge numbers of people and challenged the British capacity to maintain public order. By September, the British had more than twenty thousand troops stationed in Palestine in an attempt to quell the uprising.[29] Facing widespread and organized Arab resistance, the British government appointed a Royal Commission to investigate the causes of the unrest and make policy recommendations for improving the situation in Palestine. The members of the commission, led by the Conservative politician and former secretary of state for India Robert Peel, arrived in Palestine in November. They spent several months traveling around the country and interviewing prominent members of the Zionist and Arab political elites as well as local British government officials. In 1937 they

FIGURE 5. Members of the Peel Commission in garden of King David Hotel, Jerusalem, 1936. Matson Photograph Collection, Library of Congress LC-M33–9229.

published their findings, with a nearly four-hundred-page report detailing the increasingly violent and hostile conditions on the ground and proposing a "solution": partitioning Palestine into separate Arab and Jewish states.

This was not a new idea. Partition had been quietly discussed for some time among Zionist officials, including Chaim Weizmann, who had suggested forms of cantonization and partition both to other Zionists and to British commentators as early as 1919.[30] Both partition and transfer had played a role in Zionist proposals for achieving self-determination in the years before the revolt—Weizmann had discussed partition in some detail both with the head of the Permanent Mandates Commission and with Mussolini by 1933—and some of these discussions had drifted into the Colonial Office. In 1935, Beatrice Erskine, the director of the Palestine Information Centre in London, published a book entitled *Palestine of the Arabs,* which proposed a "cantonization" plan; in the same year a former colonial administrator in Palestine named Archer Cust wrote a memo for the Colonial Office outlining a similar idea.[31] This possibility attracted notice despite an angry denunciation from the influential district commissioner Edward Keith-Roach, who told the Colonial Office in no uncertain terms that it would represent an unconscionable violation of Arab property and civil rights.[32]

Besides Peel himself, whose role in the proceedings was limited somewhat by illness, the Royal Commission had five other members. Reginald Coupland, later regarded as the main architect of the partition idea, was a professor of colonial history at Oxford with a particular interest in India, and a former editor of the *Round Table*. Harold Morris, a lawyer and judge best known as chairman of the Industrial Court, had briefly served as a member of Parliament associated with Lloyd George's Liberal coalition government in the early 1920s. Morris Carter, a former colonial chief justice in Tanganyika, had served as chairman of the Kenya land commission in 1932–33; he and Laurie Hammond, a former governor of Assam who had chaired the Indian delineation commission the previous year, represented the colonial official perspective. Horace Rumbold, a career diplomat who had signed the Lausanne Treaty as high commissioner of Constantinople and had most recently served as the British ambassador to Berlin, completed the group. None of the six had any special knowledge of Palestine, but several— particularly Coupland and Carter—viewed themselves as experts on ethnic conflict in colonial territories. They were charged with the task of

> ascertain[ing] the underlying causes of the disturbances which broke out in Palestine in the middle of April; to enquire into the manner in which the Mandate for Palestine is being implemented in relation to the obligations of the Mandatory towards the Arabs and the Jews respectively; and to ascertain whether, upon a proper construction of the terms of the Mandate, either the Arabs or the Jews have any legitimate grievances on account of the way in which the Mandate has been or is being implemented; and, if the Commission is satisfied that any such grievances are well-founded, to make recommendation for their removal and for the prevention of their recurrence.[33]

The commission published its full report in 1937. It opened with a version of Palestine's ancient history, linking the "dispersion of the Jews" with the emergence of the modern Zionist movement, and went on to describe in some detail the various clashes among the Arabs, Jews, and British that had characterized the mandate from its inception. It offered some general observations on the nature of the mandate government, the inequities of the educational system, and the failures of public security in Palestine. In the third part of the report, entitled "The Possibility of a Lasting Settlement," it came to the commission's central recommendation:

The problem cannot be solved by giving either the Arabs or the Jews all they want. The answer to the question which of them in the end will govern Palestine must be Neither. No fair-minded statesman can think it right either that 400,000 Jews, whose entry into Palestine has been facilitated by the British Government and approved by the League of Nations, should be handed over to Arab rule, or that, if the Jews should become a majority, a million Arabs should be handed over to their rule. But while neither race can fairly rule all Palestine, each race might justly rule part of it.

The idea of Partition has doubtless been thought of before as a solution of the problem, but it has probably been discarded as being impracticable. The difficulties are certainly very great, but when they are closely examined they do not seem so insuperable as the difficulties inherent in the continuance of the Mandate or in any other alternative arrangement. Partition offers a chance of ultimate peace. No other plan does.[34]

The commission's proposal was sweeping in vision, if rather vague in terms of exact procedure and outcome. It recommended that Palestine be divided into a Jewish state encompassing the north and northwestern coast, extending from the northern border south to Tel Aviv; a British-mandated territory surrounding Jerusalem, Bethlehem, and Nazareth and with a corridor to the coast through Jaffa; and an Arab state, to be joined somehow with Transjordan, comprising the remaining territory. The northern cities of Haifa, Akka, Safed, and Tiberias were labeled "mixed" and designated for temporary inclusion in the British mandate until they could be fully incorporated into the new Jewish nation. The report emphasized the uniqueness and desperation of the situation in Palestine and the novelty of its suggested solution: "The disease is so deep-rooted that, in our firm conviction, the only hope of a cure lies in a surgical operation"[35]—a graphic medical image that would become the most dominant metaphor for partition in the British commentary.[36]

The proposed borders bore no resemblance to actual demographics on the ground, particularly in the case of the proposed Jewish state. The commission estimated that the plan would leave about 1,250 Jews in Arab territory and more than 225,000 Arabs in the Jewish state, as well as a further 85,000 Arabs in Jerusalem and Haifa. Considering this unacceptable, the commission declared, "Sooner or later there should be a transfer of land and, as far as possible, an exchange of population. . . . The existence of these minorities clearly constitutes the most serious hindrance to the smooth and successful operation of Partition. If the settlement is to be clean and final, the question must be boldly faced and firmly dealt with."[37] The members cited the Greek-Turkish exchange as a model for population exchange: "The courage of the

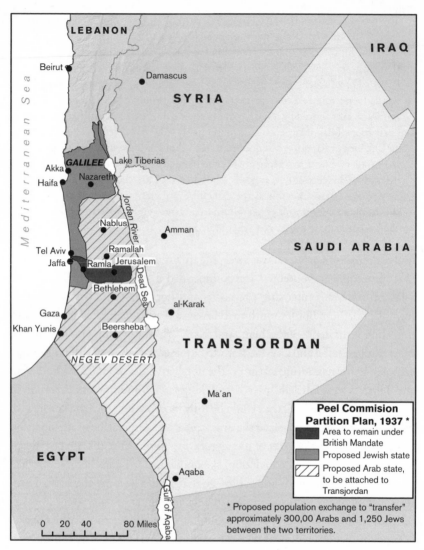

MAP 4. Rendering of the Peel Commission's proposed plan for partitioning Palestine into separate Arab and Jewish states, 1937. Map by Sachi Arakawa.

Greek and Turkish statesmen has been justified by the result. Before the operation the Greek and Turkish minorities had been a constant irritant. Now Greco-Turkish relations are friendlier than they have ever been before." [38] The mechanics of this transfer were laid out only in the sketchiest terms, suggesting that the irrigation and agricultural redevelopment of Transjordan, the Jordan Valley, and Beersheba could potentially boost the capacity of these areas to absorb large numbers of transferred Arabs. The proposal assumed that existence as a political "minority" was untenable for either Jews or Arabs in Palestine. The Arabs would be "finally delivered from the fear of being swamped by the Jews, and from the possibility of ultimate subjection to Jewish rule," while the Jews would have the National Home converted into a state and thereby "cease at last to live a minority life."[39]

From the beginning of the mandate, the emphasis on separate representation for Jews and Arabs and differentiated citizenship rights for the two "racial" groups had meant that residents of Palestine were defined above all by their ethnoreligious category. The debates over demographics and representation built a zero-sum game into Palestinian politics, but they also indicated one of the fundamental issues with the way the postwar order understood minorities as basically national: if minorities were essentially defined as national political units, the principle of self-determination could not coexist with the principle of assimilation. Now the commission was making the argument that a "minority"—here, for the first time, applying the term to a settler colonist community—could be assimilated into a nonrepresentative state, but not into a representative one. "The successful working of representative government," they wrote, "requires that the population concerned should be sufficiently homogenous. Unless there is common ground enough between its different groups of classes to enable the minority to acquiesce in the rule of the majority and to make it possible for the balance of power to readjust itself from time to time, the working basis of parliamentary government or democracy as we understand it is not there."[40] The only solution, then, was forcibly to divide the territory and population into two ethnically and nationally homogenous states.

Colonial Secretary William Ormsby-Gore advocated caution and consideration in responding to an idea "so radical, so novel and so unexpected."[41] Addressing the Permanent Mandates Commission in Geneva, he declared the necessity of recognizing "what can never be lost sight of in connection with Palestine, the deep historical roots which make it a country different from all other countries"—going on to declare that "in the light of our dual obligations, we have endeavoured to give equal weight to the interests of those two deeply divided, race-conscious, and civilisation-conscious peoples."[42] Leo Amery, speaking in the House of Commons, located partition as the final, inevitable step in a series of disasters for both Palestine and the British empire:

However much we may regret it, we have lost the situation in Palestine, as we lost it in Ireland, through a lack of whole-hearted faith in ourselves.... In Palestine, as in Ireland, we have reached a deadlock which cannot be overcome, so far as carrying out the original mandatory policy is concerned, except by measures of resolute and ruthless coercion that we, as a nation, ... are incapable of carrying out. The Commission now suggest, as an alternative line of policy, a solution which contains at any rate some reasonable hope of overcoming the difficulty.[43]

Such British interpretations of the genesis and meaning of the partition proposals were designed to suggest that partition was a radical, new, and innovative solution to what had inexplicably become an otherwise insoluble clash of ethnicities and religions specific to Palestine. But in fact, partition rested on the same set of assumptions as the practices of transfer that the British, French, and League of Nations had already applied in other regional contexts: the relevance of ethnoreligious identity to citizenship, the inevitably oppositional relationship between minorities and majorities, and the threats posed by plural ethnicities and religions within a single state. It built further on the now well-established premise that mandate governments and the League had the capacity and the responsibility to legislate, administer, and if necessary engineer ethnic, national, and religious identifications vis-à-vis state authority.

ARAB AND ZIONIST RESPONSES

The regional—and indeed global—Arab response to the Peel Commission's report was disbelief. The Lebanese-American writer Amin Rihani voiced the opinions of most of the Palestinian Arab population when he declared, "Of all the solutions of the Palestine problem this idea of cantonization is by far the worse [sic].... Cantonization, or more political divisions in a country that has suffered so much from the acquisitive and dominating passion of European imperialism is the flimsiest of all political expediencies and the most fantastic of all the ideas of exploitation."[44] From the perspective of the Palestinian Arab political elite, who had from the beginning regarded the Balfour Declaration as fundamentally illegitimate, partition appeared to be little better than outright theft.

The specifics of the plan met with outrage. The Peel Commission assigned several major Arab cities—some of which were also important centers of

Palestinian Arab nationalist activism, including Jerusalem, Nazareth, and Ramla—to either the British mandate territory or the Jewish state. Arab leaders viewed the population transfer which was to accompany the enforcement of the new borders as radically, dramatically one-sided—which indeed it was, with a proposed 300,000 Arabs (nearly a third of Palestine's Arab population) to be "transferred" versus just 1,250 Jews. The distribution of land within the new states was equally problematic, with three million dunams of Arab-owned land located in the proposed Jewish state versus one hundred thousand dunams of Jewish-owned land in the designated Arab territories.[45] But there were more general philosophical objections as well. The British and League acceptance of the Balfour Declaration, which had been imposed by force on the Palestinian Arab population even before the inception of the mandate as the basis for and legitimization of a partition plan, aroused anger; so did the commission's recommendation that what remained as Arab territory following partition should be annexed to Transjordan.

Although there were a few leading members of the political elite, mainly encompassing the moderately pro-British Nashashibi family, who were willing quietly to discuss the option of partition, Palestinian Arabs were broadly unified in opposition to any partition plan. The Arab Higher Committee (the unofficial but generally recognized institution representing the Palestinian Arab body politic) condemned the plan, as did the secularist, pan-Arab Istiqlal Party.[46] *Al-Liwa'*, the journal of the Husayni family's political organization, declared that anybody supporting the idea of partition was a "traitor";[47] it was shut down for three months in late 1937 for its vocal condemnation of the commission's recommendation.[48] Such censorship could not hide the fact that most Palestinian Arabs across the political spectrum were unequivocally opposed to partition. The Orthodox-owned newspaper *Filastin*—not usually a pro-Husayni voice—expressed backing for *al-Liwa'*'s unyielding position, declaring that "there are no moderates or radicals [on partition] . . . partition is a national catastrophe."[49]

Eventual Zionist sovereignty—a fundamental part of any partition proposal—was unimaginable to the Palestinian Arab political classes, who viewed it as overt seizure of property and an unacceptable violation of Arab civil and political rights. As the Arab Higher Committee argued in a memo to the Peel Commission, "The Arabs, further, see no benefit nor hope of reform to be gained from minor changes within the existing structure, because the evil has its roots deep within the system itself. Therefore unless the grievances fundamental to this system are themselves remedied, wholly and courageously, the evil cannot but continue, and the grievances intensify."[50] This point of view only solidified with the brutal British military response to the revolt of 1936–39, in which the Palestinian Arab political elite was systematically decapitated through arrests, imprisonment, deportations, and executions.[51]

Despite their fundamental conviction that the mandate itself represented an illegitimate authority in Palestine, the Palestinian Arab political elite had long engaged in practical negotiations with the mandatory government and Geneva, frequently making use of the League's own legal language to further the Arab cause.[52] As such, Arab objections to the proposal sought publicly to reframe the minority/majority debate as a question of religious designation unrelated to issues of nationality and governance. Declaring that Jews would be welcome in an Arab-majority Palestine, they redefined "minority" as a term of cultural rather than political difference. At a meeting in London in 1939, Palestinian nationalist leaders Jamal Husayni, 'Izzat Tannus, and Musa Alami told Colonial Secretary Malcolm MacDonald that they believed as many as half a million Jewish settlers could be accommodated in Palestine in the event of the recognition of Arab independence, and that within Palestine Arabs would plan to "exercise majority control over the Jews and simply assure them spiritual and religious liberty"—precisely the terms that the League's minorities treaties had guaranteed (and, by 1939, manifestly failed to deliver) to Jewish and other minority communities in eastern Europe.[53] But the partition debate also marked the definite emergence of more specifically ethnic and religious definitions of Palestinian Arab nationalism.[54] As Palestine became an international issue under constant discussion at the League and elsewhere, Palestinian Arab leaders began to think about how Zionism had successfully sold its message at the level of international diplomacy and look for ways to emulate that success. For some leaders, this involved making a case for the ethnically Arab nature of the territory and its people; others began to make a different case for Palestine as a site of specifically Muslim identity.

Already in 1928 the mufti of Jerusalem, Hajj Amin al-Husayni (himself an important if not always reliable associate of the British government, to whom he owed his appointment as head of the Supreme Muslim Council), had begun looking to external Muslim and Arab interests to support Palestinian nationalism against Zionism and the British mandate. A conference he convened in Jerusalem brought more than seven hundred delegates from a variety of Arab countries to discuss political strategies for combating Zionism and put together a committee "for the defence of the holy Muslim places in Jerusalem."[55] Following the violence of the riots over the Western Wall in 1929, Husayni's consciousness of the need to look to Muslims and Arabs outside Palestine for political support against British-Zionist cooperation grew. The Supreme Muslim Council under his leadership began conducting ongoing appeals to Muslim leaders outside Palestine and proposed a yearly religious conference to draw participants from across the Muslim world.[56] In 1935, al-Husayni presided over a meeting of ulama in Jerusalem at which he noted the joint fatwas issued by himself and a Shi'i notable in Iraq condemning land sales to the Zionists; the participants passed resolutions to "appeal to Moslem rulers and chiefs who are likely to assist the Palestine Arabs and to ask them to help protect the Holy Places" and "to encourage local products and use only locally manufactured goods—Egyptian, Syrian and Iraqian [sic] products to be considered as 'local.'"[57] The resolutions were disseminated through mosques across Palestine the following month, with plans to distribute the material outside Palestine "at the time of the pilgrimage," as well as including Christians by asking clerics to distribute the material to their congregations in all the major Palestinian urban centers.[58] The fatwa itself explicitly categorized Zionism as the "Judaisation of this Moslem holy country."[59] The massive rise in immigration through the 1930s and the Peel Commission's partition proposal helped solidify the case for this new vision for a "Muslim world" that al-Husayni and his partners hoped might offer a more successful set of alliances for Palestine and the Arab Middle East more generally.[60]

Other Palestinian nationalist leaders, particularly Arab Christians, responded to the new circumstances by producing a narrative of ethnic rather than religious identity for Palestine, with the continued aim of perfecting their message for the League and other "international" (i.e., European) audiences. Some of this rhetoric was deliberately modeled after Zionist language, with the explicit purpose of replicating Zionism's success in the Western public sphere and at the League. The Palestinian Christian activist 'Izzat Tannus founded the Arab Centre in London with a vision of countering Zionist ideology by imitating its tactics. "This is a frank admission," he wrote, " of our backwardness in the very important field of information and propaganda. I must admit again that it was wrong of the Arab people of Palestine to depend only on their indisputable natural rights to their country and on the Covenant of the League of Nations which decreed their right to self-determination."[61] To this end, the Arab Centre published a number of pamphlets making the case for a specifically Arab Palestinian national consciousness, one that included both Muslims and Christians but was exclusively Arab in nature. Tannus recruited Lebanese, Syrian, Iraqi, and Saudi Arabian sympathizers to his cause, "indicating that the Arabs were still one nation." [62] As the secretary of the Arab Centre, George Mansur, told Malcolm MacDonald following a meeting in London in 1939, "as an Arab, I do not talk of 'fanatical Moslems,' though I might use the word to describe our *national* convictions; we are Christian Arabs and Moslem Arabs with a common ideal." [63] This was in no way a new idea, of course, but it did indicate that activists like Mansur and Tannus had finally and definitely moved away from the concept of a decentralized greater Syria including non-Zionist Jews—as had been envisioned, for instance, by the writers of the Syrian Congress in 1919, which explicitly included non-Zionist "Jewish compatriots" in its definition of the citizen body—toward a narrower vision of an ethnically Arab national identity that more closely conformed to League visions for modern statehood. And even this secularized, ethnically oriented, and Christian-dominated organization also occasionally glanced hopefully at the Muslim world. In 1939, alongside its reproductions of the McMahon-Husayn correspondence and histories of Palestinian Arab nationalism, it also published a short "Statement of Indian Muslim Views on Palestine" indicating global Muslim support for the Palestinian case against Zionism.

Language like this found a mirror in diaspora activist communities as well. The Arab National League, an organization of Arab activists from Palestine, Lebanon, and Syria based in New York and headed by a Palestinian surgeon named Fuad Shatara, published a memorandum responding to the partition proposal and the subsequent disturbances that dealt explicitly with the majority/minority trope: "For the first time in history, a majority finds it necessary to appeal for protecting its inalienable rights against an arrogant domineering, and highly organized and financed minority. . . . This appeal is addressed to all peace loving people to raise their voices to save the land where the Prince of Peace was born, to save it as a shrine to which Christian, Moslem, and Jew may reverentially turn." [64] Such rhetoric coming from the diaspora referenced an Ottoman approach to governing religious minority communities, with their long-established rights to some degree of autonomy, alongside some of the discourse of the League's approach to minority rights outside the Middle East; but it was flavored further with language derived from a European tradition of anti-Semitism that until recently had had no real counterpart in the Arab world. [65]

By contrast, many Zionist leaders were cautiously optimistic about the possibility of dividing Palestine if the territorial and demographic issues could be worked out to their satisfaction, and strategically accepted the Peel Commission's defense of partition as an expression of minority rights. Although the initial appointment of the commission sparked intense anxiety within the Yishuv, both Chaim Weizmann and David Ben-Gurion—the two most central figures in the Zionist political establishment—saw partition as a positive step toward the foundation of a state, which they thought could be expanded territorially at a later date.

Weizmann's initial statements to the commission invoked the minority/majority distinction that the British and the League had already begun to develop. In describing the reasons for the Arab revolt, he told its members that "the Arab is a totalitarian," eliciting the response from Reginald Coupland that the Arab "does not like minorities."[66] Such portrayals hinted at a dire fate for a Zionist settler population left as a permanent "minority" in a majoritarian Arab Palestine, and left open the possibility that Weizmann might be willing to consider a partition proposal that would allow for a definite Jewish majority in part of the country. Asking for more time to consider the question of partition, and prevaricating even while suggesting Zionist opposition to the plan, gave the commission the distinct impression that Weizmann, at least, was open to further negotiation.[67]

Ben-Gurion was surprised and delighted to see a proposal for transfer in the commission's plan, as most of the leading members of the Jewish Agency Executive had thought that gaining British backing for mandatory population exchanges was not a realistic goal at this stage.[68] (The long history of Zionist enthusiasm for mass Arab "transfer" out of Palestine has been admirably detailed elsewhere.)[69] In his meetings with the commission itself Ben-Gurion was careful not to show enthusiasm and indeed to state multiple reservations and objections to the plan. But in his meeting with a Mapai (the main Labor Zionist outlet) party committee, he took a different tone: "In my opinion there is such a solution and it existed even before the Royal Commission and in my opinion this is the solution. The solution is the direction of the proposal of Sir Stafford Kripps [sic]—establishing two states in Eretz Israel, an Arab and a Jewish state.... This is not a solution under all circumstances. But if the minimum land necessary for our growth in the near future will be set aside for the Jewish state, then this is the solution."[70]

If Weizmann and Ben-Gurion were both in favor of the idea and pretending to some reluctance mainly to strengthen their negotiating positions, partition did have some real opponents within the Zionist movement. Vladimir Jabotinsky, the chief spokesman of the militant Revisionist Party, also made use of the concepts of a minority and majority, repeatedly insisting on the necessity of recreating the whole of Palestine (in which he included Transjordan) as a Jewish-majority space. For Jabotinsky, the idea of partition was anathema as it admitted the possibility of giving up some of the territory that he regarded as absolutely necessary for the Zionist cause. "I do not deny," he declared before the House of Lords in 1937, "that in the process the Arabs of Palestine will necessarily become a minority in the country of Palestine. What I do deny is that *that* is a hardship.... I fully understand that any minority would prefer to be a majority, it is quite understandable that the Arabs of Palestine would also prefer Palestine to be the Arab State No. 4, No. 5, or No. 6—that I quite understand; but when the Arab claim is confronted with our Jewish demand to be saved, it is like the claims of appetite versus the claims of starvation." [71]

After a substantial internal struggle, the issue came to the floor at the Twentieth Zionist Congress held in Zurich in August 1937. The resolution that was eventually adopted, with a vote of 300 to 158, rejected the specifics of the Peel Commission plan and condemned British efforts to restrict Jewish immigration to Palestine in the short term as a "violation of Jewish rights." But crucially, the resolution did not reject the principle of partition. "The Congress declares that the scheme put forward by the Royal Commission is unacceptable," it read, "[but] empowers the Executive to enter into negotiations with a view to ascertaining the precise terms of His Majesty's Government for the proposed establishment of a Jewish State." [72] In other words, the specific division the Peel Commission had arrived at was not adequate, but a different territorial delimitation might prove acceptable for the Yishuv.

REGIONAL RESPONSES

Immediately following the publication of the Peel Commission's report, Haj Amin al-Husayni sought to organize a broad regional response by gathering as many Arab leaders as possible from Palestine, Syria, Lebanon, and Egypt at a conference in the southern Syrian resort town of Bludan to construct a unified response to the proposal and a plan for combating it. The Bludan Congress, which was apparently funded in large part by Husayni himself, provided a forum for Arab leaders to frame partition not only as a threat to the territorial integrity and national character of Palestine but also as an effort to impose a permanent imperial legacy on the region as a whole. As historian Elie Kedourie suggested, "The Bludan Congress may be considered a landmark in the increasing involvement of the Arab world in the Palestine problem."[73]

A total of 411 delegates attended the congress: 160 from Syria, 128 Palestinians, 65 from Lebanon, 30 from Transjordan, 12 Iraqis, 6 from Egypt, and a lone representative from Saudi Arabia.[74] Most were members of the urban elites who dominated the Arab political establishment across the region, and were generally well informed about events in Palestine and the tactics and practices of the Zionist movement; even the skeptical British witness reported that "the proceedings were modeled on those of the recent Zionist congress in Zurich," and that "the order and organization of the congress appear on the whole to have been excellent and shows that talent for administration is not entirely lacking."[75]

The delegates at Bludan framed their opposition to partition in both national and international terms, making use of the League's own discourse to protest the idea of dividing Palestine. The political committee's report repeatedly noted the British failure to carry out the League's stated intentions:

> The British government also ignored the principles which she and her allies, in various ways, declared of granting liberty to the nations and allowing them their full right to decide their own destiny, as mentioned in Article 22 of the Covenant of the League of Nations . . . although the Royal Commission actually admitted in the report they made the power of the national spirit which prevailed among all Arabs . . . [and] the persistent desires of the Arabs to obtain their independence, their expression of hatred of the Mandatory power, of the refusal to be governed by it, of their unswerving opposition to a Jewish national home; although they knew perfectly well that the Arabs could govern themselves as do their brethren in Syria and Iraq, the report which this Royal Commission issued respecting the partition of Palestine, was a complete contradiction of these admissions . . . [and] was also in contradiction to the covenant and the spirit of the League of Nations.[76]

Such language indicated a thorough understanding of the discourse through which the League and the British claimed international legitimacy, and assigned partition to the category of colonial policy rather than internationally sanctioned governance. It also recognized the way the League had made minorities and minority rights a central issue in international law, noting that upon the repudiation of Jewish national claims to Palestine "the Arabs will agree that the Jews, who will be within the Arab state in Palestine, shall be treated in the same way as are minorities the world over."[77]

But while confronting the League using its own language of self-determination and minority rights, the congress also turned its attention to Arab and Muslim global constituencies who it hoped might prove a more reliable source of support. Noting the success of Zionist public outreach campaigns, the propaganda committee suggested targeting three main audiences to look for support—the Arab "home" (i.e., Palestine itself), the Muslim world, and the broader Arab world—making use of different frames of reference for each. "Propaganda in the Arab home," its report read, "should be directed to the fact that the Palestine problem is that of the Arab nation at large, and that the Zionist menace . . . is truly a most wicked one, because it prevents the Arabs from having their national ideals, universal unity, and their glory duly recognized." In the Muslim world, propaganda should rest on a framework of religious duty: "Each Moslem ought to understand the high religious position of Palestine, as well as its sanctity due to the presence of the holy places. The Moslem faith lays it down as the duty of every Moslem to fight for these shrines with all the means in his power. . . . [A Jewish state will] kill the revival of the Moslem nations, stop them from springing to free themselves from the bondage of foreign colonization, and prevent them from enjoying their religious liberty which is the most essential part of the Moslem's life." In the Arab world, propaganda should emphasize the multireligious, international effects of the fate of Palestine: "This particular campaign should also show up the endangering of people's rights and of the Christian holy places by the Zionists, as well as prove the harm done to international justice and law and order, through the support of the English of their policy. . . . Establishing a Jewish state in Palestine is harmful to the Arabs and to their independence, because it robs them of the liberty and the natural rights they so far have enjoyed."[78] An anti-Jewish pamphlet printed in Cairo and passed out to the delegates, though not part of the congress's resolutions or productions, demonstrated how such categories of religion and nation could be elided, citing an "unceasing struggle that has ever gone on between the Jews and the Moslems and of the hatred always shown by the Jews for Moslems," and adding, "The Jews send messengers to the Kurdish tribes," and "The Jews are the servants of Satan."[79] Though the text of the congress's resolutions focused primarily on the theme of self-determination, then, some of the peripheral conversations around the congress engaged in acts of slippage between religious and national categories—as, of course, the League, the

British, and the Zionists were also doing in defining a European Jewish settler community as a national minority.

At the Arab Congress in Cairo the following year, an Indian representative reemphasized partition in Palestine as an issue of concern to the Muslim world as a whole: "Muslims should treat Muslim questions from a Muslim point of view without distinction of nationality," adding the specifically national perspective and analysis that "India had come to the conclusion that British Imperialism had gone mad.... The Munich lesson of self-determination should be applied by Mr. Chamberlain to the Arabs."[80] The congress also reopened some of the questions surrounding transfer, partition, and "minority" rights. Participants cited Iraq's 1932 commitment to the protection of minorities as a precedent for establishing the Jews as a minority in an independent Arab Palestine. An Iraqi representative demanded "stoppage of Jewish immigration, creation of a national constitutional Government, conclusion of a treaty with Great Britain similar to Anglo-Iraqi Treaty and with guarantee for protection of minorities."[81] A Syrian delegate, bringing up the idea of transfer in distinctly League-inflected terms, suggested that Britain "should establish a national home for the Jews in Australia or Canada"—precisely the proposal that the League's own Michael Hansson would make in his speech accepting the Nobel Peace Prize two months later.[82]

Palestinians and their allies in the Arab world, then, attempted to recast partition as a colonial policy fundamentally irreconcilable with the League's stated aims of national self-determination. They further sought to define minority rights as essentially cultural and religious, a definition derived not only from the Ottoman past but also from the League's own postwar decisions regarding central and eastern Europe and its attempted imposition of a particular vision of minority rights on Iraq upon its independence. Their emphasis on the "minority" question proved prescient. As the Permanent Mandates Commission took up the question of partition for Palestine, this issue of the relationship between minority rights and national self-determination became paramount.

LEAGUE RESPONSES

In the summer of 1937 the Permanent Mandates Commission (PMC) met at Geneva to discuss the Peel proposals. Over the course of nearly thirty meetings, the Commission's conversation demonstrated the evolution of two new concepts concerning Palestine and its possible division. First, while the PMC's members generally accepted the British categorization of Arabs and Jews as separate races and civilizations, with the Jewish community representing a significantly more "advanced" stage than the Arabs, they also viewed the mandate government as having had no small part in perpetuating and widening this division. More radically, they began to make use of the now-enshrined categories of "minority" and "majority" to describe the Jewish settler and Arab indigenous community, discussing separation and partition as modes of ensuring a minority right to self-determination.

William Rappard, speaking on the question of a British preference for the Arabs over the Jews, drew on this civilizational distinction to analyze the three-way colonial relationship and what he perceived as a British coolness toward the Yishuv:

> Their feelings were human and natural. Colonial officials were accustomed to dealing with subject peoples at a less advanced stage of development; and, of course, the Arabs approximated more closely than did the Jews to the human material with which the colonial officials had dealt in the course of their previous careers. The development of the Jews was, if anything, more advanced than that of the members of the Mandates Commission! The Jews were peculiarly analytical and critical, and given to the discussion of political ideology; and most colonial officials—not only British officials—had an instinctive dislike for people who, instead of going about their business, were always trying to discuss theoretical problems.[83]

Generally, the Commission accepted a racialized hierarchical distinction between European Jewish settlers and the indigenous Arab population in Palestine. As Lord Hailey suggested, they had already come to believe that "the real difficulty was, perhaps, that Crown Colony government was not well suited to an advanced people like the Jews."[84] However, the Commission's members were quite critical of what they saw as the mandate government's distinct encouragement of separate political, economic, and cultural spheres for the two communities. The Portuguese representative Count de Penha Garcia identified (correctly) some of the ways in which the British had deliberately emphasized communal categories in the structure of the mandate state. In particular, he critiqued the British decision to allow representation only through communal institutions: the Jewish Agency on the one hand, and on the other the Supreme Muslim Council (whose authority was much more limited, extending only to the sharia courts and questions of *waqf* property):[85]

Possibly not enough attention had been paid to the creation of independent administrative institutions and of economic organisations in which the interests of Jews and Arabs would have been combined. Perhaps no sufficient attempt had been made to create an Arab authority outside the strictly religious sphere.

In reality, authority had been entrusted in the case of the Jews to a colonisation agency of a confessional character; and in the case of the Arabs, to a Committee administering religious property and intervening in certain other cases. Thus, the religious aspect of the two sections of the population had been accentuated, and no attempt had been made to create a national feeling. The difference in economic power and even in civilisation between the two sections of the population had become more and more pronounced.[86]

Other members criticized the bifurcated educational system and advocated a bilingual curriculum that required students to learn something of both Jewish and Arab history, a suggestion to which the British Colonial Office representative responded defensively: "The Commission must realise that the two races disliked one another, and that there was an irreconcilable conflict between them. . . . The children might be forced to read the 'little manual' in school; but they would go back to an atmosphere of hatred in their homes."[87] And although the Commission expressed criticism of the mandate government's approach, it accepted the British claim that Jews and Arabs were separated by a racial and civilizational gulf. This racial differentiation now took on a new aspect in the PMC's discussions as the Commission's members began to make use of the League's already-extant legal framework of minority and majority and apply it to Palestine's settler and indigenous communities.

The discussions made a long-overdue acknowledgment: that the initial vision for Palestine as enshrined in the mandate text had always anticipated an eventual Jewish majority with an Arab minority, governed by Zionists with certain guarantees for the Arabs. The Dutch lawyer and judge Frederik Mari Baron van Asbeck stated this in frank terms:

A Jewish National Home, in short, with self-governing institutions, was taken . . . as the final aim to be attained after an intervening period of development—self-governing institutions in which minority groups would, of course, have their due share as guaranteed minorities. . . . If, therefore, the League reverted to the mandate as it was conceived of in 1917 and the following years, it would be deciding for a policy of "de-arabisation" of the country. There would, in the end, be a Jewish majority capable of administering a

Jewish State, with an Arab minority guaranteed within the framework of the League of Nations. The attainment of that end would require government by force, which would have to last until, by gradual evolution, a Palestinian nation had come into being.[88]

Van Asbeck was acknowledging, finally, that the League from the beginning of the mandate had never thought of Palestine as a space for the assimilation of a Jewish settler minority to an Arab majority, but rather had always assumed the eventual development of a Jewish majority.

The chairman of the PMC, Pierre Orts, now deployed this civilizational distinction in new terms to explain why the assimilation of what he was now calling a "minority" and a "majority" would be impossible. "The story of Palestine," he declared, "was a succession of broken illusions: the illusion that it would prove possible to set up a State composed of two elements, the Arab already occupying the country, and the Jew who had introduced himself there, and that they would live together in harmony; the illusion that, in such a country, the majority would see, in the liberal form of government proffered, anything but a weapon with which to crush the minority and to destroy the mandate—that was to say, the very constitution of the territory."[89] Putting aside the radically disingenuous claim about the "liberal" nature of a government that had relied almost solely on force to maintain its authority throughout the mandate period, this analysis matched up the concept of civilization with the idea of minority rights. The Arabs, in this view, could not be trusted to carry out the responsibilities of a majority toward a minority population. Equally, as Count de Penha Garcia noted, "the Arabs would oppose on principle any arrangement which did not preserve Arab independence and leave the Jews in a minority"[90]—just as the Jews, as Ormsby-Gore pointed out, "wished to be, not a minority, but a majority in that State."[91]

The PMC, then, was carefully overlaying the legal categories of majority and minority—defined in international law through the minorities treaties for eastern Europe in the previous decade—onto the categories of indigenous people and settler colonists to advocate for the idea of partition. As one member put it toward the end of the Commission's deliberations:

The value of the report of the Royal Commission lay in this, that it had forced us at last to consider whether Arabs should be subordinate to Jews or Jews to Arabs. That issue had never been fairly faced before.... If the Jewish National Home meant anything, it meant a Jewish State, and the Jews could not be subordinate to the Arabs; but Lord Hailey also felt, for his part, that the British public would never with any conviction support a scheme which involved the subordination of an indigenous Arab population to a new population largely consisting of Polish and German colonists.

The Mandates Commission must therefore envisage some solution which did not involve subordination either of Jews to Arabs or of Arabs to Jews; and any solution on those lines postulated some form of partition.[92]

Orts agreed, declaring that partition "possessed the merit of granting each of the two sections of the population self-governing institutions which, if they remained together, would have the effect of enabling the existing majority to crush the minority."[93] Such language camouflaged the essentially colonial nature of the settlement of Palestine and reinforced the idea that the burden of decision making lay with the League, for whom the questions of "minority" rights had emerged as a central concern in the process of adjudicating postwar territorial claims in central and eastern Europe.

This categorization of the issue as a minority/majority conflict also allowed for an extensive discussion of transfer, voluntary or mandatory, as a part of any proposed partition plan—something the League viewed itself as having unique authority to execute. While Ormsby-Gore was careful to state that Britain had not yet formally accepted the principle of mass transfer proposed in the Peel Commission report, he commented optimistically on its possibilities with reference to the "ease" of the League-supported Greek-Turkish population exchange of the previous decade. "If it were a case of moving the Arabs long distances to a strange country," he mused, "transfer would indeed be difficult. But these people . . . would be going literally only a comparatively few miles away to a people with the same language, the same civilisation, the same religion; and therefore the problem of transfer geographically and practically was easier even than the interchanges of Greeks and Turks between Asia Minor and the Balkans."[94]

The PMC's members ultimately agreed to continue their consideration of partition on an ongoing basis—an inconclusive decision in part arising from an emerging consensus that the British government itself would reject the Peel Commission's proposal, which it did the following year. By 1939, the revolt, though put down brutally, had achieved one of its central goals: convincing the British government that the expense and difficulty of enacting partition or maintaining its current defense of mass Jewish immigration would be enormous. That year the famous "White Paper" essentially repudiated the Balfour Declaration, asserting that "His Majesty's Government believe that the framers of the Mandate in which the Balfour Declaration was embodied could not have intended that Palestine should be converted into a Jewish State against the will of the Arab population of the country" and setting out the goal of an independent Arab-dominated Palestine within ten years.[95] The question of partition was closed, for the moment; but the 1937 plan would represent a central model when the idea of separate Jewish and Arab states was revived, this time very seriously indeed, after the Second World War.

PARTITION AT THE UNITED NATIONS

In February 1947, an increasingly embattled and financially strapped British government, pressed not only by ongoing Arab opposition to the continuation of the mandate but also by Zionist militias engaging in terrorist activity against British civilian and military targets, announced its intention to withdraw from Palestine and turn over the question of its future to the newly formed United Nations. (Not coincidentally, the British also almost simultaneously declared their intention to withdraw from India and began discussions about partitioning India along Hindu-Muslim lines.)[96] In May, the United Nations announced the formation of a new commission—the United Nations Special Commission on Palestine, briefly known as UNSCOP—to investigate the situation and make recommendations on the future of the state. UNSCOP had eleven members, none of whom represented nations with a voice on the Security Council (they came from Australia, Canada, Czechoslovakia, Guatemala, India, Iran, the Netherlands, Peru, Sweden, Uruguay, and Yugoslavia), and none of whom had significant previous knowledge of Palestine. The Jewish Agency pressed hard not to include British or Arab representatives on the commission, successfully lobbied for its members to visit "displaced persons" camps in Germany and Austria as part of its investigation, and won Zionist representation on the political subcommittee. The Arab Higher Committee, representing the Palestinian Arab political establishment, saw the resolution as a violation of their right to self-determination and boycotted the proceedings on the grounds that the transition of authority to the United Nations was illegal and the question should go to an international court.[97]

Zionist arguments to UNSCOP drew on all the tropes of transfer and partition that had been well established across the Middle East in the previous three decades. A memo from the Revisionist group Lohamei Herut Yisrael (Fighters for the Freedom of Israel, also known as LEHI) condensed many of these arguments. In their view, Jewish settlement and nationhood would lead to mass agricultural and industrial development; transfer of Arab populations out of the territory followed on a long history of effective and successful nation-building exchanges such as the postwar expulsion of ethnic Germans from Poland and Czechoslovakia (described in astoundingly anodyne fashion as "population exchanges between friendly countries"); and a pluralistic state was impossible because the majority would eventually "demand a majority in the government for the majority of the population."[98] This was not merely a right-wing perspective. In his remarks to UNSCOP, Ben-Gurion echoed these well-established points, declaring that the creation of a Jewish state could "realize the maximum development of all the potentialities of Palestine; to cultivate as many millions of dunams as possible out of the 18 million which are at present uncultivated; to irrigate instead of 40,000 dunams as at present, at least 4,000,000."[99] He too focused on the minority/majority question, emphasizing the impossibility of European Jews living under an Arab government: "A Jewish minority in an Arab State, even with the most ideal paper guarantee, would mean the final extinction of Jewish hope, not in Palestine alone, but for the entire Jewish people, for national equality and independence, with all the disastrous consequences so familiar in Jewish history. . . . The fate of the Jewish minority in Palestine will not differ from the fate of the Jewish minority in any other country, except that here it might be much worse."[100] (How the Palestinians would have acquired the capacity to inflict mass violence "much worse" than the extermination of a great majority of Europe's Jews and the permanent displacement of nearly all the survivors was a question left unanswered.)

UNSCOP's research included a few weeks' travel in Palestine, where the members noted the military apparatus of the British mandate state—"barbed wire defences, road blocks, machine-gun posts and constant armoured patrols are routine measures"[101]—and met with representatives of Irgun as well as with the Hagana and the Zionist political establishment. They also investigated the Jewish refugee situation in Europe and made a brief trip to Beirut, where they met with delegates from a number of neighboring Arab countries to ascertain Arab views on the question of partition in lieu of speaking with Palestinians.[102] Following lengthy debate, the committee finally produced its conclusion: "The claims to Palestine of the Arabs and Jews, both possessing validity, are irreconcilable . . . among all of the solutions advanced, partition will provide the most realistic and practicable settlement." [103]

The committee's majority report proposed a partition plan clearly inspired by the 1937 Peel Commission. It envisioned a three-way division of Palestine, with an Arab state comprising 43 percent of the mandate territory, including the highlands and one-third of the coastline; a Jewish state encompassing 56 percent of the territory and including the northern coast, eastern Galilee, and most of the Negev; and a "Corpus Separatum" including Jerusalem and its surrounds, which would be subject to some form of international authority. In describing the plan, the commission members noted that it suffered from many of the same problems the Peel Commission's proposal had encountered—most centrally, the presence of large numbers of Arabs in the proposed Jewish state. One of the subcommittees set up to investigate the viability of the proposal, criticizing the reliability of the population figures UNSCOP had used, predicted that "at the outset, the Arabs will have a majority in the proposed Jewish State." [104] However, unlike the Peel Commission, UNSCOP did not feel able to include some form of mandatory transfer in the plan. Further, not all the committee's members supported partition; three of them, representing India, Iran, and Yugoslavia, proposed a different solution that would link the two communities in a "federal" state and give the UN permanent control of Palestine's most important religious sites. [105]

UNSCOP's partition plan essentially represented a continuation of League concerns, policies, and approaches. It accepted the idea that pluralism was inherently problematic and that the United Nations, like its precursor, had a special responsibility to ensure "minority" rights, "including the protection of the linguistic, religious and ethnic rights of the people"—further referencing the long-established colonial trope that this was somehow especially true for Palestine, "in view of the fact that these two people live physically and spiritually apart, nurture separate aspirations and ideals, and have widely divergent cultural traditions." Indeed, its reports included a "Memorandum on Rights of Minorities in Palestine," which explicitly advocated for maintaining the mandate's "status quo" approach and the remnants of the Ottoman system that gave religious communities control over personal status law. [106] It supported the premise of Jewish nationhood and mass resettlement of what was left of Europe's Jews as a "solution" to what was still being called "the Jewish problem." And finally, it carried on the League's claim that such ethnonational conflicts indicated its successor's right and indeed responsibility to intervene to protect "peaceful relations in the Middle East," declaring that "taking into account the charged atmosphere in which the Palestine solution must be effected, it is considered advisable to emphasize the international obligations with regard to peaceful relations which an independent Palestine would necessarily assume." [107] The new United Nations, far from representing a new voice, had taken up the League's now decades-old legitimization of the principle of ethnonational separation as well as its claim of the right to administer it.[108]

REFUGEES REDUX

The subsequent tale of the partition vote, the outbreak of war, and the eventual Zionist expulsion of most of the Palestinian Arab population to the West Bank, Gaza, and the surrounding Arab countries is now a familiar narrative.[109] (The level of violence—encompassing thousands of deaths and the displacement of approximately 750,000 Palestinians Arabs—paralleled the even more brutal loss of life and property in the almost simultaneous partition of India, in which an estimated million people were killed and some fourteen million displaced in the name of ethnoreligious nation building.)[110] In the aftermath of the war, the regional and international organizations overseeing the construction, administration, and maintenance of camps for displaced Palestinians in Lebanon, Jordan, Iraq, Syria, and Egypt began to constitute a new refugee regime, reflecting many of the assumptions, ideologies, and political goals of the refugee camps set up for displaced Armenians and Assyrians more than three decades earlier but now on a much bigger scale.

Concepts of transfer and resettlement loomed large in the international discourse of refugee humanitarian aid. Howard Wilson, a representative of the American Friends Service Committee in Geneva, described an ongoing discussion of resettlement in the immediate postwar response to the problem of Palestinian displacement:

> I have gradually become troubled by the fairly general reports in the press and elsewhere to the effect that resettlement schemes will be established for refugees in the underpopulated neighboring Arab States of Transjordan and Iraq. It has been my impression that this type of solution to the problem is very appealing to Americans especially. . . . There is obviously a great appeal in the idea of a new TVA [Tennessee Valley Authority] in the Tigris-Euphratis [sic]

valley, reorganization thereby of "backward" Arab agriculture, reclaiming of land, the establishing of photogenic subsistence homelands.

He added,

This type of solution has apparently been advocated by the Zionists for many years. . . . The long-term Zionist program of public education in this regard has been so effective that resettlement is perhaps becoming the generally accepted "solution." [111]

But resistance from both the refugees themselves and the Arab states now hosting them meant that resettlement would not in fact be implemented. With the exception of Jordan, which had long hoped for an absorption of some Palestinian territory and population and offered its refugees citizenship almost immediately, these countries did not want to absorb hundreds of thousands of refugees and reify and legitimize the state of Israel in the process. As Israel confirmed its position that the refugees would not be allowed to return to their homes and property, the UN decided to maintain its philosophical commitment to the principle of return rather than pressing for Palestinian resettlement elsewhere. Amid the flurry of resolutions and declarations that the new state of Israel must allow the refugees to return to their land if they wished and compensate those who chose not to return,[112] the UN faced the first of many reminders of its almost total impotence in the face of Israeli intransigence.[113] So in 1949, having failed to resolve the question of return for the 750,000 Palestinian refugees scattered across the Arab Middle East, the UN established the United Nations Relief Works Agency (UNRWA) to provide services in the new refugee camps that would now become a permanent part of the political landscape of the Middle East.

UNRWA was premised on the theoretical assumption that repatriation was imminent; but the idea of resettlement and transfer died hard. In the first six years following its founding, the organization came up with a number of schemes for at least partial resettlement as an alternative to repatriation. In the years 1951–53, a program encouraging skilled workers from the camps to emigrate moved tiny numbers of refugees to new homes in Iraq and Libya. Such schemes proved expensive for the agency, met with resistance from local populations, and were broadly resented by the refugees themselves, many of whom returned to the camps rather than continue to live in this second exile. UNRWA's representative to Egypt reported that out of thirteen "artisans" who had been resettled in Libya after 1951, eight had returned to Lebanon, "7 because they desired return and 1 because he was an agitator and because he was frequently intoxicated and creating disturbances."[114] This did not represent a promising model for a broader settlement of the refugee questions. UNRWA next engaged in much larger-scale efforts to "reclaim" large swathes of territory for the refugees in Jordan and Egypt by engaging in massive irrigation and water development schemes funded by the European powers and especially the United States. Such schemes reflected earlier modes of thinking about refugees as potential tools for claiming and developing unproductive or uninhabited land, simultaneously creating newly controlled territory and solving the problem of mass displacement. But competing Israeli water development schemes, demands from the Arab countries over water access, and rising Cold War tensions meant that these plans were never implemented. By 1955, out of a projected budget of $200 million, the agency had spent only about $5.6 million on preliminary work, with no prospects of being able to move forward on any of their development proposals.[115]

By the end of the 1950s, UNRWA had abandoned the possibility of resettlement and instead accepted the UN's position that the refugees should be allowed to return. This meant that the agency maintained the hypothetical assumption that the refugees would be repatriated, while in practice it tried to improve conditions for the refugees largely by making their accommodations more permanent. By 1961, UNRWA had replaced all the tents in the camps across the region with shelters, established more enduring medical services, and set up school facilities and curricula.[116] UNRWA's approach to categorizing, formalizing, "rehabilitating," and educating Palestinian refugees in these designated spaces through particular, bureaucratized programs had the effect of further nationalizing the camp populations. The highly secularized nature of the education offered in UNRWA schools, in particular, had the unintended consequence of providing an intellectual framework for new forms of Palestinian nationalism. As anthropologist Julie Peteet has put it, "UNRWA inadvertently prepared a generation of educated youth for secular, militant nationalist activities."[117]

Their accidental nationalization in UNRWA camps stood in especially sharp contrast to the emerging international consensus, at the UN and elsewhere, that Palestinian refugees would not be treated as a national entity but as a large-scale humanitarian problem. This was evident from the earliest UN resolutions on the subject, which repeatedly called for the "repatriation, resettlement, economic and social rehabilitation of the refugees and the payment of compensation" without mentioning the question of Palestinian statehood.[118] In 1948, the newly formed United Nations Conciliation Commission for Palestine issued a gloss on this position declaring that compensation was owed both to refugees returning to their land and those who chose not to return, but it did not address the outstanding questions of nationality and statehood.[119] Jewish refugees in Europe were also being evaluated for nationhood during the same period, with substantially different outcomes. In 1945 the UN formally declared Jewish refugees stateless and therefore eligible for a new set of resettlement services, and in 1948 the International Refugee Office threw its support behind mass refugee immigration to Israel as a solution to the problem of postwar Jewish displacement—thus, as historian Gerard Daniel Cohen has put it, "acknowledging the legitimacy of Jewish nationhood claims . . . [and fostering] the emergence of philosemitism in international politics."[120]

Thus as Europe's "displaced persons" camps were gradually dismantled and their inhabitants resettled according to new criteria of nationality, the Palestinian refugee camps were gradually and without fanfare incorporated into a settled international regime of extraterritorial aid and administration. Indeed, Palestinian refugees became one of the major institutional preoccupations of the United Nations during the 1950s, a state of affairs that persists today. Just as the post–First World War camps for Armenians and Assyrians had served to coalesce refugee populations around gestures of nationalism and self-determination unsupported by actual international practice, the UNRWA camps now served (albeit less intentionally) to produce an intensified Palestinian nationalism that would quickly find itself at odds with the political decision making of the reigning global powers.

Further, just as Armenian and Assyrian camps of the previous generation were conceived and developed to serve as evidence of the League's importance to the preservation of minority nationalisms, Palestinian refugees now became a raison d'être of the new United Nations. The UN's inability to force a political resolution of the issue became evident alongside its gradual solidification of institutions like UNRWA (the only UN organization since its inception devoted to a single national refugee group) as foundational to the United Nations mission. UNRWA would eventually become one of the UN's largest agencies, with thirty thousand employees working across five regions advertising their role in providing "assistance and protection" for Palestinian refugees "to help them achieve their full potential in human development."[121] Its refugee camps quickly became permanent features of the Middle Eastern political landscape, standing as a visible, tangible argument for the importance of international institutions and as proof of the international community's theoretical sympathy for Palestinian national self-determination against all the available political evidence.

. . .

The idea of partition—dividing a territory by edict and then devolving power onto separate, newly established "national" governments—did not represent a new solution borne of desperation over the dire situation in Palestine. In fact, partition had been under discussion for years before the Peel Commission formally proposed it and reflected central principles of the imperial state system the mandate governments and the League were building across the Middle East.[122]

The particular trajectory of the partition proposals for Palestine rested on some new interpretations of the minority/majority discourse that had emerged out of the League's oversight of eastern Europe and the Eastern Mediterranean. Initially, the minorities treaties and the League's early visions of minority rights made it possible to create a governing structure enshrined in the text of the mandate for Palestine that recognized the Yishuv as a national entity and the Arabs as religious communities. As the mandate wore on, the League also began to describe the Jewish settler colonial community as a "minority"—a novel use of the term that allowed the League and the British to superimpose a postwar minority/majority discourse on a much older imperial vision of racial and civilizational hierarchy. By the 1930s, the British and the League were suggesting that territorial partition could serve as a mode of minority protection—safeguarding a settler colonial "minority" from rule by a majority indigenous population at a lower stage of political and cultural development.

Palestinians, and many non-Palestinian Arabs, bitterly opposed partition as an imperial scheme to permanently place colonial collaborators in a privileged position on stolen land; and the UN's eventual acceptance of the partition solution spoke to the radical exclusion of indigenous interests from the "international" arena. But these schemes of ethnic engineering that eventually led to the territorial division of Palestine were not merely imposed from the League down. Rather, they were embedded in the new postwar international order of which the League was a primary representative, but which had another major player that helped to shape the emergence of this discourse of ethnic homeland and national purity. For while schemes of transfer, resettlement, and now partition often sought to serve imperial interests, they were also closely aligned with the interests of diaspora populations. As we shall see in the next chapter, partition in Palestine was enabled at least in part by the political activism and support of a global diaspora network with a deeply self-interested commitment to supporting an ethnic "homeland" they would most likely never visit.

FIVE

Diasporas and Homelands

Even as ethnically based transfer and partition schemes were meeting with opposition and anger on the ground in Iraq, Syria, and Palestine, they were often hailed by minority diaspora communities scattered through the world. Throughout the interwar period Armenian, Assyrian, and Jewish activists in Europe and the United States lobbied at the national and international levels for the creation of minority ethnic "homelands" supported by the international community—campaigns that became important sources of legitimacy for British, French, and League attempts to remake the demographic order of the Middle East over the protests of local actors.

Few Jews, Armenians, or Assyrians in diaspora actually planned to relocate to an emergent Israel, Armenia, or Assyria. Their support for ethnic nationalisms in regions they had left (or, in many cases, never visited) largely arose from the difficulties of their domestic contexts. Finding themselves in liminal and sometimes precarious positions in their host countries, these communities sought public guarantees of membership in the ingathering of civilized peoples as a means of assimilation. Armenian, Assyrian, and Jewish diaspora representatives, driven by a conviction that ethnic "homelands" represented desirable markers of membership in the modern world, attended the peace talks in force and advocated vigorously for the creation of ethnonational states to protect vulnerable minorities seeking a secure place in the new world order. Following the establishment of the League, its ad hoc petitions committees fielded hundreds of letters advocating for ethnic "homelands" from minority diaspora groups and largely interpreted such documents as international approbation for the concept of ethnonational separation. During the 1930s, as Assyrian, Armenian, and Jewish states failed to materialize, diaspora organizations from the United States to France to

South Africa turned their attention to promoting other modes of ethnic separation like transfer and partition—advocacy that was all the more valuable to the League precisely because it often directly countered the approaches and desires of local populations in the Middle Eastern mandate states.

DIASPORAS AT THE PEACE TALKS

The role of minority diasporas in the creation and support of this rhetoric of ethnic separation began early. Following on the Zionist model, Armenian and Assyrian diaspora groups across the globe saw in the peace talks after the First World War an opportunity to develop an international audience for their claims to nationhood and lobby for the creation of an ethnic "homeland" that they hoped would bolster their standing within their new host nations. Armenian and Assyrian diaspora activism drew on a highly colored rhetoric of ancient nationhood and claims of racially advanced status vis-à-vis Muslim Arab and Turkish populations. Such ideas, which often had their origins in late nineteenth-century encounters with Western missions, intersected in powerful ways with the sorts of claims being made by Zionists for Jewish historical nationhood in Palestine and the civilizational and political advantages of creating a European Jewish nation-state there. Jewish, Armenian, and Assyrian petitions to the peace conference thus collectively set the tone and the agenda for three decades of intensive diaspora engagement with the League of Nations over the question of creating exclusive ethnic homelands for the war's displaced minorities.

As we have already seen, the Jewish presence at the Paris peace conference was sharply divided by political and regional affiliation. On one end of the political spectrum were Zionists who wanted both Jewish national rights in eastern Europe and the creation of a Jewish state in Palestine.[1] The Zionists organized themselves into the Comité des Delegations Juives, comprising primarily Russian and eastern European activists, alongside an American Jewish delegation led by Julian Mack. On the other end, western European Jews, epitomized by the British diplomat Lucien Wolf and his Joint Foreign Committee of British Jews along with the French leaders of the Alliance Israélite Universelle, tended toward an assimilationist and often actively anti-Zionist position. They advocated for legal language in the treaties that would protect and advance the full participation of secularizing Jewish communities in the emerging states of the postwar order.[2]

American Jews' approach to Zionism arose out of their domestic political experience in early twentieth-century America, where they faced an increasingly xenophobic political atmosphere and a multiplicity of both governmental and private organizations calling for restrictions on immigration. The National Americanization Committee, founded in 1915, listed more than a hundred organizations involved in the promotion of "Americanization" across the country in 1918.[3] Supported by leading political figures like Theodore Roosevelt and Woodrow Wilson, the government passed significant anti-immigration measures three times between 1917 and 1924, citing the need to protect a nativist American identity against the cultural incursions of what Roosevelt dismissively called the "hyphenates."[4] Lacking a secondary national identity, and reluctant either to expose themselves to anti-Semitism by making use of a "Jewish-American" moniker or to be identified, as African Americans were, as a racial category, many American Jewish intellectuals and activists began during these years to self-identify as a distinct ethnicity and put forth theories of ethnic difference that simultaneously defended Jewish whiteness, Americanness, and cultural distinctiveness.[5] As political scientist Victoria Hattam has put it, they sought to reject Wilson's and Roosevelt's attacks on plural identifications by reinventing "hyphenation" as "*the* distinctive mark of being American."[6]

Such a conception of ethnicity required defenses of two different types of separatism: a degree of cultural distinctiveness within American society, and the existence of a geographical "homeland" elsewhere. The well-known judge and Jewish activist Louis Brandeis, writing in the first issue of the Harvard Menorah Society journal in 1915, harnessed these two interests together as the essential twin pillars of American Jewish identity:

> Assimilation is national suicide. And assimilation can be prevented only by preserving national characteristics and life as other peoples, large and small, are preserving and developing their national life. Shall we with our inheritance do less than the Irish, the Serbians, or the Bulgars? And must we not, like them, have a land where the Jewish life may be naturally led, the Jewish language spoken, and the Jewish spirit prevail? Surely we must, and that land is our fathers' land; it is Palestine. . . . The glorious past can really live only if it becomes the mirror of a glorious future; and to this end the Jewish home in Palestine is essential. We Jews of prosperous America above all need its inspiration.[7]

This particular vision of American commitment to Zionism had little to do with the actual remaking of Jewish life in Palestine and everything to do with creating a "hyphenated" ethnic identity that would mark Jews as full participants in a fundamentally American project of pluralistic national belonging, along the same lines as other white nationalities now naturalized as American. In a speech in 1917, Brandeis further emphasized this logic: "Every Irish-American who contributed towards advancing home rule was a better man and a better American for the sacrifice he made. Every American Jew who aids in advancing the Jewish settlement in Palestine, though he feels that neither he nor his descendants will ever live there, will likewise be a better man and a better American for doing so."[8] Many other American Jewish leaders accepted this logic—for instance, the well-known jurist and activist Felix Frankfurter, who was equally explicit about the American loyalties tying him to the Zionist platform in Paris and about his interpretation of the issue as a moment for the expression of American power and political values. In a letter to Wilson he wrote, "As a passionate American . . . I cannot forbear to say that not a little of the peace of the world depends upon the disposal before you return to America of the destiny of the people released from Turkish rule."[9]

The American Jewish delegation to the peace conference presented a pro-Zionist perspective influenced by advocates like Louis Brandeis, Julian Mack, Felix Frankfurter, and Stephen Wise, all of whom had just helped to formulate the political position of the new American Jewish Congress at its inaugural meeting in Philadelphia in 1918. The AJC associated Zionism with specifically American political ideas, casting its resolutions claiming rights to internal cultural autonomy and proportional representation as a "Jewish Bill of Rights" for Jews in eastern Europe.[10] Despite some internal opposition from prominent American Jews like Louis Marshall, who strongly disapproved of the Zionist remaking of Jewish identity as national, American Jewish representation at the peace conference tried to convince Wilson to support the Balfour Declaration and broadly conceived maximalist interpretations of the Zionist position.[11]

Jewish petitions coming from further afield, outside the strongholds of either Zionism or European movements for assimilation, tended to support the Zionist position and to express Jewish identity as "national," though often in rather vague terms. Jewish organizations as far-flung as Uruguay and Shanghai wrote to the peace conference representatives to urge the "re-establishment of a Israelite national home [*rétablissement foyer national Israélite*]" in Palestine.[12] A petition from Jews in Greece demanded that the conference recognize a Jewish nation in Palestine that would participate in the League on the same basis as other emerging nations of Europe.[13] Such petitions often demonstrated a rather abstract and absolutist grasp of the Zionist claim; the South African Zionist Conference, for instance, declared that "the Jewish people will not be satisfied with anything less than undivided Palestine coincident in area with the fullest historical extent."[14] Such imprecise but maximalist language was quite different from the language of Zionists from eastern Europe and Palestine itself, who cast their goals in much more concrete and specific (and usually better informed) terms.[15]

Like the Jewish presence, Armenian representation at the Paris peace conference was politically, culturally, and ideologically fragmented, with diaspora representatives often supporting a broader and more territorially ambitious version of the ethnic "homeland." The official representatives of the Armenian cause were the members of the Armenian National Delegation, headed by the Egyptian Armenian leader Boghos Nubar Pasha, claiming to represent ex-Ottoman Armenians in the Middle East but also various Armenian settlements across the diaspora; he himself had never been to the territory now being discussed as Armenia.[16] The new Republic of Armenia was represented by a competing leader, Avetis Aharonian, and did not receive official recognition from the Allied powers at the negotiating table. Beyond these two groups, there were also forty other independent Armenian lobbyists attending the talks as representatives of various individual Armenian diaspora groups, mainly in the United States and Europe. One observer recorded the Armenian presence as overwhelming: "They held conferences and meeting at which hundred of journalists, writers, singers, professors, senators, and ex-ministers, made long speeches in support of the Armenian cause. The Armenian delegates followed Wilson, Lloyd George, and Clemenceau, reminding them every minute of the debt they owed Armenia."[17]

Survivors of the Armenian genocide, by contrast, were largely absent from the peace negotiations. As we have seen, many were now concentrated in Syria, where they were gradually making use of local and French government contacts to move out of the wartime refugee camps and into more permanent settlements in French-designated areas around the cities. For the most part, their concerns were immediate: shelter, employment, and, as the possibility of return to eastern Turkey receded, citizenship, which the French unilaterally granted to Armenian refugees resident in Syria in 1924. Few such refugees had the means to travel to Paris to represent Armenian interests at the negotiating table. Consequently, the Armenian presence at the peace talks was almost entirely made up of diaspora activists broadly focused on a goal of claiming a maximum amount of space for an ethnic homeland, out of the former Ottoman lands that now appeared to be subject to all manner of territorial claims.

The peace conference was flooded with correspondence from Armenian diaspora groups across the globe advocating for Armenian independence, sometimes alongside proposals for an American mandate over Armenia.[18] As one historian with a nationalist bent has put it, "The Armenian world was delirious with visions of a resurrected fatherland."[19] Initial Armenian diasporic visions at the talks were ambitious, encompassing an Armenian state that would include not only the Republic of Armenia but also the Turkish territories of Van, Bitlis, Diyarbekir, Kharput, Sivas, Erzerum, and Trebizond as well as Cilicia—a territorial maximalism that the representatives of Russian Armenia under Avetis Aharonian's leadership did not share.[20] (Some philo-Armenian visions went even further; James Barton, foreign secretary of the American Board of Commissions for Foreign Missions, promoted the cause by declaring, "Give the Armenian capital and a righteous government and he will turn the whole of Turkey into a Garden of Eden in ten years."[21]) An Armenian group in Yonkers, New York, telegraphed the conference, "It is the ardent wish and desire of the Armenians residing at the city of Yonkers NY that the United States accept a mandate over integral liberated and independent Armenia."[22] The Society of Danish Friends of Armenia demanded Armenian national representation at the peace conference.[23] A meeting of Armenians and sympathizers in the Swiss town of Bale expressed sympathy for the goal of an Armenian nation, with "equal sympathies to other Christian peoples oppressed by Turkey."[24] A similar gathering in Lausanne called for the "recognition [*reconnaissance*]" of the "legitimate" nation of Armenia.[25]

Some Armenian diasporic activists saw Zionism as a model and a potential source of support for the sorts of national and territorial claims they hoped to advance. As historian Yair Auron has pointed out, the Zionist and Armenian diaspora presses in London and Paris were in conversation and promoted the idea that Armenian and Zionist political platforms were mutually reinforcing. In 1917, *Palestine,* the journal of the British Zionist movement published in London, made a case for the essentially national qualities of both communities and their shared political goals:

> Between the Armenian and the Jew there are notable points of community. The persistence of Armenian nationality through long generations of oppression is one; the fellowship of suffering is another; a certain harmonising of

East and West is a third. The survival of the Armenian nation is a political miracle only second in wonder to that of the Jews. If the Jews have maintained their national quality in exile from their land, the Armenians have maintained the life and the hold of theirs under the heel of a foreign tyrant and sundered from the kindred West by a surrounding ocean of different and often hostile elements. Only a high moral fortitude and a rare spiritual virtue could sustain a nation under such circumstances.[26]

Following the Balfour Declaration in November 1917, Boghos Nubar Pasha wrote to leading Zionists in London to offer his congratulations, declaring that it "strengthens our hope that the victory of those fighting for the liberation of the oppressed peoples will bring the realization of the Armenian hope, at the same time as the Jewish People achieves the establishment of its nationality."[27]

In the United States, too, the Armenian diaspora and its allies who put together significant lobbying efforts to encourage Wilson and his administration to press the Armenian issue at the peace talks and beyond sometimes made use of Zionist-derived language and arguments. An Armenian American lawyer in New York named Vahan Cardashian, who had affiliations with the Dashnak Party and had written pieces for an Armenian newspaper in Boston, followed up an unsuccessful wartime proposal that the United States invade the Cilician coast from a British base in Cyprus (an idea considered with interest, albeit only briefly, by Teddy Roosevelt) by founding the American Committee for the Independence of Armenia (ACIA) in 1918.[28] Its goal was to ensure an independent homeland in Armenia, overseen by an American mandate. Most of the ACIA's founding members were wealthy Protestant elites drawn from the worlds of industry, politics, and higher education, though the group also included the early American Zionist activist Stephen Wise.[29] Cardashian's colleague and cofounder of ACIA, a former ambassador to Germany named James Gerard, argued for Armenian nationalism in terms that precisely recalled Herzl's declaration two decades earlier that Zionists in Palestine would represent "part of a wall of defense for Europe in Asia, an outpost of civilization against barbarism":[30]

The Armenian, an Alpine Aryan like the Swiss, North Italian, and most Greeks, since his emigration to Asia Minor over 3,000 years ago, has been a stumbling block in the way of Asiatic invaders toward the West and has kept aflame in the New East the light of Western civilization and Christianity amidst hardships that would have ground to the dust a weaker nation. . . . If we take the Armenian mandate, Armenia will become the outpost of American civilization in the East.... [If not,] we shall have thus lost a great opportunity for the propagation of Anglo-Saxon civilization in the Near East.[31]

Such language would become fundamental to the diasporic memorialization of a lost Armenian homeland. Peter Balakian's memoir recorded his aunt's use of such language decades later in the United States: "Had the Treaty of Sevres [with its promise of an independent Armenia] passed, it would have said: The civilized world cares about the most ancient Christian nation of the Near East.... We were left to the perverted barbarism of the Turks."[32] Further echoing Zionist language, by the early 1920s the newly formed Armenia America Society (whose membership overlapped with the ACIA and which counted both Gerard and Wise as representatives on its national committee) was calling for an Armenian "national home" in Cilicia, conceived as a semiautonomous space under external protection that would serve as a first step toward sovereign statehood.[33]

Promoting Armenian nationalism and the cause of an Armenian ethnic homeland by linking it to Zionism and to a specifically American version of Western "civilization" represented a diaspora tactic that was not generally reflected in the activism of Armenians still in Soviet Armenia or the various Armenian encampments across the Middle East. The Soviet Armenian leadership drew primarily on the language of revolutionary socialism and was largely uninterested in making claims to "civilization,"[34] while Armenian refugees in the camps remained focused on immediate questions of survival within Syria, Lebanon, and Iraq.[35] Diasporic territorial goals were also significantly more expansive than those of more local actors, to the extent that one ACIA official sponsored a Senate resolution in 1918 calling for an Armenia encompassing "Russian Armenia, the six vilayets of Turkish Armenia, and even a district in North Persia claimed neither by the Armenian republic nor by the Armenian National Delegation."[36] As was also true for Assyrian and Zionist claims, the diasporas had ambitious territorial goals for their envisioned "homelands" not shared by many local representatives.

The Assyrian presence at the peace conference, while significantly smaller than the Armenian or Jewish, reflected a similar divergence between diaspora activists and local communities. Refugee Assyrians' political activism was limited both by the dire postwar economic and political situation and by their desire, unsupported by any Allied members of the peace conference, to be repatriated to their former homes in Hakkari even if it meant living under the Turkish state. The American Assyrian diaspora, on the other hand, sent a delegation to Paris headed by the longtime activist, writer, and translator Joel Werda to present explicitly national and separatist claims. Werda explained the relations between the Assyrians in Iraq and his delegation thus:

> Shortly after it became known that the Peace Conference would be held in Paris, the writer, as the President of the "Assyrian National Associations of America," which he had organized, sent a cable through the courtesy of the Department of State to the American consul in Bagdad, requesting of the latter to ascertain the wishes of the Assyrian national leaders with reference to their national claims, to be presented at Peace Conference in Paris. Of the three sectarian groups, into which the Assyrian people are divided, the Nestorian element, because of the great and courageous role it played in the war had the first right to speak. And yet, for the sake of the Assyrian national unity, it was deemed advisable by the writer to ascertain the wishes of the other two Assyrian Patriarchs as well. The American Consul, through the Department of State, replied that the Jacobite Patriarch, being then in the territory still occupied by the Turks, could not be communicated with; that the Roman Catholic Patriarch has a desire to go to Paris in person; but the wish of the Nestorian Patriarch is, "All Assyrians united, and under the protectorate of Great Britain!" This was precisely the policy advocated by the Assyrian American Courier, which was then as still is, the only national organ of the Assyrian people.[37]

These claims, as presented in a pamphlet for distribution to the delegates at the peace conference, revolved around the demand that "the Assyrians, as a historic people, both in the interests of history, and for the perpetuation of that history, should be created into a separate state . . . bounded roughly by Tikrit (below Zaba) in the south, and the province of Dearbeker in the north; and by a straight line running parallel with the banks of Euphrates in the west, to the mountains of Armenia in the east," this expansive territory to be placed under the supervision of a mandatory power that would retain its role for at least twenty-five years.[38] Werda declared that this was a universal desire among Assyrians across the globe, including the refugee communities in Iraq: "These claims are in perfect accord with the wishes of Mar Shimon and men of war and the leaders of the Assyrian nation as expressed through the cables transmitted through the department of State in Washington to the President of the Assyrian National Associations of America"[39]—a seriously doubtful claim, made just as local activists in Mosul and Baghdad tried to organize their communities for a move back to Hakkari or look for some sort of reformulation of the millet status they had enjoyed under the Ottomans.

Nevertheless, Werda's organization, the New York-based Executive Committee of Assyrian National Associations of America, repeated these assertions in other letters, petitions, and documentation addressed to the delegates. Its members argued to the peace conference that an independent Assyrian state was a straightforward idea: "The lines of nationality are fairly clear and the claims of the delegates will not involve any complication between her neighbors." Their writings also clearly presented Assyrian identity as oppositional to Turkish backwardness and barbarism: "The Assyrians in Mesopotamia and Urmia in Salmas and Khay have fought the battles of the Allies with Russia and English Armies. Their heroic fights and brave deeds were recognized by the Allied Commanders. . . . The history of Turkish government and its cruel deeds are known to the world; fertile lands lie sterile under the dead hand of the Turk, whereas Assyrians in their country are successful in every branch; they are an intelligent, industrious and prolific race." [40] This Assyrian American program thus drew on a now-standard set of diaspora claims: that the Assyrians constituted a clearly identifiable Christian nation, loyal to the Allies and enemies of Muslim Arabs and Turks alike, who (like the Zionists) were uniquely capable of developing the land they would be given. Far from reflecting the interests of Assyrian communities existing in a state of limbo in refugee camps in Mesopotamia, such language primarily reflected the anxieties and needs of a diaspora community trying to demonstrate its whiteness, Christianity, and "civilization" in the context of an often xenophobic and hostile host country that tended to understand Middle Eastern immigrants as part of an undifferentiated Muslim barbarism. [41]

This narrative of Assyrian and Armenian Christian civilization versus Turkish Muslim barbarism, alongside vividly expressed fears of racial annihilation, represented an especially prominent trope for diaspora activists. The Assyrian National Associations of America advocated for an independent Assyrian state to be carved out of Kurdistan and Mesopotamia on precisely these grounds:

> The centuries have proved that the Turks are incapable of reform, and the Arabs are not accustomed to any form of government . . . .
>
> Assyrians have lived under centuries of cruelty and persecution. Their faithfulness to their nationality and religion have saved them from extermination. [42]

For Armenian and Assyrian diaspora communities in the West, this rhetoric of ancient Christian nationhood represented a crucial mode of assimilation. By accepting and promoting ideas of Turkish Muslim barbarism set beside Assyrian and Armenian national and religious commitment, they could claim a space in "Western civilization" that would make absorption into the United States, France, England, and Australia (among others) an easier task. In some cases, particularly in the United States, this claim to Christian nationhood could also pave the way to claiming the legal category of "white" and its corresponding legal and political privileges.[43]

Despite their vagueness, such petitions received serious attention from Allied powers looking for partners in their claims over the Middle East while trying to fit the fate of the region into the rhetorical framework of self-determination being constructed at the talks. Diplomatic discussions of the question of "homelands" for Jewish, Armenian, and Assyrian populations thus often accepted the diasporic framing of ethnic homelands as a humanitarian cause that would also carry political benefits for the sponsoring powers. They also tended to group together Jewish, Armenian, and Assyrian diasporas as representatives of "civilization" and modernity in regions generally lacking both. The British statement of policy on the Middle East summed up these essentially imperial assumptions about the uses of large "minority" immigrant populations into newly built ethnic homelands:

> Non-Turkish populations formerly subject to Turkey, or populations in which the Turkish element is in a minority, ought to be liberated completely from Turkish rule, and from all political connection, even nominal, with the Ottoman Government.... [But] "self-determination," as provided for above, is subject to certain inevitable limitations. There may be cases where the area inhabited by a population that wishes to form an independent unit does not constitute a geographical unity that can be administered separately. There are areas, such as Thrace, Constantinople, Armenia, in which the population cannot speak with a united voice, and in which the assisting Power will have to be chosen by the Conference rather than by the people themselves. There are elements, like the Armenians and the Zionist Jews, which, for historical reasons or on account of future possibilities, have a claim to special consideration out of proportion to their present numerical strength in the Middle Eastern countries they inhabit. And, finally, there are world interests such as the "permanent opening of the Black Sea Straits as a free passage to the ships

and commerce of all nations under international guarantees," or access to Holy Places in Palestine for all religions or denominations legitimately interested in each of them, which are so important that they must, if necessary, take precedence over the wishes of the inhabitants of the localities in which they are situated.[44]

Mass voluntary immigration from Armenian and Jewish diasporas could, in this reading, play a central role in the demographic remaking of the postwar order. This became a recurring theme particularly in British commentary on the peace talks, which sometimes specifically predicted this role for the Armenian diaspora. "The Armenians are at present the most progressive and prolific element in the population," one memo ran, adding that "there will be an immigration of Armenians from abroad and they are likely to play a leading role in the future"[45]—a concept derived from Armenian advocates like Avetis Aharonian, who told the British government that "to the united country there would come back great numbers of Armenians from all over the world."[46] Very similar language appeared in their descriptions of Zionist activities in Palestine: "The Jewish agricultural colonists in Palestine, like the Armenians and Greeks in the areas above-mentioned, are a minority which, on account of its historic past, its superior vigour and ability, the barbarous methods by which its numbers have recently been reduced, and its reservoirs of potential immigrants, from which its losses can be made good, is certain of a future which entitles it to consideration out of proportion to its present numbers."[47] Some British commentary explicitly linked Armenian and Jewish diasporic national claims, as in one Foreign Office document declaring that "it should be laid down in Armenia that the dead and exiles should be taken into account, and Armenian immigrants from other parts of the world into Armenia should be given the same facilities as Jewish immigrants into Palestine for settling down in their ancestral home."[48] Assyrians came in for very similar treatment: "The sufferings of this people, and their services to the Allied cause, during the war give them some claim to special consideration."[49]

A handbook prepared by the India Office on "Armenia and Kurdistan" went still further by drawing a genealogical connection among all three groups, describing Armenians as having arisen from "an admixture of Assyrian and Jewish elements fused with the Aryan peoples.... These elements, together with the subarctic climate of a highland home, have contributed to produce a remarkably vigorous and virile stock, a people who had maintained a distinct national consciousness for 2,500 years."[50] Such a description stood in direct contrast to that of the Kurds, who were described in much briefer and less flattering terms as "tent-dwelling nomads" [51]—reflecting Arnold Toynbee's declaration just a few years earlier that the genocide had been all the more appalling because Armenians were not "nomadic shepherds like their barbarous neighbours the Kurds." [52] British officialdom thus distinguished Christians and Jews from Muslim populations claiming similar "national" rights, an approach that drew considerable support from European Christian organizations. One Christian coalition in Manchester, for instance, sent a resolution to the peace conference calling for "the emancipation of the Christian races in the Turkish Empire . . . as of the utmost importance to the future of Christian civilization and the freedom of the world." [53] The conversations around the peace talks were beginning to produce a narrative of a few favored "races" with very similar sets of claims to nationhood and land in the former Ottoman territories. Diaspora Assyrian, Armenian, and Jewish groups were conscious of the success of this narrative and anxious to further it through claims about their simultaneously ancient and modern collective national identities.

Arab activists in the diaspora also made their case that the peace arrangements should create particular national formulations, especially with regard to Syria, but much less successfully—largely because rather than drawing on the tropes of race, civilization, and development that Zionist, Armenian, and Assyrian diaspora groups emphasized, they advocated for political formulations partially inspired by earlier Ottoman models. The kind of ethnic cleansing practiced by the late Ottoman state in the Balkans and eastern Anatolia had no real counterpart in the Arab provinces, where a prosperous Christian middle class had emerged as a major element in Syrian and Palestinian nationalist movements by the early 1920s.[54] From the nineteenth century, Syrian Christians had also become a significant diasporic element, working in Europe, the United States, and Latin America while often maintaining ties to land, family, and business interests in the homeland.[55] The largely Christian expatriate Syrian groups writing from Europe and the United States therefore viewed the question from the perspective of a relatively functional late Ottomanism.[56] They mainly advocated for the maintenance of a decentralized but unified Syria that would include Palestine, disagreeing primarily on the question of whether France, Britain, or the United States should be charged with Syria's supervision on the road to independence.

R. Haddad, who headed the Syrian National Committee of North America based in Brooklyn, encapsulated the areas of both broad agreement and conflict within the Syrian American community in a letter to the British consul general in New York. He described three main factions: one pro-French and essentially a branch of similar organizations based in Paris; one pro-American and backed by a set of Protestant missionary interests; and one, his own, pro-British. All three backed the principle of a multinational and multireligious unified Syrian state (including Palestine, its "sacred heart"), "in order to preserve the unity of Syria and to place all Arabic-speaking countries of the Orient under one protection and influence," and asked the conference "to apply self-determination to Syria and to give her self government under a guardianship or supervision conforming to the wishes and demands of the majority of her own people." [57] Nearly all the diasporic petitions coming from Syrian communities in the United States and Europe made the case for Syrian unity, including Palestine as a central part of a historic Syrian Arab state—a position often upheld by Palestinian diaspora groups as well.[58] Many explicitly disputed the case for separating Lebanon from Syria on the basis of religious difference, arguing that diverse communal identities did not preclude political unity.[59] One such petition from a group of Syrians in Paris labeled this as a regrettable partition that would deal a mortal blow (*coup mortel*) to Syrian national interests and directly contradicted Allied and American "principles of right and justice." [60] Some, like a Syrian congress writing from Brazil, appealed to Wilsonian principles by making the case for a united Syria under an American mandate: "Pray help us attain this end." [61]

In some ways, these visions of a pluralistic, decentralized Syrian state including Lebanon and Palestine bore a resemblance to Lucien Wolf's anti-Zionist proposals in 1917 for a postwar federation of Poland, Lithuania, and Ukraine under some form of Russian oversight, with defined rights for minorities—an argument that a pluralistic state with certain protections and guarantees could represent a successful modern formulation. As historian Mark Levene has noted, Wolf "was implicitly arguing from a Jewish point of view that there was nothing seriously at fault with a German[-inspired] *Ostimperium*," [62] just as these far-flung Arab nationalists were declaring that there was nothing seriously wrong with a basically Ottoman conception of Syria. Some diaspora activists made quite an explicit case for maintaining continuity with the Ottoman sphere; one group of Muslims in London, including Indian and Persian as well as Arab activists, wrote to Balfour to suggest precisely this:

We welcome the proposal to create self-governing institutions in the occupied Provinces of Turkey and in Armenia under the guarantee of the League of Nations but we most strongly deprecate the suggestion to sever them absolutely from the Turkish Empire. Our reasons for this submission are not sentimental; they are founded on ground of expediency and policy.... We hope that with the disappearance of the two Empires that had hitherto exploited Asiatic unrest and misgovernment to their own advantage, with a view to final political or economic absorption, the new Peace would assure the pacific development of Western and Middle Asia on durable lines.

On the question of a Jewish state in Palestine (to which they objected strongly), they added, "History proves that the Jews can live in the closest amity with their Mussulman fellow-subjects under Moslem rulers and enjoy exceptional privileges not conceded to them even now by many European nations." [63]

Such advocacy for pluralistic states maintaining some of the political foundations of the toppled empires could not be successfully advocated in the postwar context. The idea of a multifarious Syrian nationalism as the basis for a new state received almost no hearing at the peace talks—partly because its vision conflicted with the already-determined strategic goals of Britain and France, but also precisely because it presented a view of nationhood and political identity linked with Ottoman precedent. A handbook prepared for the Allies on "Syria and Palestine" in 1919 summed up the prevailing attitude toward this looser interpretation of national belonging: "Even if Burton's gibe, that the Lebanese hide their weapons at the call of patriotism, be too bitter, it may be owned that they have turned their arms ninety-nine times in a hundred on one another, and have allowed Arabs, Turks, and Egyptians to ride roughshod over them, unopposed by any local patriotism worthy to be mentioned in the same breath with that of the Armenians, the Greeks, and any Balkan race." [64]

Diaspora activism, then, was already a significant component of the international conversation about the fate of the Middle East by the time of the peace negotiations. Indeed, the emergence of the Paris conference as a venue for the expression of diasporic political goals and ambitions set a precedent for the relationship between the League of Nations and diaspora groups throughout the West. The diaspora voices that were most successful hewed closely to already-established narratives: ancient nationhood and racial distinctiveness, opposition to Muslim power, commitment to modernization and development, and loyalty to particular European (and in some cases American) sponsors. These narratives, in turn, reappeared in Allied restatements of their strategic goals as evidence that the communities under discussion themselves supported the imperial restructuring of the region that was underway.

ASSYRIAN, ARMENIAN, AND JEWISH DIASPORA RESPONSES TO TRANSFER AND PARTITION PLANS

Already well established before 1914, Assyrian, Armenian, and Jewish diaspora communities across the United States and Europe expanded significantly after the war as a consequence of wartime dislocation and the slow but substantial refugee resettlement efforts undertaken by the League and its allies. The fledgling "minority" diaspora activism evident at the peace talks now solidified into more definite movements advocating for international recognition of Jewish, Armenian, and Assyrian identities as national through the creation of ethnically based homelands. Such advocacy strove to normalize immigrant communities by distancing them from the negative associations around the ghetto, the Muslim world, and the "Orient."

Jewish, Armenian, and Assyrian diasporic advocacy for the "recreation" of an ancient ethnic homeland emerged out of an increasingly hostile atmosphere for immigrants. In both France and the United States, the Western host countries who received the largest numbers of Armenian immigrants in the interwar period, the 1920s and 1930s saw a major rise in xenophobic, anti-immigrant, and antiminority commentary and increasingly draconian limits on immigration and citizenship. In the United States, the so-called National Origins Formula enshrined in the Immigration Act of 1924 introduced a quota system intended to ensure the maintenance of the current ethnic makeup of the country and sharply restricted Jewish and Armenian immigration from central and eastern Europe and the Middle East.[65] In France, relatively simple requirements that French immigrants over the age of fifteen carry identification cards had given way to dramatic and brutal crackdowns in 1934–35 as the government expelled large numbers of refugees.[66] Xenophobic language sometimes explicitly linked Armenians and Jews as permanent, malevolent outsiders. In 1935, for instance, the French journalist Lucien Rebatet described the two communities as sharing "the same aptitude, the same absence of an attachment to any territory (all left without any thought of returning), the same promiscuity in the ghettos, where they seem crushed, where the same pogroms decimated them, and from where they suddenly emerged just as cliquish and as congested as they had been previously. The Armenian is, with the Jew, the same type of foreigner."[67] Support for movements of an ethnic "homeland," then, represented a way for minority ethnicities in France and the United States to demonstrate precisely such an attachment to a territory and prove their belonging in a world of nation-states.

Because of this new hostility, support for Zionism among both French and American Jews went during the interwar period from virtually nonexistent to representing a significant though still minority interest. Until the 1930s, Zionism had never attracted much interest among French Jews, who by and large subscribed to the state's joint commitment to secularization and assimilation. Indeed, Jewish leaders in France during the first decades of the twentieth century tended to view Zionism with suspicion, as presenting a threat to full Jewish citizenship and political participation. But in the 1930s, as the French public sphere increasingly included overtly anti-Semitic and xenophobic commentary and Jews in France became increasingly concerned about the fate of their coreligionists in central and eastern Europe, some began to regard Zionism in a more favorable light. Without endorsing its goals altogether, the Jewish intelligentsia in France began more seriously to consider Zionism's framing of Jewish identity as essentially ethnonational rather than religious, and to support some Zionist efforts to resettle threatened eastern European Jews in Palestine.[68]

Even the Alliance Israélite Universelle, fervently anti-Zionist almost since its inception, began to view Palestine as a potential haven for eastern European Jews during the 1930s. By 1947 René Cassin, the president of the AIU and a member of Charles de Gaulle's provisional government (and now best known as a primary architect of the United Nations Universal Declaration of Human Rights), had reversed his previous opinion and begun to advocate for 100,000 Jews to be immediately resettled in Palestine and for the UN to take over the mandate from the British.[69] Further, he associated this change of approach with the organization itself, saying that the AIU would support a solution involving "massive immigration and colonization as well as the free development of a Jewish state in Palestine" if negotiations between Jews and Muslims and all other interested parties proved unsuccessful.[70] This represented a major shift from the AIU's long-held position of hostility to Zionism as a dangerous and damaging interpretation of the nature of Jewish identity in the modern world.

Interest in Zionism took a similar trajectory in the United States. In 1914, of the approximately three million Jews in the United States, about twelve thousand (less than 0.5%) belonged to some kind of Zionist organization. But in the 1920s and 1930s a new and especially hostile form of anti-Semitism began to emerge in the United States, epitomized especially by the new prominence of the Ku Klux Klan. As the quota system entrenched immigration restrictions and American Jews faced increasing hostility in the public sphere, Zionism seemed to offer a mode of support for persecuted European Jews that would not arouse further tension within American domestic politics. As one Zionist historian has put it, "The fear of creating an anti-Semitic backlash stifled the urge to attack restrictive immigration laws.... Among American Jews, Zionism became a comforting substitute for the domestic political agitation in which they did not dare indulge."[71] This approach was made easier by the fact that as early as the 1920s there was already significant support among the American Christian political establishment for Zionism, both on evangelical Protestant grounds and on a more specifically American understanding of the Jewish settler project in Palestine as analogous to the American conquest of the frontier.[72] Beginning in 1930, American Zionists began to set up some more public-facing organizations to promote the cause of Jewish resettlement in Palestine from an American perspective, including the Pro-Palestine Federation of America and the American Palestine Committee. These diaspora organizations made the most of the high levels of evangelical Christian support for their cause by using terms like "Holy Land" to describe Palestine and constructing narratives of ancient nationhood as a backdrop to the idea of a European Jewish "return" to an ethnic homeland. They also began to spend significant amounts of money on lobbying efforts directed at Christian organizations in the United States to "crystallize the sympathy of Christian America," as the Zionist Organization of America put it.[73]

By the late 1930s, then, Zionists in the United States had significantly raised the profile of their movement, within the confines of their reading of American public opinion. They focused on the immediate plight of Jewish communities in Germany and eastern Europe, avoiding discussion of Labor Zionism's socialist platform that many were loath to support. They also carefully rejected any suggestion of the creation of a broadly based Jewish communal bloc within American politics. A proposed resolution at a 1938 meeting of all the main American Jewish organizations advocating "a union of all American Jewish groups ... a single, all-inclusive [Jewish] agency organized on a democratic, representative basis," failed in the face of resistance from the American Jewish Committee, the Jewish Labor Committee, and B'nai B'rith, all of which stamped the concept of a Jewish bloc as antiassimilationist.[74] The extensive petitions, pamphlets, and letters American Zionists sent to the League and the British government during the 1930s—mainly protesting restrictions on immigration into the mandate state—reflected their commitment to cultural, political, and economic assimilation within the United States rather than an interest in immigration to a potential Jewish "homeland."

Diaspora petitions coming from Armenian communities during the interwar period indicated a similar disconnect between the stated goal of a "homeland" and underlying attempts to address pressing domestic concerns in their host countries. Through the 1920s, as the fate of Armenian refugees was debated at the League of Nations, Armenian diaspora groups—largest and most active in the United States and France, where large numbers had settled after the massacres of the 1890s and again following the First World War—continued to lobby for some form of independent statehood. The crisis over Alexandretta in 1938 and 1939, which resulted in its absorption into the Republic of Turkey, led to claims that Armenians were fleeing from the region and again brought up the question of an Armenian ethnic homeland.[75] By the following year renewed calls for an international consensus on the borders of Armenia could be heard in London and Paris, but such discussion often masked a rather different underlying agenda. In London, for instance, one Armenian representative made use of broad rhetorical claims to a national homeland to advocate for other, more local and specific forms of assistance:

> The Armenian Delegation wish to convey to you the earnest desire of the Armenian people for the creation of an independent Armenian State whose frontiers should include the territories of Soviet Armenia and those provinces of Turkish Armenia which were assigned to them under the Treaty of Sèvres. We submit that the principle of self-determination of nations as well as political and strategical considerations entitles us to the recognition of our right to a separate national states within the confines of our original homeland. An independent Armenia would be the safeguard for the preservation of peace in the Near East and a bulwark against the expansionist aims of certain powers.
>
> We are, however, aware that the existing international situation presents difficulties that make the fulfillment of this purpose impossible at the moment. There are, however, other aspects in our national life in which Great Britain could be of great help.[76]

FIGURE 6. Meeting of Armenian General Benevolent Union in Buenos Aires, 1932. Courtesy of AGBU Nubar Library, Paris.

The national claim, then, actually served as a tactic for the promotion of other agenda items: opposition to the proposed French withdrawal from Alexandretta, anxiety over relationships with Soviet Armenia, and funding and support for Armenian military units.

Throughout this period, many Armenian diaspora groups continued to draw on Zionist models to produce their narratives of ancient nationhood and the recreation of an ethnic homeland, responding both to Zionist successes and to the way anti-immigrant sentiment tended to link criticisms of Armenians and Jews. To demonstrate their theoretical attachment to the idea of an ethnic homeland, Armenian activist and community groups in France developed networks of compatriotic unions and societies that celebrated the idea of an Armenian "motherland" (though with considerable disagreement about the extent to which this formulation should be attached to what had now become Soviet Armenia).[77] Some of these diaspora organizations opened branches in Lebanon and Syria, where they advocated for specifically nationalist visions of Armenian identity. The Armenian Relief Cross, founded in Boston in 1910, dedicated itself to health and educational work but also to the nationalist vision of the Dashnak Party when it expanded into Lebanon in 1929.[78] Similarly, the Howard Karagheuzian Commemorative Corporation, a private Armenian American charitable organization established in New York in 1921, opened new branches in 'Anjar and Beirut after the French ceded Alexandretta to Turkey in 1939, as an expression of Armenian national solidarity.[79] The Armenian General Benevolent Union, founded in Cairo in 1906 under the leadership of Boghos Nubar Pasha, had branches in Europe, the United States, and Latin America and moved its main office to Paris in 1922. Its branches raised substantial amounts of money in the early 1930s to support building a model village for resettled refugees near Yerevan, as well as funding Armenian schools in Bulgaria, Egypt, France, Iraq, Greece, Lebanon, Syria, Palestine, and Cyprus. Throughout the 1920s and 1930s, Armenian expatriates not only supported such diaspora organizations and their outreach activities in Lebanon and Syria but also sent significant amounts of money to support settlements in the "homeland," usually without any indication of interest in personally relocating.

Like their Zionist parallels, these sorts of diasporic social organizations supported the concept of a homeland primarily as a way consciously to perpetuate a specifically Armenian diasporic identity in the Middle East and Europe. They were thus simultaneously a source of international legitimacy for the Armenian national cause and, sometimes, a weakness for its actual implementation. Monte Melkonian, an Armenian American turned militant Armenian nationalist, noted this contradiction in his writings:

> Take, for example, the common claim that since we are all Armenians, we are all motivated to struggle for our right to live in our homeland. Such a notion was perhaps emotionally satisfying for many, but in practical terms it hindered our political and organizational development. . . . Although none but a handful of these people are ever likely to place themselves on the front line of the struggle, they can and should be a source of support for the vanguard. . . . [But] the vanguard should guide the struggle. It should never compromise its political and ideological independence to less committed supporters, no matter how much material assistance the latter may rally.[80]

Diaspora actors supported the concept of ethnic "homelands" for reasons other than the interests of compatriots on the ground and maintained distinct political goals within such ethnic nationalist movements.

This discrepancy became especially visible in the Assyrian case in the 1930s, as diasporic Assyrians committed themselves to supporting a plan for mass Assyrian relocation in Brazil that had almost no support among those actually slotted to be moved. Diaspora narratives about the Assyrians privileged their nationhood over all else, abandoning specific land claims in favor of pleas for international resettlement, recognition, and independence and presenting the community as a persecuted outpost of Western-affiliated Christians who just happened to be in Iraq. By the mid-1930s, Mar Shimun, operating from Cyprus and London, had transformed his office into a political institution arguing for Assyrian nationhood. Assyrian diasporic churches and social organizations worked alongside the patriarchate to lobby the international community for recognition and support for an independent Assyrian national entity, presenting the idea as a humanitarian as well as a political cause. Although their ultimate goal was an independent, internationally recognized Assyrian state, Assyrian communities in London, Chicago, Marseilles, and Los Angeles saw resettlement in an altogether different context—like Brazil—as an opportunity for the Assyrians to be recognized as a Christian partner to the Western nations rather than be regarded primarily as a Middle Eastern refugee problem. Beginning in 1933, diasporic groups flooded the British government and the League of Nations with correspondence supporting the League's new proposal to resettle Assyrians in Brazil.

Their letters, speeches, pamphlets, and petitions tended to feature three main lines of argument. First, they argued for an understanding of Assyria as a nation with an unbroken line of descent from the ancient Assyrian empires. A petition from the Assyrian community in Greece beseeched the League to go forward with resettlement, "not only to prove to the civilized world the existence of the League of Nations' human love towards the persecuted and suffering people, but to preserve the existence of the Assyrians—the world's oldest and historical nation that once was known as Shepherd dog of the civilized world," [81] and to place the Assyrians "in a country that we may not be persecuted and massacred again, by our religious and political enemies." An Assyrian diaspora group in Geneva wrote to the League,

> Although they [the Assyrians] have fought more than any other people for their freedom and as a Christian and civilized people have more claim to a national home in their country that has been their abode since time immemorial, the Assyro-Chaldean people is the only one of all the Near Eastern people which up to the present time has not been granted what is their just and legitimate claim. The Arabs, the Lebanon Christians, the Druzes, the Allaouites, and the Jews have all secured their independence and a national home, while the Assyrians ... have been victims of all sorts of insults, ill-treatment, and wholesale massacres by Iraqui [sic] fanatics. [82]

As well as this trope of ancient Christian nationhood and explicit comparison to the Zionists among others, Assyrian diaspora activists deployed the language of the minorities treaties to remind the League of its international obligations to protect minority communities in its member states. Many also voiced anti-Arab and anti-Muslim sentiments, accusing the Iraqi government of barbarity and representing the Assyrian position as a total unwillingness to continue to live under Arab or Muslim rule. Diasporic Assyrian activists neatly related the Islamophobic language of British imperialism to the new internationalist language of minority rights within the League to argue for Assyrian resettlement outside Iraq. From Marseille, one Assyrian writer described the community as "unfortunate people . . . compelled to become subjects of the uncivilized Arabs of Iraq." [83] Another spoke of "the absolute impossibility for a Christian minority to flourish and prosper in a Muslim state." [84] The vice president of the Assyrian National Federation in Yonkers, New York, wrote to the League to protest keeping the Assyrians in Iraq, saying that a recent report "that the Assyrians are willing to live under Arab rule is false and unfounded." [85] The Assyrian National League in Chicago wrote to the League that resettlement would save "an ancient nation and church," and reminded the committee that "the Assyrians are the League's ward, and as such they are entitled to its protection . . . since the League has assumed full responsibility for the protection of the minority groups." [86]

Finally, these diaspora groups drew on the theme of racial extinction as the natural consequence of the League's failure to come up with a satisfactory resettlement scheme. "The political situation in the regions where the Assyrians are now located is so grave," the Chicago branch declared, "that an immediate decision on the part of the League is absolutely imperative if the Assyrians are to be saved from complete extinction." [87] A secular constitutional government would not answer the problem, since "for then, the minority through intermarriage and so-called equality, in a short time will be absorbed by the Muslim majority, which would mean the extinction of our language and national existence." [88] A wide variety of Christian organizations in the West, from the archbishop of Canterbury to mission groups to American Midwestern churches, echoed this language in a series of petitions and letters to the League. The World Alliance for International Friendship Through the Churches passed a resolution in 1933 calling for Assyrian resettlement, to "secure to this minority the protection which was assured to them when the State of Iraq was admitted to the League of Nations." [89] The

Assyrian National Union, based in Boston, made an appeal to the League typical of these diaspora efforts: "We beg of you, in the name of humanity to prevent any further outbreaks and similar outrages and most humbly pray that the League of Nations give this matter due consideration with the ultimate purpose of finding a suitable homeland for these Christian Assyrians where they may live peacefully without fear of religious or racial prosecution [sic] in the future."[90]

As we have already seen, this diaspora support for transfer was generally not echoed in Iraq, where many Assyrians actively opposed resettlement and those who did support it much preferred Syria as a destination over far-flung locales like British Guiana or Brazil. Even Mar Shimun, who strongly favored the idea of resettlement once it had become clear that the Iraqi government would under no circumstances cede land for an autonomous Assyrian enclave, admitted that "the Assyrian emigration to Syria—due to its proximity to Iraq—would be far less objectionable than any other remote country."[91] The concept of mass resettlement in a faraway land appealed primarily to already exiled migrants as a solution for other people.

DIFFERENTIATIONS

Despite the best efforts of Armenian and Assyrian diaspora groups to make use of the Zionist model to press their case for statehood, there remained a divide between European diplomatic views of European Zionists and the Christians of the former Ottoman Empire. In the view of many European officials, long accustomed to thinking of Ottoman Christians as beleaguered recipients of humanitarian assistance and sites of international intervention, Armenians and Assyrians would necessarily require political tutelage and financial and military propping, in contrast to European Jewish settlers who they imagined would be largely self-supporting. Final decisions about Armenian, Assyrian, and Jewish "homelands" ultimately rested on diplomatic assessments of the usefulness of such creations to the postwar British and French imperial projects in the former Ottoman territories, and diasporic lobbying would be used primarily to justify and defend decisions made on strategic grounds.

In part, American, British, French, and League encounters with Armenian and Assyrian refugee populations in the postwar camps had served to produce a view of these diasporas as primitive political communities that would require investment, training, and military protection if they were to be reconstituted as independent nation-states. Building on nineteenth-century depictions of Ottoman Christians as picturesque but backward, officials at camps like Baʿquba emphasized processes of nationalization and civilization as necessary and long-term training for eventual independence. As historian Jo Laycock has noted, Western Armenophiles had long "lamented the detrimental effect of Ottoman rule upon the development of the Armenians, suggesting that with the help of European intervention the Armenians could eventually be a civilising force in the region."[92] The refugee camps, intended partly as spaces for nationalization, thus also deliberately produced the tutelary relationship later formalized in the League of Nations' mandate system. James Barton, director of Near East Relief, believed that any potential mandate over Armenia would have to last for at least thirty years before Armenia could be self-governing—a view supported by the British undersecretary and Near East advisor Louis Mallet, who declared in 1919, "You may call the country Armenian and make it independent, but the moral is that the tutelary power will have to govern it for a long time to come."[93]

Even diaspora groups advocating for statehood produced narratives of long-term Armenian and Assyrian dependence on some kind of mandate-style oversight. One British Armenia Committee pamphlet declared that Armenians would not be capable of immediate independence: "Only by the wise guidance of a powerful and impartial external authority can the peoples themselves hope to establish a stable political community."[94] Assyrian diaspora groups likewise sometimes emphasized the importance of European oversight; as one American group wrote, "All Assyrians united, and under the protectorate of Great Britain!"[95] Notably, Armenians on the ground tried to persuade the Allies that little would be required of a mandate authority. Aram Dildilian met with American representatives in Samsun in September 1919, and remembered the local insistence on this point: "Everywhere [the Americans] went, the Armenians in groups or in person tried to inform General Harbord's party that the United States of America's name is enough to keep the Turks in line, and to do that, a few thousand American soldiers are more than enough.... On the contrary, the other group, including our missionary friends, reported that it is necessary to have several hundred thousand U.S. soldiers.... So we lost our cause because of our friends."[96] Jewish diaspora groups, by contrast, often advocated for an ethnic homeland as a positive contribution to the structures of European imperial rule in Palestine that would require little or nothing in the way of military or financial support from the mandate authorities (though ultimately, of course, the Yishuv would be heavily dependent on British backing for its establishment in Palestine). As Felix Frankfurter wrote to Wilson during the peace talks, "I am, of course, most eager that the Jew should be a reconstructive not a disruptive force in the new world order."[97]

From the beginning of the peace talks, colonial officials sometimes openly acknowledged the actual strategic rationales behind the creation of such minority states, as in Curzon's discussion of British support for a potential Armenian state in late 1918:

> Our reasons for desiring [an independent Armenia] are, it seems to me, three in number. In the first place, adopting the terminology which has become popular with regard to Palestine, we desire to provide a national home for the scattered peoples of the Armenian race. As long as they are diffused in helpless and hopeless minorities, in areas inhabited for the most part by the Kurds and Turks, every man's hand is raised against them, and any chance of settled life or autonomous existence cannot be said to exist. Secondly, we want to set up an Armenian State as a palisade, if I may use the metaphor, against the Pan-Turanian ambitions of the Turks, which may overflow the Caucasian regions and carry great peril to the countries of the Middle East and East. Thirdly, we want to constitute something like an effective barrier against the aggression—if not now, at any rate in the future—of any foreign Powers, impelled, by ambition or by other motives, to press forward in that direction. That, I think, is a fair statement of the reasons for which probably all of us here desire the erection of an independent Armenian State.[98]

While this imperial rationale for supporting a settler colonial project in Palestine continued to hold water for the time being, it quickly disintegrated in the Armenian case. Sober assessments of the postwar situation in the Caucasus, the Levant, and Mesopotamia recognized the weakness of the Allied military position in and around Armenian and Assyrian areas in the Caucasus, eastern Turkey, and Mesopotamia. One British diplomat summed up his conclusions following lengthy discussions of the possibilities for Armenian "repatriation": "Our withdrawal means we can't take on such a job. We should need in Armenia six times the troops we are withdrawing from the Caucasus."[99] The American government was equally dismissive, viewing plans for an American-backed independent Armenia as fundamentally impractical. Indeed, the specter of mass transfer was soon raised in this context as well, as Wilson's secretary of state Charles Evan Hughes suggested that Armenian refugees be resettled in the Aegean islands or Cyprus in lieu of an Armenian state.[100]

From an early date, then, the British, French, and American governments all came to think of the idea of Armenian and Assyrian "homelands" as making impossible practical and logistical claims on the Allied powers. The Zionist project, by contrast, seemed to offer imperial assistance at a relatively low cost. In the final analysis, diaspora advocacy for ethnic homelands could not successfully override imperial considerations; it could only legitimize political and military decisions already made on other grounds.

. . .

The project of an Armenian homeland did not become a reality until a truncated independent Armenia emerged from the collapsed Soviet Union in 1991. The idea of an Assyrian nation remains unfulfilled. By contrast, of course, the eventual expulsion of most of Palestine's Arabs did make possible the emergence of a new Jewish nation-state in Israel, a development hailed with delight by diaspora activists in the United States and elsewhere. "Within the framework of American interests," declared the executive committee of the American Jewish Congress in 1949, "we shall aid in the upbuilding of Israel as a vital spiritual and cultural center and in the development of its capacity to provide a free and dignified life for those who desire to make it their home." [101] Although diaspora activists attempted to participate in the drawn-out negotiations over the end of the 1948 war and the armistice lines drawn in 1949, they did not have a measurable effect on the outcomes.[102] Nevertheless, 1948 marked the beginning of a long period of significant and continually increasing diasporic contributions to the international discourse about the Palestinian-Israeli conflict and the nature of the newly realized Jewish state, a state of affairs correctly predicted by the leading American Zionist Abba Hillel Silver, who told the Jewish Agency in 1948 that "for years—perhaps for generations—the State of Israel will be dependent on the Diaspora." [103]

Despite their massive public efforts and the visibility of their campaigns in service of ethnic "homelands," neither Jewish, Armenian, nor Assyrian diaspora communities had a notable impact on the actual emergence of particular states. Instead, their activities largely served to endorse and sanction concepts of ethnically specific and separate homelands, both in theory (as in the League's proposals for transfer, resettlement, and partition for Armenians, Assyrians, and Jews in the interwar period) and in practice (as in the ex post facto international support and recognition for the new state of Israel after

1948). Diasporic voices became important partners for the League in legitimizing schemes of ethnic separation that failed to win adherents among their largely unwilling participants. Ironically, then, by the post-1945 period many diaspora activists attempting to ease their communities' assimilation into their pluralistic host societies had come to play an important role in the promotion of exclusionary ethnic nationalisms on the international stage.

Epilogue

During their interwar occupation of Iraq, Syria, and Palestine, the British and French mandate governments and the League of Nations undertook a series of varied but linked campaigns of ethnic transfer, resettlement, and partition. Their somewhat haphazard efforts to construct regimes of ethnic division across the ex-Ottoman Arab provinces sought to buttress struggling colonial administrations in practical ways, while also legitimizing European imperial rule as a mode of international governance promoting national sovereignty and minority rights. The struggles on the ground over implementing these ragged schemes of ethnonational separation would cast a long shadow over the twentieth-century Eastern Mediterranean.

We can understand this history in a number of ways: as a coda to the final dissolution of Eurasia's pluralistic land empires; as the first manifestations of a twentieth-century global ideological commitment to the nation-state; as a consequence of the mass dislocations and traumas of the First World War. But it is also a story about the rapid and dramatic expansion of state and international power. Between the late nineteenth century, when the Ottoman Empire's centralization began to speed up as a response to both internal and external pressures, and the end of the 1940s, when the mandate system finally came to an end, the ambitions and capacities of state and international authority expanded exponentially. Seen in this light, the dramatic use of ethnic transfer and partition throughout this period appears not so much a strategy for actually achieving more homogenous national states across the Middle East as a mode of channeling and legitimizing state and international power for its own sake.[1]

Declaring the necessity of moving populations around was a way for the Ottomans to consolidate state authority, make use of refugee communities to support centralization, and establish the reach of the state in previously lightly governed areas. In the postwar era the British and French mandate governments, struggling with highly resistant subject populations and major questions of legitimacy, used concepts of ethnoreligious nationalism and practices of ethnic separation to justify and maintain a violent colonial order. The League relied even more heavily on these tropes. Needing a raison d'être beyond its actual commitment to maintaining the nineteenth-century liberal imperial order, it seized on the issues of minority rights and ethnonational self-determination—and concomitant practices of transfer and partition—to legitimize the mandatory regimes in the Middle East as a form of modern internationalism.

The idea of using transfer and partition as tools for creating a modern state order served both rhetorical and practical agendas. Rhetorically, the mandate governments and the League could represent such demographic engineering as politically necessary and requiring a neutral external organizer. Supporting some form of ethnonational space for Assyrians in Iraq, Armenians in Syria and Lebanon, and Jews in Palestine thus all became ways to build postimperial rationales for an ongoing European presence in the Eastern Mediterranean. The sometimes violent resistance that transfer and partition plans engendered among colonial subject populations, far from disrupting the process, could be used as further evidence for the necessity of an external force to regulate and oversee Middle Eastern state building. And in practical terms, creating mobile, disconnected, dependent communities out of the war's migrants, refugees, and victims gave mandate governments new capacities to deploy entire ethnic communities in the service of the colonial state. Using Assyrians as shock troops against Arab and Kurdish uprisings in Iraq, relocating Armenians to difficult border areas in Syria, and furthering large-scale Jewish resettlement in Palestine were all ways to extend colonial authority in unwelcoming territory. Local opposition to such schemes often rested on Ottoman-inflected concepts of authority and representation that could not gain a hearing in Europe—because they challenged contemporary British and French territorial ambitions in former Ottoman territory and the emerging European cult of the nation-state, to be sure, but also because Ottoman pluralism had lost all international legitimacy following the state's genocidal campaign against its Armenian and Assyrian subjects during the war. Ethnic separation thus emerged as a way of simultaneously legitimizing and exerting newly emboldened forms of state and international authority over the interwar Middle East and beyond.

This history helps explain why international support for the principle of ethnic separation—despite its manifest historical failure to resolve ethnic conflict anywhere—seemed only to intensify as the century wore on. The first years after the Second World War saw two of the largest population transfers along ethnic lines in modern history, both sanctioned by outside authority and both accompanied by unspeakable violence and mass death. Stalin's and the postwar Polish and Czech governments' expulsion of some twelve million ethnic Germans from Poland, Czechoslovakia, and the Soviet Union received active support from Britain and the United States, both of whose leaders invoked the precedent of the Greek-Turkish exchange as a rationale for their actions. Addressing the House of Commons in December 1944, Churchill declared his belief that "expulsion is the method which, so far as we have been able to see, will be the most satisfactory and lasting.... A clean sweep will be made"—a sentiment echoed by Roosevelt, who told Anthony Eden that "the Prussians will be removed from East Prussia in the same manner as the Greeks were removed from Turkey after the last war." [2] Just a few years later, the partition of India and Pakistan along (imagined) Muslim-Hindu lines—which displaced somewhere on the order of fourteen million people, caused as many as a million deaths, and left the remaining Hindus and Sikhs in Pakistan and Muslims in India permanently saddled with the label of "minority"—was similarly celebrated by its architect Lord Mountbatten as one of "the greatest administrative operations in history." [3]

After 1945 the new United Nations, made up of not only the "Great Powers" of the past but also the new superpowers of the United States and the Soviet Union alongside dozens of nations emerging from colonial rule in Asia and Africa, likewise continued the League's tradition of privileging ethnic nationalism as the fundamental building block of the modern state. Although post-Nuremberg international law declared the forced removal of civilians illegal, the international community—often supported by diaspora nationalist voices—continued to allow for the possibility of partition as a potential solution to ethnonational discord, proposing and sometimes helping implement or maintain ethnically based divisions of territory in a variety of conflict zones. [4] The United Nations Peacekeeping Force in Cyprus, for instance, committed in 1974 to maintaining a "buffer" zone between the Greek- and Turkish-controlled territories, a mission that the UN defined as "a vital element in preventing a recurrence of fighting" and has since continued periodically to reapprove. [5] As late as 1995, the Dayton Accords that ended the Bosnian war rested on a framework of ethnic division of territory and an ex post facto legitimization of the expulsions and transfers that had taken place during the struggle.[6] And even more recently, the specter of new forms of externally supported ethnoreligious transfer and partition began to reappear in the Middle East itself.[7]

This post-1945 atmosphere of quiet approval for various iterations of ethnonational separation did not reflect an ideological commitment to transfer and partition as an answer to ethnic conflict. Rather, it represented a continuation of an earlier strategy of creating externally monitored regimes of ethnic separation to justify and channel international intervention. In the interwar period, remaking the Middle East as a collection of "states of separation" helped to inscribe a new global order, one that used new ideological premises of ethnic nationalism and minority self-determination to legitimize political formulations that looked rather like the old order. The astonishing longevity of the idea that transfer and partition could represent solutions to global problems of ethnic pluralism suggests that this process is still ongoing.

NOTES

INTRODUCTION

1. Summary of article in "À Noite," November 2, 1933, LNA C1533 20A/80617/19093.

2. Memo on the Possibilities of Assyrian Settlement in the Rupunini District of British Guiana, September 1934, LNA R3945 4/20316/13763.

3. "The Nansen International Office for Refugees—Nobel Lecture," Nobelprize. org, www.nobelprize.org/nobel_prizes/peace/laureates/1938/nansen-lecture.html. Emphasis added.

4. For an especially useful examination of the new categorization of European Jewish communities as "minorities" in the eighteenth and nineteenth centuries, see Aamir Mufti, *Enlightenment in the Colony: The Jewish Question and the Crisis of Postcolonial Culture* (Princeton, N.J.: Princeton University Press, 2007).

5. The literature on this is too extensive to cite in total here, but for a useful overview, see particularly A. Dirk Moses, "Empire, Colony, Genocide: Keywords and the Philosophy of History," in *Empire, Colony, Genocide: Conquest, Occupation, and Subaltern Resistance in World History* (New York: Berghahn Books, 2008), 3–54.

6. Garvey's movement had an antecedent in the abolitionist-led nineteenth-century movement to restore African slaves to Africa, just as some nineteenth-century evangelical Protestants in Britain and the United States had envisioned "restoring" the Jews to Palestine. On Protestant concepts of "restorationism," see especially Donald Lewis, *The Origins of Christian Zionism: Lord Shaftesbury and Evangelical Support for a Jewish Homeland* (Cambridge and New York: Cambridge University Press, 2010); Shalom Goldman, *Zeal for Zion: Christians, Jews, and the Idea of the Promised Land* (Chapel Hill: University of North Carolina Press, 2009); and Michael Oren, *Power, Faith, and Fantasy: America in the Middle East, 1776 to the Present* (New York: Norton, 2007). Of course, the idea of an African "restoration" differed significantly from the Zionist model in that there had in fact been some examples of actual returns by individuals escaping from slavery and coming back to their homelands.

7. Eugene M. Kulischer, *Europe on the Move: War and Population Changes, 1917–1947* (New York: Columbia University Press, 1948), 18–23.

8. Aristide R. Zolberg, "The Formation of New States as a Refugee-Generating Process," in *The Global Refugee Problem: U.S. and World Response, Annals of the American Academy of Political and Social Sciences* 467 (1983): 24–38; Nathaniel Berman, "'But the Alternative Is Despair: European Nationalism and the Modernist Renewal of International Law," *Harvard Law Review* 106 (1992–93): 1792.

9. The terms "resettlement" and "transfer" bleed into each other in the British, French, and League sources. Broadly speaking, "resettlement" is more frequently encountered, and is used to describe both individual and collective settlement practices and proposals. The term "transfer" is more frequently used to mean removal of a whole community, or a large part of it, to a new location. It should be emphasized, though, that such distinctions are not rigorously observed.

CHAPTER 1

1. Andrew Porter notes that this replaced an eighteenth-century imperial framework that assumed adaptable cultural, rather than immutable racial, difference; see his "Introduction" to *The Oxford History of the British Empire: The Nineteenth Century,* ed. W. Roger Louis and Andrew Porter (Oxford and New York: Oxford University Press, 2009), 24.

2. Nadia Abu El-Haj, *The Genealogical Science: The Search for Jewish Origins and the Politics of Epistemology* (Chicago: University of Chicago Press, 2012), 68

3. There is a large literature on this, among which might especially be noted Sadiah Qureshi, *Peoples on Parade: Exhibitions, Empire, and Anthropology in Nineteenth-Century Britain* (Chicago: University of Chicago Press, 2011).

4. Saliha Belmessous notes that the disillusionment of French colonial officials in the Americas whose project to assimilate Amerindians to French society had failed led directly to the racialization of a colonial system of governance, arguing that "race was therefore very much the fruit of colonialism; it arose directly out of the political experience of colonization"—an argument that could also be applied to British imperial expansion. See *Assimilation and Empire: Uniformity in French and British Colonies, 1541–1954* (Oxford: Oxford University Press, 2013), 57.

5. Jones to Governor-General, March 19, 1788, quoted in George Rankin, "Custom and the Muslim Law in British India," *Transactions of the Grotius Society* 25 (1939): 97. Rankin points out that the "sincerity of this belief is shown by the action of Warren Hastings in having the Hedaya translated into Persian.... Also by the elaborate proposals of Jones for a digest of Hindu and Mahomedan law and by his own work on the *Sirajiyyah* and *Sharifiyyah*."

6. See especially the discussion of Jones in Joel Beinin, "Knowing the 'Other': Arabs, Islam, and the West," in *Doing Race: 21 Essays for the 21st Century,* ed. Hazel Rose Markus and Paula M. L. Moya (New York: Norton, 2010), 207.

7. This began with the Morley-Minto Reforms, which were eventually incorporated into the Government of India Act of 1935.

8. Sugata Bose and Ayesha Jalal, *Modern South Asia: History, Culture, Political Economy,* 2nd ed. (New York: Routledge, 2004), 84. Broadly, this question of the colonial enforcement of communal identities has been a major feature of South Asia historiography; see particularly Partha Chatterjee, *The Nation and Its Fragments: Colonial and Postcolonial Histories* (Princeton, N.J.: Princeton University Press, 1993), and *Nationalist Thought and the Colonial World: A Derivative Discourse?* (London: Zed Books, 1986); Gyan Pandey, *The Construction of Communalism in Colonial North India* (Delhi: Oxford University Press, 1990); Ayesha Jalal, "Exploding Communalism: The Politics of Muslim Identity," in *Nationalism, Democracy and Development: State and Politics in India,* ed. Ayesha Jalal and Sugata Bose (Delhi: Oxford University Press, 1998); Thomas Metcalf, *Ideologies of the Raj* (Cambridge: Cambridge University Press, 1997); Bernard Cohn, *Colonialism and Its Forms of Knowledge: The British in India* (Princeton, N.J.: Princeton University Press, 1996); and C. A. Bayly, *Indian Society and the Making of the British Empire* (Cambridge: Cambridge University Press, 1988).

9. This was John Ward, fellow of the Society of Antiquaries, in a book entitled *Pyramids and Progress* published in 1890; cited in C. A. Bayly, "Representing Copts and Muhammadans: Empire, Nation, and Community in Egypt and India, 1880–1914," in *Modernity and Culture from the Mediterranean to the Indian Ocean,* ed. Leila Tarazi Fawaz and C. A. Bayly (New York: Columbia University Press, 2002), 172.

10. Cited in Bayly, "Representing Copts," 180. Bayly further notes that "Jews were, indeed, a point of reference for practically every discussion of race and politics during this period."

11. W. Wigram, *The Assyrians and Their Neighbors* (London: Bell Press, 1929), 178–79; also cited in Madawi al-Rasheed, *Iraqi Assyrian Christians in London: The Construction of Ethnicity* (Lewiston, N.Y.: Edwin Mellen Press, 1998), 42.

12. On the violence of this process, see especially Ben Kiernan, *Blood and Soil: A World History of Genocide and Extermination from Sparta to Darfur* (New Haven, Conn.: Yale University Press, 2009). Kiernan includes a discussion of Algeria in his chapter on "Settler Genocides in Africa," 364–92.

13. For a detailed examination of this process, see Guy Perville, *De l'empire français à la decolonization* (Paris: Hachette, 1991), 35–6; and John Ruedy, *Modern Algeria: The Origins and Development of a Nation,* 2nd ed. (Bloomington: Indiana University Press, 2005), ch. 3.

14. Michael Brett, "Legislating for Inequality in Algeria: The Senatus-Consulte of 14 July 1865," *Bulletin of the School of Oriental and African Studies* 51, 3 (1988): 440–61.

15. The Alliance's first major campaign promoted Jewish rights in Romania, which in its first years of independence had introduced a number of restrictions on Jewish citizenship and political representation. Crémieux viewed the Alliance as a way to force the "civilized nations" to intervene on behalf of Romania's Jews and

enforce Jewish emancipation there and elsewhere across eastern Europe. His eventual success, in 1878, in incorporating a clause into the Treaty of Berlin guaranteeing "the freedom and outward exercise of all forms of worship" to all residents of Romania provided an important boost to the idea that international diplomatic agreements could serve to legislate Jewish emancipation.

16. On the Alliance's educational practices, see especially Aron Rodrigue, *Jews and Muslims: Images of Sephardi and Eastern Jewries in Modern Times* (Seattle: University of Washington Press, 2003); and Michael M. Laskier, *The Alliance Israélite Universelle and the Jewish Communities of Morocco: 1862–1962* (Albany: State University of New York Press, 1983).

17. On this development, see especially Joshua Schreier, *Arabs of the Jewish Faith: The Civilizing Mission in Colonial Algeria* (New Brunswick, N.J.: Rutgers University Press, 2010).

18. For a useful overview of genocidal settler colonialism, see Kiernan, *Blood and Soil,* as well as Moses, *Empire, Colony, Genocide,* and Mark Levene, *Genocide in the Age of the Nation State: The Meaning of Genocide* (London: Tauris, 2005). For a comparative approach to such colonial settlement practices, see especially Benjamin Madley, "Patterns of Frontier Genocide, 1803–1910: The Aboriginal Tasmanians, the Yuki of California, and the Herero of Namibia," *Journal of Genocide Research* 6, 2 (2004): 167–92.

19. On the immense numbers of Jewish emigrants out of southern and eastern Europe during the late nineteenth and early twentieth centuries, see Walter Nugent, *Crossings: The Great Transatlantic Migrations, 1870–1914* (Bloomington: Indiana University Press, 1994); Jack Glazier, *Dispersing the Ghetto: The Relocation of Jewish Immigrants across America* (Ithaca, N.Y.: Cornell University Press, 1998); Gur Alroey, *Bread to Eat and Clothes to Wear: Letters from Jewish Migrants in the Early Twentieth Century* (Detroit: Wayne State University Press, 2011); and Rebecca Kobrin, *Jewish Bialystok and Its Diaspora* (Bloomington: Indiana University Press, 2010).

20. Dawn Chatty, *Displacement and Dispossession in the Modern Middle East* (New York: Cambridge University Press, 2010), 74.

21. Cited in David Vital, *Zionism: The Formative Years* (Oxford: Clarendon Press, 1982), 65.

22. Theodor Herzl, *Diaries of Theodor Herzl,* vol. 2, ed. Marvin Lowenthal (New York: Dial Press, 1956), 644.

23. Lewis, in *The Origins of Christian Zionism,* offers a useful discussion of nineteenth-century support for Zionism among Protestant evangelicals in Britain, focusing particularly on missionary institutions intent on converting the Jews.

24. Such anti-Semitic rhetoric coalesced particularly around Benjamin Disraeli's rise to power. See Mufti, *Enlightenment in the Colony,* 109.

25. Hobson letter to C. P. Scott, September 2, 1899, cited in Bernard Porter, *Critics of Empire: British Radicals and the Imperial Challenge* (London: Tauris, 2008), 201–2.

26. See Jill Pellew, "The Home Office and the Aliens Act, 1905," *Historical Journal* 32, 2 (1989): 369–85; and Vital, *Zionism,* 134–36.

27. Laura Robson, "Archeology and Mission: The British Presence in Nineteenth-Century Jerusalem," *Jerusalem Quarterly* 10, 1 (2010): 5–17.

28. Cited in Vital, *Zionism*, 155–56.

29. Discussed in greater detail in chapter 3.

30. Vital, *Zionism*, 143.

31. Shlomo Avineri, "Theodor Herzl's Diaries as a Bildungsroman," *Jewish Social Studies* 5, 3 (1999): 34. Consistent with other Zionist scholars, Avineri refers to the Uganda plan as a "blunder" from which he says Herzl never recovered. For a useful look at Nordau's idea of *Nachtasyl*, see Allen Arkush, "Max Nordau: The Post-Herzl Years," in *The Festschrift Darkei Noam: The Jews of Arab Lands*, ed. Casten Schapkow et al. (Leiden: Brill, 2015), 235–54.

32. "The goal of our present endeavors," he wrote, "must be not the Holy Land, but a land of our own." See Leon Pinsker, *Auto-emancipation*, trans. D. S. Blondheim (London: Federation of Zionist Youth, 1937), 32.

33. Chaim Weizmann, *Trial and Error* (New York: Harper and Brothers, 1949), 84.

34. More than three thousand Jews were killed in pogroms in southern Russia between 1903 and 1905.

35. Gur Alroey, "Zionism without Zion? Territorialist Ideology and the Zionist Movement, 1882–1956," *Jewish Social Studies: History, Culture, Society* 18, 1 (2011): 6. Alroey has provided our most complete scholarly picture to date of the territorialist movement, which he views as an important shadow movement to early Zionism that retained its significance through the 1920s. See his several articles on the subject, including two recent pieces: "Mesopotamia—'The Promised Land': The Jewish Territorial Organization Project in the Bilad al-Rafidayn and the Question of Palestine, 1899–1917," *Middle Eastern Studies* 50, 6 (2014): 911–35, and "Angolan Zion: The Jewish Territorial Organization and the Idea of a Jewish State in Western Africa, 1907–1913," *Journal of Modern Jewish Studies* 14, 2 (2015): 179–98.

36. Decrees reiterating this principle were issued in 1884, 1887, and 1888; see Chatty, *Displacement and Dispossession*, 75. There is debate about the extent to which Ottoman officials viewed Zionism as a threat to the empire. Most scholars consider that the Ottoman state did not think of Zionism as analogous to the national movements threatening Ottoman imperial control in the western reaches of the empire, viewing it instead as primarily a cultural movement which could be encompassed within Ottomanism; see, for instance, M. Sükrü Hanioğlu, "Jews in the Young Turk Movement to the 1908 Revolution," in *The Jews of the Ottoman Empire*, ed. Avigdor Levy (Princeton, N.J.: Darwin Press, 1994), 523; and Ilber Ortayli, "Ottomanism and Zionism during the Second Constitutional Period," in *Jews of the Ottoman Empire*, 532. Michelle Campos, though, observes that there is disagreement on this point, citing a Zionist report from 1908 that portrayed the Ottoman view on Zionism as analogous to Armenian nationalism: "[The Young Turks] consider us as separatists, if not today, then at any rate tomorrow. And they do not wish to let people enter [Palestine] who 'will create a new Armenian question' for them." See Michelle Campos, *Ottoman Brothers: Muslims, Christians, and Jews*

in Early Twentieth-Century Palestine (Stanford, Calif.: Stanford University Press, 2010), 299–300 n48. It is likely that this divergence of scholarly opinion reflects an equally wide variety of opinions among the Ottoman leadership.

37. Cited in Campos, *Ottoman Brothers,* 209.

38. Chatty, *Displacement and Dispossession,* 75.

39. This is probably high, but certainly there had been significant growth. On the debates over population figures in late Ottoman Palestine, see especially Justin McCarthy, *The Population of Palestine: Population History and Statistics of the Late Ottoman Period and the Mandate* (New York: Columbia University Press, 1990).

40. Cited in Vital, *Zionism,* 51.

41. Cited in Campos, *Ottoman Brothers,* 212.

42. Carole Fink, *Defending the Rights of Others: The Great Powers, the Jews, and International Minority Protection, 1878–1938* (Cambridge and New York: Cambridge University Press, 2004), 88.

43. The most recent thorough assessment of the Balfour Declaration is Jonathan Schneer, *The Balfour Declaration: The Origins of the Arab-Israeli Conflict* (New York: Random House, 2010). Among the enormous literature dealing with the topic, see also Avi Shlaim's recent chapter on the declaration in *Israel and Palestine: Reappraisals, Revisions, Refutations* (London: Verso, 2009).

44. Among them Lloyd George, whose Welsh Methodist upbringing had instilled in him a romantic vision of biblical Palestine and a sense of destiny concerning the "return of the Jews." See Lewis, *Origins of Christian Zionism,* as well as Lloyd George's own account of the diplomatic machinery of the war and its aftermath, *Is It Peace?* (London: Hodder and Stoughton, 1923).

45. Fink, *Defending the Rights of Others,* 88.

46. Memorandum of Edwin Montagu on "The Anti-Semitism of the Present Government," August 23, 1917, CAB 24/24.

47. It is also worth noting that throughout the Ottoman sphere the boundaries between Muslim, Christian, and Jewish communities often remained blurry, with all three sharing certain religious practices, shrines, holidays, and superstitions. For a recent investigation of this phenomenon, see James Grehan, *Twilight of the Saints: Everyday Religion in Syria and Palestine* (Oxford: Oxford University Press, 2014), which argues that denominational divides were often less meaningful than shared local folk practices through the early modern period.

48. This was partly because Islamic law and philosophy did not press proselytization, but also—probably more importantly—because, as Mark Mazower has succinctly put it, "Christians paid higher taxes, and mass conversion would have impoverished the empire." See his *The Balkans: From the End of Byzantium to the Present Day* (London: Phoenix, 2000), 58.

49. Suhnaz Yilmaz and Ipek Yosmaoglu make the important point that whatever the millet system's later political uses, it originated in "the operating logic of a pre-modern state . . . [and] was devised first and foremost to serve the tax collection needs of the central state." See their "Fighting the Spectres of the Past: Dilemmas of Ottoman Legacy in the Balkans and the Middle East," *Middle Eastern Studies* 44,

5 (2008): 682. For an overview of the various meanings of the word "millet" from the early modern period to the *tanzimat*, see the entry for "Millet" in *Encyclopedia of Islam*, 2nd ed. (Leiden: Brill, 2006), http://referenceworks.brillonline.com/entries /encyclopaedia-of-islam-2/millet-COM_0741?s.num = 0&s.f.s2_parent = s.f.book .encyclopaedia-of-islam-2&s.q = millet.

50. As Aron Rodrigue has put it, "Nothing in the political system of the Ottoman Empire called for different groups to merge into one. . . . That particular arrangement, therefore, renders invalid all our terms for debate about minority/ majority, which are all extraordinarily Europe-centered." See Aron Rodrigue interview with Nancy Reynolds, "Difference and Tolerance in the Ottoman Empire," *Stanford Electronic Humanities Review* 5, 1 (1996), www.stanford.edu/group /SHR/5–1/text/rodrigue.html. Benjamin Thomas White makes a very similar point, noting that "in a religiously-legitimated monarchy, whether or not the ruler shares the language or 'ethnicity' of the ruled is irrelevant." See *The Emergence of Minorities in the Middle East: The Politics of Community in French Mandate Syria* (Edinburgh: Edinburgh University Press, 2011), 31.

51. There is extensive literature (and debate) on the millet system. For more detailed discussions, see Benjamin Braude and Bernard Lewis, eds., *Christians and Jews in the Ottoman Empire: The Functioning of a Plural Society*, 2 vols. (New York: Holmes and Meier, 1982); Bruce Masters, *Christians and Jews in the Ottoman Arab World: The Roots of Sectarianism* (Cambridge: Cambridge University Press, 2001); Youssef Courbage and Phillipe Fargues, *Chrétiens et juifs dans l'Islam arabe et turc* (Paris: Fayard, 1992); and Xavier de Planhol, *Minorités en Islam: Geographie politique et sociale* (Paris: Flammarion, 1997), as well as descriptions in broader histories of the empire like Donald Quataert, *The Ottoman Empire, 1700–1922* (New York: Cambridge University Press, 2000); Halil Inalcik et al., eds., *An Economic and Social History of the Ottoman Empire, 1300–1914*, 2 vols. (Cambridge: Cambridge University Press, 2004); Fadil Bayat, *al-Dawla al-'Uthmaniyya fi al-majal al-'Arabi: dirasa tarikhiyya fi al-awd a' al-idariyya fi daw' al-watha'iq wa-al-masadir al-'Uthmaniyya asran* (Beirut: Markaz Dirasat al-Wahdah al-'Arabiyya, 2007); and Caroline Finkel, *Osman's Dream: The Story of the Ottoman Empire 1300–1923* (New York: Perseus, 2005). Halil Inalcik, "The Status of the Greek Orthodox Patriarch under the Ottomans," *Turcica* 21–23 (1991): 407–36, offers a periodization of the history of the millet system with regard to the relationship between the Ottoman state and the Greek Orthodox Patriarchate. Saba Mahmood looks at this issue from a contemporary anthropological perspective in her "Religious Freedom, the Minority Question, and Geopolitics in the Middle East," *Comparative Studies in Society and History* 54, 2 (2012): 418–46.

52. Ryan Gingeras notes this especially as a consequence of the American Board of Commissioners for Foreign Missions representatives operating among Armenians and Greeks in the area he calls the South Marmara; see his *Sorrowful Shores: Violence, Ethnicity, and the End of the Ottoman Empire, 1912–1923* (Oxford: Oxford University Press, 2009), 23.

53. On this point, see Chatty, *Displacement and Dispossession,* 51, and the first three chapters of Keith Watenpaugh, *Being Modern in the Middle East: Revolution,*

Nationalism, Colonialism, and the Arab Middle Class (Princeton, N.J.: Princeton University Press, 2006). On the impact of European and American missions, see particularly Ussama Makdisi, *Artillery of Heaven: American Missionaries and the Failed Conversion of the Middle East* (Ithaca, N.Y.: Cornell University Press, 2008); Heather Sharkey, *American Evangelicals in Egypt: Missionary Encounters in an Age of Empire* (Princeton, N.J.: Princeton University Press, 2013); Eleanor H. Tejirian and Reeva Spector Simon, *Conflict, Conquest, and Conversion: Two Thousand Years of Christian Missions in the Middle East* (New York: Columbia University Press, 2012); Heleen Murre-van den Berg, ed., *New Faith in Ancient Lands: Western Missions in the Middle East in the Nineteenth and Early Twentieth Centuries* (Boston and Leiden: Brill, 2005); and Inger Marie Okkenhaug, "Christian Missions in the Middle East and the Ottoman Balkans: Education, Reform, and Failed Conversions, 1819–1967," *International Journal of Middle East Studies* 47, 3 (2015): 593–604.

54. Such that by the early 1920s an exit visa from Turkey could use "Armenian" to denote both ethnicity and religion (see Gingeras, *Sorrowful Shores,* 1), and in 1905 the Ottoman government allowed the Romanian Christian Vlachs to claim legal status and recognition as a separate millet. See Ipek K. Yosmaoglu, "Counting Bodies, Shaping Souls: The 1903 Census and National Identity in Ottoman Macedonia," *International Journal of Middle East Studies* 38, 1 (2006): 65.

55. Dimitris Livanios, "Beyond 'Ethnic Cleansing': Aspects of the Functioning of Violence in the Ottoman and Post-Ottoman Balkans," *Southeast European and Black Sea Studies* 8, 3 (2008): 193. On this figure of "bandit, terrorist, and/or nationalist rebel," see also Isa Blumi, *Ottoman Refugees: Migration in a Post-Imperial World* (London: Bloomsbury Academic, 2013), 44.

56. On the emergence of Balkan nationalisms in the nineteenth-century Ottoman sphere, see Benjamin Fortna et al., eds., *State-Nationalism in the Ottoman Empire, Greece and Turkey: Orthodox and Muslims, 1830–1945* (London: Routledge, 2013); Hannes Grandits et al., eds., *Conflicting Loyalties in the Balkans: The Great Powers, the Ottoman Empire and Nation-Building* (London: Tauris, 2011); and Keith Brown, *Loyal unto Death: Trust and Terror in Revolutionary Macedonia* (Bloomington: Indiana University Press, 2013).

57. Mazower, *Balkans,* 95.

58. Two useful investigations of the comparative trajectories of the Habsburg, Ottoman, and Russian empires during this period are Omer Bartov and Eric D. Weitz, eds., *Shatterzone of Empires: Coexistence and Violence in the German, Habsburg, Russian, and Ottoman Borderlands* (Bloomington: Indiana University Press, 2013); and Karen Barkey and Mark Von Hagen, *After Empire: Multiethnic Societies and Nation-Building: The Soviet Union and the Russian, Ottoman, and Habsburg Empires* (Boulder, Col.: Westview Press, 1997).

59. To illustrate this point, it is worth noting that the largest ethnoreligious bloc in Macedonia's capital city, Salonica, was actually made up of Sephardic Jews. See Mark Mazower, *Salonica, City of Ghosts: Christians, Muslims and Jews 1430–1950* (New York: HarperCollins, 2004).

60. As Ipek Yosmaoglu points out, "The early subscribers of nationalism in Ottoman Macedonia . . . understood well the need to recast it in a new and overtly religious language." See her *Blood Ties: Religion, Violence, and the Politics of Nationhood in Ottoman Macedonia, 1878–1908* (Ithaca, N.Y.: Cornell University Press, 2014), 5. On this point, see also Livanios, "Beyond 'Ethnic Cleansing,'" 193–94.

61. Ipek Yosmaoglu notes that the classifications also triggered conversation in Istanbul, where the Ottoman administration considered replacing them with simpler religious categories of Muslim, Christian, and Jew, as well as the possibility of more explicitly national labels like Serb. "It seems that in the case of the 1903 census," she writes, "the central state's desire to obtain an accurate count of its population, vertically ordered, and to preserve a common census policy across the empire overrode concerns about the problems that might arise from this distinction in a politically volatile area." See "Counting Bodies, Shaping Souls," 64.

62. Resat Kasaba, *A Moveable Empire: Ottoman Nomads, Migrants, and Refugees* (Seattle: University of Washington Press, 2009), 109.

63. See Gingeras, *Sorrowful Shores*, 24; Kemal Karpat, *Ottoman Populations, 1830–1914: Demographic and Social Characteristics* (Madison: University of Wisconsin Press, 1985), 69; and Ehud Toledano, *Slavery and Abolition in the Ottoman Middle East* (Seattle: University of Washington Press, 1998), 84.

64. Kasaba, *Moveable Empire*, 109.

65. Blumi, *Ottoman Refugees*, 45; Kasaba, *Moveable Empire*, 111; Gingeras, *Sorrowful Shores*, 25–26.

66. See Gingeras, *Sorrowful Shores*, 26–27.

67. Kasaba, *Moveable Empire*, 110.

68. Blumi, *Ottoman Refugees*, 178–79 n7.

69. Kasaba, *Moveable Empire*, 111–14.

70. Kemal Karpat, "Muslim Migration," in *Studies on Ottoman Social and Political History: Selected Articles and Essays* (Leiden: Brill, 2002), 311–23.

71. Livanios, "Beyond 'Ethnic Cleansing,'" 196.

72. For a detailed look at the "Christianization" of the Pomaks, see Fatme Myuhtar-May, "Pomak Christianization (Pokrastvane) in Bulgaria during the Balkan Wars of 1912–1913," in *War and Nationalism: The Balkan Wars, 1912–1913, and Their Sociopolitical Implications*, ed. M. Hakan Yavuz and Isa Blumi (Salt Lake City: University of Utah Press, 2013), 316–60. This is also discussed briefly in Justin McCarthy, *Death and Exile: The Ethnic Cleansing of Ottoman Muslims, 1821–1922* (Princeton, N.J.: Darwin Press, 1995), 153.

73. McCarthy, *Death and Exile*, 156.

74. Chatty, *Displacement and Dispossession*, 82.

75. Halide Edip, *Turkey Faces West* (New Haven, Conn.: Yale University Press, 1930), 115; cited in Nesim Seker, "Demographic Engineering in the Late Ottoman Empire and the Armenians," *Middle Eastern Studies* 43, 3 (2007): 464–65.

76. Seker, "Demographic Engineering," 467.

77. The mandate system extended outside the Middle East as well; alongside the "Class A" Middle Eastern mandate states (Syria, Lebanon, Iraq, Palestine) the trea-

ties created "Class B" mandates out of Germany's former colonial holdings in Africa, and "Class C" mandates out of the German colonies of the South Pacific. See Susan Pedersen, "The Meaning of the Mandates System: An Argument," *Geschichte und Gesellschaft* 32, 4 (2006): 560–82, for a useful overview of the system as a whole.

78. On this point and the effects of this Wilsonian language on anti-imperial nationalist movements around the globe, see especially Erez Manela, *The Wilsonian Moment: Self-Determination and the International Origins of Anticolonial Nationalism* (Oxford: Oxford University Press, 2009).

79. See Eric D. Weitz's important article "From the Vienna to the Paris System: International Politics and the Entangled Histories of Human Rights, Forced Deportations, and Civilizing Missions," *American Historical Review* 113, 5 (2008): 1330. Crucially, these last two found themselves working in Ottoman territory as well as European, where multiple actors were simultaneously reformulating the communal distinctions that were crucial to Ottoman governance as (proto-) minority-majority divisions. For examples of this, see Aron Rodrigue, *French Jews, Turkish Jews: The Alliance Israélite Universelle and the Politics of Jewish Schooling in Turkey, 1860–1925* (Bloomington: Indiana University Press, 1990), and *Images of Sephardi and Eastern Jewries in Transition: The Teachers of the Alliance Israélite Universelle, 1860–1939* (Seattle: University of Washington Press, 1993); S. Goldstein-Sabbah, "Jewish Education in Baghdad: Communal Space vs. Public Space," in *Modernity, Minority, and the Public Sphere: Jews and Christians in the Middle East,* ed. S. Goldstein-Sabbah and H. Murre-van der Berg (Leiden: Brill, 2016); and Schreier, *Arabs of the Jewish Faith.* On international reformist groups, see especially Davide Rodogno, *Against Massacre: Humanitarian Interventions in the Ottoman Empire, 1815–1914* (Princeton, N.J.: Princeton University Press, 2012).

80. The emergence of this minority-majority discourse is chronicled in some detail in Weitz, "From the Vienna to the Paris System," 1329–33; and Mark Mazower, "Minorities and the League of Nations in Interwar Europe," *Daedalus* 126, 2 (1997): 47–65. Wilson's revision of "self-determination"—which had emerged as an established socialist idea about collectivist political expression within multiethnic states—led the phrase to mean, as Eric D. Weitz puts it, "free white men coming together consensually to form a democratic political order." See his "Self-Determination: How a German Enlightenment Idea Became the Slogan of National Liberation and a Human Right," *American Historical Review* 120, 2 (2015): 485.

81. Cited in Mazower, "Minorities and the League of Nations in Interwar Europe," 50.

82. Liliana Riga and James Kennedy, "Tolerant Majorities, Loyal Minorities and 'Ethnic Reversals': Constructing Minority Rights at Versailles, 1919," *Nations and Nationalism* 15, 3 (2009): 471.

83. Comite des Delegation Juives de la Conference de la Paix to President and Members of the Peace Conference, May 10, 1919, CZA L6/80; cited in David Vital, *A People Apart: The Jews in Europe, 1789–1939* (Oxford: Oxford University Press, 1999), 743.

84. Mark Levene, *War, Jews, and the New Europe: The Diplomacy of Lucien Wolf* (Oxford: Oxford University Press, 1992), 225.

85. Ibid., 226.

86. Mark Mazower, "The Strange Triumph of Human Rights, 1933–1950," *Historical Journal* 47, 2 (2004): 383. In terms of numbers, Germans represented the single largest ethnic minority in Europe, representing 8–9 million of the 36 million people classified as "national minorities" in eastern Europe. See also Mark Mazower, *Hitler's Empire: How the Nazis Ruled Europe* (New York: Penguin, 2008), 32–40.

87. See Weitz, "From the Vienna to the Paris System," 1330.

88. The various drafts of the minorities treaties are discussed in Athanasia Spiliopoulou Åkermark, *Justifications of Minority Protection in International Law* (London: Kluwer Law International, 1996), 102–4 (quote on 103).

89. Cited in Fink, *Defending the Rights of Others*, 211.

90. Cited in Vital, *People Apart*, 753.

91. Mazower, "Strange Triumph of Human Rights," 382.

92. James Wycliffe Headlam-Morley, *A Memoir of the Paris Peace Conference, 1919* (London: Methuen, 1972), 112–13.

93. League of Nations, Information Section, LN Secretariat, *The League of Nations and the Protection of Minorities of Race, Language, and Religion* (Geneva: League of Nations, 1927), 16. This is also discussed from a legal history perspective in David Wippman, "The Evolution and Implementation of Minority Rights," *Fordham Law Review* 66, 2 (1997), 601.

94. Historian Samuel Moyn describes the system as a "search for guarantees of subnational citizenship"—a precise and accurate description of how the League understood the concept of minorities. See Samuel Moyn, *The Last Utopia: Human Rights in History* (Cambridge, Mass.: Belknap Press, 2010), 33.

95. Thus, for instance, the French High Commission in Syria would refuse to recognize the Kurds or Circassians as "minorities," arguing that they constituted ethnic rather than communal groupings and thus did not qualify for minority status—an idea also supported in some instances by Syrian Arab nationalists. See White, *Emergence of Minorities*, 52–53 and 57–60.

96. League of Nations Council, *Protection of Linguistic, Racial or Religious Minorities by the League of Nations: Resolutions and Extracts from the Minutes of the Council* (Geneva: League of Nations, 1929), 45.

97. The many scholars who have viewed the minorities treaties as a basically well intentioned but fundamentally flawed first attempt at an international system have, by and large, failed to recognize the ways in which these treaties essentially represented an extension of the Ottoman capitulations treaties and a further elaboration of the principles of ethnoreligious subjecthood in the context of empire, repackaged as humanitarian internationalism. This is especially true of Fink, *Defending the Rights of Others*, and Vital's work on Zionism and the peace treaties.

98. Nathaniel Berman, *Passion and Ambivalence: Colonialism, Nationalism, and International Law* (Leiden: Nijhoff, 2012), 58.

99. Jacob Robinson et al., *Were the Minorities Treaties a Failure?* (New York: Institute of Jewish Affairs, 1943), 41.

100. "Protection of Minorities," Report by the Sixth Committee to the Assembly of the League of Nations, September 20, 1922 (Geneva: League of Nations, 1922), 3.

101. Mark Mazower, "An International Civilization? Empire, Internationalism, and the Crisis of the Mid-Twentieth Century," *International Affairs* 82, 3 (2006): 560. For a useful though somewhat overgenerous estimation of the treaties' impact, see Carole Fink, "The League of Nations and the Minorities Question," *World Affairs* 157, 4 (1995): 197–205.

102. Catriona Drew, "Population Transfer: The Untold Story of Self-Determination," presentation at Global Fellows Forum, New York University, 2006, 6, www.law.nyu.edu/sites/default/files/upload_documents/gffdrewpaper.pdf.

103. Weitz, "From the Vienna to the Paris System," 1313.

104. Mark Sykes, memo, "Our Position in Mesopotamia in Relation to the Spirit of the Age," n.d. [1919], FO 800/22.

105. On the mandates system in the interwar Middle East, see particularly Peter Sluglett and Nadine Meouchy, eds., *The British and French Mandates in Comparative Perspective* (Leiden: Brill, 2004); and Cyrus Schayegh and Andrew Arsan, eds., *The Routledge Handbook of the History of the Middle East Mandates* (Abingdon and New York: Routledge, 2015); see also Susan Pedersen, "Meaning of the Mandates System," 560–82, and *The Guardians: The League of Nations and the Crisis of Empire* (Oxford: Oxford University Press, 2015).

106. Michael Callahan, *Mandates and Empire: The League of Nations and Africa, 1914–1931* (Brighton: Sussex Academic Press, 1999), 3. The text of the Berlin conference is available at http://courses.wcupa.edu/jones/his312/misc/berlin.htm.

107. Covenant of the League of Nations, part 1, article 22.

108. Legal scholar Balakrishnan Rajagopal makes the important point that nineteenth-century international law sanctioned violence against native populations largely through the deliberate absence of a legal vocabulary for anti-imperial resistance. "No matter how much 'resistance' the natives posed—for example the Mau Mau rebellion in British Kenya—international law had no vocabulary for understanding and accommodating it," he writes, adding, "This enabled the colonial authorities to treat anticolonial resistance as criminal acts and deal with them through law enforcement measures, especially through the doctrine of emergency"—an analysis that applies with equal validity to the League-overseen British and French mandate governments facing rebellion in interwar Palestine, Syria, and Iraq. See Balakrishnan Rajagopal, "International Law and Third World Resistance," in *The Third World and International Order: Law, Politics and Globalization,* ed. Antony Anghie et al. (Leiden: Nijhoff, 2003), 145–72, 160. The nineteenth-century positivist legal defense of colonial violence is also discussed in some detail in Anthony Anghie, "Finding the Peripheries: Sovereignty and Colonialism in Nineteenth Century International Law," *Harvard International Law Journal* 40, 1 (1999): 1–80.

109. Text of mandate is at http://avalon.law.yale.edu/20th_century/palmanda.asp.

110. Ibid.

111. League of Nations, *Mandat pour la Syria et le Liban* (Geneva: League of Nations, 1922).

112. League of Nations, *Mandates: Final Drafts of the Mandates for Mesopotamia and Palestine, for the Approval of the Council of the League of Nations* (London: HMSO, 1921), 2.

113. On this point, see particularly Martin Bunton, "Inventing the Status Quo: Ottoman Land Law during the Palestine Mandate, 1917–1936," *International History Review* 21, 1 (1999): 28–56; and Laura Robson, *Colonialism and Christianity in Mandate Palestine* (Austin: University of Texas Press), ch. 2.

114. Radhika Mongia has traced how central migration was to producing new narratives of state sovereignty in this period, arguing that the idea of state sovereignty proved a useful mechanism for "manag[ing] that liminal space between 'external' and 'internal' sovereignty where inter-*national* migration resides . . . and legitimat[ing] a state monopoly over migration in the discourse of equivalent state sovereignty and security." See her "Historicizing State Sovereignty: Inequality and the Form of Equivalence," *Comparative Studies in Society and History* 49, 2 (2007): 384–411.

115. Some recent literature has begun to address the construction of this category of "expertise" among imperial internationalists; see, for instance, Sean Andrew Wempe, "From Unfit Imperialists to Fellow Civilizers: German Colonial Officials as Imperial Experts in the League of Nations, 1919–1933," *German History* 34, 1 (2016): 21–48; Yann Decorzant, "The League of Nations and the Emergence of a New Network of Economic-Financial Expertise (1914–1923)," *Critique internationale* 3 (2011): 35–50; and Patricia Clavin, *Securing the World Economy: The Reinvention of the League of Nations, 1920–1946* (Oxford: Oxford University Press, 2013).

116. Susan Pedersen accurately describes these League institutions as "mechanisms for generating talk . . . [requiring] the imperial powers to engage in a protracted, wearisome, and public debate about how undemocratic rule over alien populations (accepted before the Wilsonian era as an entirely normal state of affairs) could be justified." See Pedersen, "Meaning of the Mandate System," 571.

117. For a useful recent example of scholarship exploring this relationship between mandatory subjects and the bureaucratic mechanisms of the League, see Natasha Wheatley, "Mandatory Interpretation: Legal Hermeneutics and the New International Order in Arab and Jewish Petitions to the League of Nations," *Past and Present* 227 (2015): 205–48.

118. It is certainly true, as Keith Watenpaugh has recently noted, that the League archive is "still very much a colonial archive" that "tends to flatten the historical experience of the peoples in the Eastern Mediterranean at whom its programs and policies were directed" (*Bread from Stones: The Middle East and the Making of Modern Humanitarianism* [Berkeley: University of California Press, 2015], 23).

Nevertheless, the structures of its information collection and its bureaucratic machinery meant that it served as a repository for extensive engagement on the part particularly of local elites from a variety of institutions, organizations, and communities across the mandate territories. As such, it represents an enormously valuable though still underused archival source for historians of the modern Middle East; Watenpaugh himself mines it to good effect to reconstruct the lives of Armenian genocide survivors who came in contact with League relief efforts in postwar Syria, in chapter 5 of his *Bread from Stones.*

CHAPTER 2

1. For a detailed recent look at the impact of the war on the region as a whole, see Kristian Ulrichsen, *The First World War in the Middle East* (London: Hurst, 2014).

2. Elizabeth Thompson, *Colonial Citizens: Republican Rights, Paternal Privilege, and Gender in French Syria and Lebanon* (New York: Columbia University Press, 2000), 23. For further discussion of wartime population losses in the Ottoman Arab provinces, see Justin McCarthy, *The Ottoman Peoples and the End of Empire* (New York: Oxford University Press, 2001), 165.

3. The question of precisely how many Armenians died in the genocide remains a contentious one. With his estimate of 600,000 Armenian casualties between 1912 and 1922, Justin McCarthy is on the low end of the spectrum of estimates and agrees with much earlier estimates of Arnold Toynbee; see his *Ottoman Peoples and the End of Empire,* 193. (McCarthy's rather apologist interpretations of the violence against the Armenians have come under considerable scholarly fire.) For recent alternative calculations and discussions of the numbers, see Ronald Suny et al., eds., *A Question of Genocide: Armenians and Turks at the End of the Ottoman Empire* (New York: Oxford University Press, 2011); and Taner Akçam, *The Young Turks' Crime against Humanity: The Armenian Genocide and Ethnic Cleansing in the Ottoman Empire* (Princeton, N.J.: Princeton University Press, 2012). The latter argues that the Turkish government mapped out and executed a policy of reducing the Christian population of Anatolia to between 5 and 10 percent of the population; he estimates 1.2 million Armenians were deported, of whom approximately 200,000 survived the war. Norman Naimark, in *Fires of Hatred: Ethnic Cleansing in Twentieth Century Europe* (Cambridge, Mass.: Harvard University Press, 2001), 40–41, notes that many Turkish historians who accept the Ottoman census figure of 1.3 million Armenians living in the prewar empire have come to a figure of approximately 800,000 killed in the genocide.

4. A number of recent scholarly works have advocated for labeling this violence an "Assyrian genocide" to be acknowledged alongside the Armenian genocide. On this point and on the numbers of Assyrians deported and massacred, see especially David Gaunt, *Massacres, Resistance, Protection: Muslim-Christian Relations in Eastern Anatolia during World War I* (London: Gorgias Press, 2006); Hannibal Travis, *Genocide in the Middle East: The Ottoman Empire, Iraq, and Sudan*

(Durham, N.C.: Carolina Academic Press, 2010), and "The Assyrian Genocide: A Tale of Oblivion and Denial," in *Forgotten Genocides: Oblivion, Denial, and Memory,* ed. Rene Lemarchand (Philadelphia: University of Pennsylvania Press, 2011); Cathie Carmichael, *Genocide before the Holocaust* (New Haven, Conn.: Yale University Press, 2009); and Sébastien de Courtois, *Le génocide oublié: Chrétiens d'orient, les derniers araméens* (Paris: Ellipses, 2002).

5. The French explicitly did not use the term "minority" to describe the Armenians, even after the term had become common currency in the 1930s to describe other communal entities in Syria like the 'Alawis and the Druze (the so-called compact minorities). The Armenians' refugee origins meant that they came to occupy a different space within the French mandate state than indigenous groups who could be identified as religious minorities but who were Arabic speakers. In Iraq, the British and the League did use the term "minority" to identify Assyrian refugees from quite an early date, and their incorporation into the state was often placed within the framework of "minority protection." On the use of the term "minority" in French mandate Syria, see especially White, *Emergence of Minorities in the Middle East,* ch. 2.

6. This relates closely to Michelle Tusan's analysis of the "ethnographic mapping" of the "Near East" in the late nineteenth century, which she argues "offered a canvas on which to map geopolitical priorities" and create a space for economic and political imperial intervention. See *Smyrna's Ashes: Humanitarianism, Genocide, and the Birth of the Middle East* (Berkeley: University of California Press, 2012), ch. 2. On this point, see also Keith Watenpaugh, "The League of Nations' Rescue of Armenian Genocide Survivors and the Making of Modern Humanitarianism, 1920–1927," *American Historical Review* 115, 5 (2010): 1315–39.

7. Cited in Sam Kaplan, "Territorializing Armenians: Geo-Texts and Political Imaginaries in French-occupied Cilicia, 1919–1922," *History and Anthropology* 15, 4 (2004): 405.

8. Kaplan, "Territorializing Armenians," 406.

9. J. F. Coakley, *The Church of the East and the Church of England: A History of the Archbishop of Canterbury's Assyrian Mission* (Oxford: Clarendon Press, 1992), 5. Until the early twentieth century, the Assyrians generally referred to themselves as *nestoryaye,* the Nestorian millet, an Ottoman designation that had no national or ethnic overtones. Protestant missionaries were especially anxious to erase the designation "Nestorian" from the community they had decided to champion, as it referred to a "heretical" theology. For the dual Assyrian/missionary making of this new version of Assyrian nationalism, see particularly Heleen Murre-van den Berg, "Chaldeans and Assyrians: The Church of the East in the Ottoman Period," in *The Christian Heritage of Iraq,* ed. Erica Hunter (Piscataway, N.J.: Gorgias Press, 2009), 157–61.

10. On this point, see especially Michel Chevalier, *Les montangnards chrétiens du Hakkari et du Kurdistan septentrional* (Paris: Departement de Geographie de l'Université de Paris-Sorbonne); and Heleen Murre-van den Berg, "Light from the East (1948–1954) and the De-territorialization of the Assyrian Church in the East,"

in *Religion Beyond Its Private Role in Modern Society,* ed. Wim Hofstee and Arie van der Kooij (Leiden: Brill, 2013), 115–34.

11. For detailed accounts of the Assyrian encounter with Western missions, see particularly John Joseph, *The Modern Assyrians of the Middle East: Encounters with Western Christian Missions, Archeologists, and Colonial Powers* (Leiden: Brill, 2000); and Coakley, *Church of the East and the Church of England.*

12. Murre-van den Berg, "Chaldeans and Assyrians," 158.

13. Discussed further in chapter 5.

14. Sargon Donabed, *Reforging a Forgotten History: Iraq and the Assyrians in the Twentieth Century* (Edinburgh: Edinburgh University Press, 2015), 64.

15. These mechanisms would remain weak throughout the mandate period. As Peter Sluglett has recently put it, "The framers of the mandate system thought they were improving on colonialism, but given the fact that they all had 'conventional' colonial empires of their own, and given the poverty of the regulatory machinery, the outcome was not all that different from the colonized countries." Peter Sluglett, "An Improvement on Colonialism? The 'A' Mandates and Their Legacy in the Middle East," *International Affairs* 90, 2 (2014): 425. The question of the degree to which the mandates system represented a genuinely new form of government versus a repackaged European imperialism has received extensive notice. Some scholars have viewed it as little more than a fig leaf for the continuation of earlier forms of British and French imperial rule; for some examples, see particularly Sluglett and Méouchy, *British and French Mandates in Comparative Perspective;* Philip Khoury, *Syria and the French Mandate: The Politics of Arab Nationalism, 1920–1945* (Princeton, N.J.: Princeton University Press, 1987); Daniel Neep, *Occupying Syria under the French Mandate: Insurgency, Space, and State Formation* (Cambridge: Cambridge University Press, 2012); Thompson, *Colonial Citizens;* Robson, *Colonialism and Christianity in Mandate Palestine;* Jacob Norris, *Land of Progress: Palestine in the Age of Colonial Development, 1905–1948* (Oxford: Oxford University Press, 2013); and Daniel Silverfarb, *Britain's Informal Empire in the Middle East: A Case Study of Iraq, 1929–1941* (New York: Oxford University Press, 1986). Others have assigned more importance to the distinction between colonial and mandate governments; see, for example, Pedersen, *Guardians,* and "Meaning of the Mandates System."

16. On the creation of the modern state of Iraq, the widespread revolt of 1920, and the reformulation of the mandate into the Hashemite monarchy, see particularly Reeva Simon and Eleanor Tejirian, eds., *The Creation of Iraq, 1914–1921* (New York: Columbia University Press, 2004); Charles Tripp, *A History of Iraq,* 2nd ed. (Cambridge: Cambridge University Press, 2000); and Toby Dodge, *Inventing Iraq: The Failure of Nation Building and a History Denied* (New York: Columbia University Press, 2003).

17. J. M. Yonan and Pera Mirza, memo on "The Assyrian People and Their Relations with the Allies in the Present War," December 1918, FO 608/274.

18. Memo from Political Bureau Baghdad to London, March 11, 1919, FO 608/274.

19. This is broadly true of many of the semiseparatist movements lobbying the delegates of the Paris Peace Conference for independence. For its applicability to the Kurdish question, see David McDowall, *A Modern History of the Kurds* (London: Tauris, 2003), chs. 6–8.

20. Surma Khassan to Matran, May 5, 1920, T 1/12603.

21. *Claims of the Assyrians as Presented to the Paris Peace Conference,* 1919, reproduced in Joel Werda, *The Flickering Light of Asia: Or, the Assyrian Nation and Church* (n.pub., 1924), 199–202, www.aina.org/books/fla/fla.htm#c31. Obviously this definition, beyond demonstrating a broad and flexible understanding of Assyrian belonging, also had the purpose of trying to present the Peace Conference representatives with the highest possible estimate of global Assyrian numbers.

22. Minute on Political Bureau Baghdad memo, March 11, 1919, FO 608/274.

23. Northcote, letter to "Mamma," September 13, 1919, NP.

24. On the League's lukewarm reaction to Kurdish claims, see especially McDowall, *Modern History of the Kurds.*

25. On this, see especially Seda Altug, "Sectarianism in the Syrian Jazira: Community, Land and Violence in the Memories of World War I and the French Mandate (1915–1939)," Ph.D. diss. (Utrecht University, 2011); and Nelida Fuccaro, *The Other Kurds: Yazidis in Colonial Iraq* (London: Tauris, 1999).

26. Cited in Jo Laycock, *Imagining Armenia: Orientalism, Ambiguity, and Intervention* (Manchester: Manchester University Press, 2009), 168.

27. Ibid.

28. H.H. Austin, *The Baqubah Refugee Camp: An Account of Work on Behalf of the Persecuted Assyrian Christians* (London: Faith House, 1920), 42. Emphasis added.

29. Northcote to "Mamma," December 3, 1918, NP.

30. Northcote to "Papa," December 11, 1918, NP.

31. Memoranda, cited in Laycock, *Imagining Armenia,* 158.

32. Austin, *Baqubah Refugee Camp,* 20.

33. Ibid., 24.

34. Levon Shahoian, *On the Banks of the Tigris* (London: Taderon Press, 2012), 50.

35. Peter Balakian, *Black Dog of Fate: A Memoir,* 2nd ed. (New York: Basic Books, 2009), 189.

36. This was in direct contrast to the approach the French would take in their resettlement of the Assyrians, who were encouraged to look for employment beyond the settlements themselves, with penury or starvation as the alternative. This was intended to force those who had opposed resettlement in Syria to come to terms with the permanence of their situation and commit themselves to their new lives in the Jazira. See chapter 3 for more details; also see Benjamin Thomas White, "Refugees and the Definition of Syria, 1920–1939," *Past and Present* (forthcoming, 2017).

37. Austin, *Baqubah Refugee Camp,* 57.

38. Ibid., 58.

39. Ibid., 54–55.

40. Qasha Yokhannan Eshu, Secretary of the National Assyrian Committee, memo on "Thanksgiving," December 2, 1919, printed in *The Near East*, January 16, 1920.

41. Ibid.

42. Memo by Northcote, "Concerning the Proposed Dispersal of the Armenian Refugees in Mesopotamia," July 15, 1921, NP.

43. Cunliffe-Owen, "Memorandum Regarding Administration of Refugee Camp at Ba'qubah," 1920, T 1/12603.

44. "Memorandum on the Subject of Agha Petros," December 3, 1924, reprinted in R. Schofield, ed., *Arabian Boundary Disputes*, vol. 9 (Cambridge: Cambridge Archive Editions, 1992), 144; see also Wigram, *Assyrians and Their Neighbors*, 220–29.

45. The question of the degree to which the Iraqi revolution can be categorized as a nationalist one has been divisive, but certainly nationalist discourse represented an important element. The quote here comes from Muhsin Abu Tabikh, one of the most prominent leaders of the revolt, who described it without reservation as a nationalist revolution in his memoirs; see his *Mudhakkirat al-Sayyid Muhsin Abu Tabikh, 1910–1960* (Beirut: al-Mu'assassa al-'Arabiyya lil-Dirasat wa-al-Nashr, 2001), 175. For broader discussions of the revolt, see especially Simon and Tejirian, *Creation of Iraq;* and Abbas Kadhim, *Reclaiming Iraq: The 1920 Revolution and the Founding of the Modern State* (Austin: University of Texas Press, 2012).

46. Rafa'il Batti, *Al-Sihafa fi al-'Iraq* (Cairo: Jami'at al-Duwal al-'Arabiyya-Muahadat al-Dirasat al-'Arabiyya, 1957), 77.

47. For more detail on the British recruitment of Assyrians into the Levies, see Laura Robson, "Peripheries of Belonging: Military Recruitment and the Making of a 'Minority' in Wartime Iraq," *First World War Studies* 7, 1 (2016): 1–20.

48. Rs. 120, or approximately 9 British pounds, according to Stafford; see R. S. Stafford, *The Tragedy of the Assyrians* (London: Allen & Unwin, 1935), 42.

49. Some settled in villages around northern Iraq with the severance money they had received. Stafford reports that by the autumn of 1921, about 6,950 refugees had settled north of Amadiyya, 1,100 in Amadiyya itself, and 7,450 had settled in Dohuk, Akho, Aqra, and Sheikhan; Stafford, *Tragedy of the Assyrians, 42.*

50. On the making of Hashemite Iraq, see especially Reeva Spector Simon, *Iraq Between the Two World Wars: The Militarist Origins of Tyranny,* 2nd ed. (New York: Columbia University Press, 2004); and Orit Bashkin, *The Other Iraq: Pluralism and Culture in Hashemite Iraq* (Stanford, Calif.: Stanford University Press, 2009). Ja'far al-'Askari's memoirs give a number of details about the process of forming the new Iraqi army; see his *A Soldier's Story: From Ottoman Rule to Independent Iraq,* trans. Mustafa Tariq al-'Askari, ed. William Facey and Najdat Fathi Safwat (London: Arabian Publishing, 2003).

51. al-'Askari, *Soldier's Story,* 241. For a gloss of al-'Askari's broader views on Iraqi nationalism, see 'Ala Jasim Muhammad, *Ja'far al-'Askari was-dawruhu al-siyasi wa-al-'askari fi tarikh al-'Iraq hatta 'am 1936* (Baghdad: Maktabat al-Yaqzah al-'Arabiyya, 1987), especially 71–140.

52. Solomon (Sawa) Solomon, *The Assyrian Levies* (Chicago: Atour, 2006), 2.

53. R. S. Stafford, "Iraq and the Problem of the Assyrians," *International Affairs* 13, 2 (1934): 164.

54. This creation of an ethnically distinct military force had clear precedents elsewhere in the British empire, including the use of Sikh and Gurkha troops as imperial forces in India. On the comparison, see Sami Zubaida, "Contested Nations: Iraq and the Assyrians," *Nations and Nationalism* 6, 3 (2000): 367.

55. High Commissioner of Iraq to Minister of the Interior, Baghdad, June 14, 1923, AIR 23/449.

56. Donabed, *Reforging a Forgotten History*, 74. This reluctance recalled an earlier episode in 1920 when some of the Armenian refugee men who had been recruited as irregular troops refused to formally sign on to the British army for fear of being pressed into imperial service overseas, and were stripped of their weaponry as a consequence. See Austin, *The Baqubah Refugee Camp*, 47–48.

57. Solomon, *Assyrian Levies*, 5.

58. Ibid., 6.

59. *Report of the Committee on Asiatic Turkey*, June 30, 1915, reprinted in Schofield, *Arabian Boundary Disputes*, 3–48.

60. Cited in J. Joseph, "The Turko-Iraqi Frontier and the Assyrians," in *The World of Islam: Studies in Honour of Philip K. Hitti*, ed. James Kritzeck and R. Bayly Winder (London: Macmillan, 1959), 259.

61. League of Nations, *Question de la frontière entre la Turquie et l'Irak; rapport présenté au Conseil par la commission constituée en vertu de la résolution du 30 septembre 1924* (Lausanne: Imprimeries réunies, 1925). This is also discussed in Percy Sykes, "Summary of the History of the Assyrians," *Journal of the Royal Central Asian Society* 21, 2 (1934): 262.

62. *Rejoinder to the Memorandum submitted by the Turkish Government to the Council of the League of Nations at Geneva*, December 3, 1924; reprinted in Schofield, *Arabian Boundary Disputes*, 131. This idea that the problems of "minority" and "majority" were even more explosive and required greater external intervention and engineering in non-European territories would return with force in discussions of partition in Palestine; see chapter 4.

63. Final diary of the British assessor to the League of Nations Frontier Commission, enclosure in H. Dobbs to L. Amery, April 15, 1925; reprinted in Schofield, *Arabian Boundary Disputes*, 167.

64. Amery, "Memorandum on the Mosul Question at the League of Nations," September 30, 1925; reprinted in Schofield, *Arabian Boundary Disputes*, 196.

65. Amery speech in House of Commons, December 21, 1925; reprinted in Schofield, *Arabian Boundary Disputes*, 226.

66. Sykes, "Summary of the History of the Assyrians," 263.

67. League of Nations, *Decision Relating to the Turco-Irak Frontier, Dec 16 1925* (London: HMSO, 1925), 4.

68. On the commission and the determination regarding Mosul, see especially Sarah Shields, "Mosul Questions: Economy, Identity, and Annexation," in Simon

and Tejirian, *Creation of Iraq,* 50–60; and Richard Schofield, "Laying It Down in Stone: Delimiting and Demarcating Iraq's Boundaries by Mixed International Commission," *Journal of Historical Geography* 34, 3 (2008): 397–421.

69. Sykes, "Summary of the History of the Assyrians," 263.

70. The Z Plan is detailed in *Military Report on Iraq (Area 9) Central Kurdistan,* Air Ministry, 1929, 196–98; it is also discussed in Donabed, *Reforging a Forgotten History,* 78–79.

71. Stafford, "Iraq and the Problem of the Assyrians," 162.

72. Ibid., 164.

73. "Baghdad Intelligence Report," September 16, 1931, IOR/L/PS/10/1313; Stafford, *Tragedy of the Assyrians,* 43.

74. "Baghdad Intelligence Report," September 16, 1931, IOR/L/PS/10/1313.

75. Ernest Main, *Iraq from Mandate to Independence* (London: Allen & Unwin, 1935), 147; also cited in Vahram Petrosian, "The Assyrians of Iraq," *Iran and the Caucasus* 10, 1 (2006): 132.

76. Mar Shimun to the League of Nations, October 23, 1931, LNA R2318 6A/22528/655.

77. Iraqi Minister for Foreign Affairs to Secretary-General of League of Nations, October 26, 1934, LNA R3927 4/15523/3314.

78. Mar Shimun to Hikmat Suleiman, Baghdad Minister of Interior, June 1933, LNA R3923 4/6523/3314.

79. *Al-Istiqlal,* April 13, 1931.

80. Petition from Bishop Mar Yuwalaha and villagers of Barwari Bala to Baghdad Minister of the Interior for transmission to the League, Baghdad Intelligence Report, September 19, 1931, IOR/L/PS/10/1313. The petition states that the signatories were speaking for about 2,400 families living in the region.

81. Khalil Azmi Bey, speech at Mutassarif residency in Mosul, July 10, 1933, LNA R3923 4/6523/3314.

82. Ellen Lust-Okar, "Failure of Collaboration: Armenian Refugees in Syria," *Middle Eastern Studies* 32, 1 (1996): 55.

83. It is worth remembering that Armenians had only ever made up about 35 percent of the population of Cilicia, and that any effort to constitute an Armenian "homeland" would have been bitterly contested by the remaining large populations of Turks, Kurds, Greeks, and Arabs in the region. On this point, see particularly Chatty, *Displacement and Dispossession,* ch. 4.

84. Benjamin Thomas White, "A Grudging Rescue: France, the Armenians of Cilicia, and the History of Humanitarian Evacuations" (unpublished paper, 2015).

85. Lust-Okar, "Armenian Refugees in Syria," 60.

86. Nicola Migliorino, *(Re)constructing Armenia in Lebanon and Syria: Ethnocultural Diversity and the State in the Aftermath of a Refugee Crisis* (New York: Berghahn Books, 2008), 74–75.

87. Bayard Dodge, "Foreword," in *The Lions of Marash,* by Stanley Kerr (Albany: State University of New York Press, 1973), xi.

88. For a look at the evolution of the Nansen Passport, see Otto Hieronymi, "The Nansen Passport: A Tool of Freedom of Movement and of Protection," *Refugee Survey Quarterly* 22, 1 (2003): 36–47; and Bruno Cabanes, *The Great War and the Origins of Humanitarianism, 1918–1924* (New York: Cambridge University Press, 2014), especially ch. 3.

89. "Arrangement of 30 June 1928 Concerning the Extension to Other Categories of Refugees of Certain Measures Taken in Favour of Russian and Armenian Refugees," United Nations Treaty Collection, *League of Nations Treaty Series* 89, 63, https://treaties.un.org/doc/Publication/UNTS/LON/Volume 89/v89.pdf.

90. Keith Watenpaugh, "Between Communal Survival and National Aspiration: Armenian Genocide Refugees, the League of Nations, and the Practices of Interwar Humanitarianism," *Humanity* 5, 2 (2014): 165.

91. Cited in Claudia Skran, *Refugees in Interwar Europe: The Emergence of a Regime* (Oxford: Clarendon Press, 1995), 115.

92. This arrangement was terminated in 1929 when the ILO's refugee-related responsibilities were turned back over to the high commissioner; the following year the independent Nansen International Office for Refugees was established as an autonomous body. For more on these transitions, see Michael Marrus, *The Unwanted: European Refugees from the First World War through the Cold War* (Philadelphia: Temple University Press, 1985), 112–13; and Atle Grahl-Madsen, *The Land Beyond: Collected Essays on Refugee Law and Policy* (Leiden: Brill, 2001), 130–31.

93. Grahl-Madsen, *Land Beyond*, 130.

94. "Report by Fridtjof Nansen of an Enquiry by a Committee of Experts Made in Armenia under the Auspices of the International Labour Office, July 1925," in League of Nations, *Scheme for the Settlement of Armenian Refugees: General Survey and Principal Documents* (Geneva: League of Nations, 1927), 66.

95. Thomas Greenshields, "The Settlement of Armenian Refugees in Syria and Lebanon, 1915–1939," Ph.D. diss. (Durham University, 1978), 238.

96. Cited in Watenpaugh, "Between Communal Survival and National Aspiration," 173–74.

97. For more on this, see chapter 5.

98. Greenshields, "Settlement of Armenian Refugees," 234.

99. Altug, "Sectarianism in the Syrian Jazira," 159. This rural resettlement is discussed in greater detail in chapter 3.

100. "Report by M. Carle on the Present Position of Armenian Refugees in Syria, 1925," in League of Nations, *Scheme for the Settlement of Armenian Refugees*, 77–78.

101. On the revolt, see especially Michael Provence, *The Great Syrian Revolt and the Rise of Arab Nationalism* (Austin: University of Texas Press, 2005).

102. Migliorino, *(Re)constructing Armenia*, 57.

103. British consular report, December 1925, cited in Provence, *Great Syrian Revolt and the Rise of Arab Nationalism*, 131. On Armenian roles supporting French forces against the Syrian revolt, see particularly Provence, *Great Syrian Revolt and the Rise of Arab Nationalism;* and Lust-Okar, "Failure of Collaboration," 61.

104. Stephen Longrigg, *Syria and Lebanon under French Mandate* (New York: Octagon Books, 1972), 159.

105. For photographic records of this transformation, see especially Vardan Terunean, *Mémoire arménienne: photographies du camp de réfugiés d'Alep, 1922–1936* (Beirut: Presse de l'Université Saint-Joseph, 2010).

106. See Watenpaugh, "Between Communal Survival and National Aspiration," 173–75.

CHAPTER 3

1. See Susan Pedersen, "Samoa on the World Stage: Petitions and Peoples before the Mandates Commission of the League of Nations," *Journal of Imperial and Commonwealth History* 40, 2 (2012): 237, for a detailed breakdown of the sources and dates of petitions to the PMC.

2. For a sense of how this fits into a *longue durée* of local uses of colonial legal systems to defend the rights of the colonized, see especially Saliha Belmessous, "The Problem of Indigenous Claim Making in Colonial History," in *Native Claims: Indigenous Law against Empire, 1500–1920*, ed. Saliha Belmessous (Oxford: Oxford University Press, 2011).

3. As Natasha Wheatley (writing specifically on Palestine) has pointed out, the extensive and committed engagement of local actors with the League—which she calls "a jurisprudence of the League's colonial jurisdiction written at cross purposes to the system's framers and caretakers"—has been largely ignored in the scholarship thus far but offers a centrally important source for an "international history from below"; see her "Mandatory Interpretation," 205–7. As we will see in chapter 5, such petitionary engagement also formed an important strategy for diaspora populations, who often found themselves taking rather different positions vis-à-vis the League's plans for various kinds of demographic engineering and national definition. On the centrality of such petitions for Middle Eastern diaspora communities, see especially Andrew Arsan, "'This is the Age of Associations': Committees, Petitions, and the Roots of Interwar Middle Eastern Internationalism," *Journal of Global History* 7, 2 (2012): 166–88.

4. This was an idea that had parallels in British and French desire to ring Germany and the emerging Soviet Union with smaller "buffer" states in central and eastern Europe, using the rhetoric of national self-determination but with the real goal of protecting imperial interests.

5. Leon Pinsker, "Autoemancipation!" in *The Zionist Idea: A Historical Analysis and Reader,* by Arthur Hertzberg (New York: Doubleday, 1959), 194.

6. Theodor Herzl, *The Jewish State* (New York: Dover, 1988), 95.

7. Gur Alroey, "Journey to New Palestine: The Zionist Expedition to East Africa and the Aftermath of the Uganda Debate," *Jewish Culture and History* 10, 1 (2008): 31–32.

8. Hill to Greenberg, August 14, 1903, cited in Alroey, "Journey to New Palestine," 32.

9. Alroey, "Journey to New Palestine," 33.

10. Israel Zangwill, speech to the Sixth Zionist Congress, in *Speeches, Articles, and Letters of Israel Zangwill* (Westport, Conn.: Hyperion Press, 1976), 186.

11. Richard Waller, "Emutai: Crisis and Response in Maasailand, 1883–1902," in *The Ecology of Survival: Case Studies from Northeast African History,* ed. Douglas Johnson and David Anderson (Boulder, Colo.: Westview Press, 1988), 73–111.

12. St Hill Gibbons, Alfred Kaiser, and Nahum Wilbusch, *Report on the Work of the Commission Sent Out by the Zionist Organization to Examine the Territory Offered by H.M. Government to the Organization for the Purposes of a Jewish Settlement in British East Africa* (London: Wethimer, Lea & Co., 1905), 81.

13. Eitan Bar-Yosef, "Spying Out the Land: The Zionist Expedition to East Africa, 1905," in *The Jew in Late-Victorian and Edwardian Culture: Between the East End and East Africa,* ed. Eitan Bar-Yosef and Nadia Valman (Houndmills, Basingstoke: Palgrave Macmillan, 2009), 197.

14. Mark Levene, "Herzl, the Scramble, and a Meeting That Never Happened," in Bar-Yosef and Valman, *Jew in Late-Victorian and Edwardian Culture,* 212.

15. Cited in Bar-Yosef, "Spying Out the Land," 184.

16. Levene, "Herzl, the Scramble, and a Meeting That Never Happened," 216.

17. Derek Penslar, "Zionism, Colonialism, and Postcolonialism," in *Israeli Historical Revisionism: From Left to Right,* ed. Derek Penslar and Anita Shapira (Portland, Ore: Frank Cass, 2003), 86.

18. Zangwill, speech to the Sixth Zionist Congress, *Speeches, Articles, and Letters,* 195.

19. Levene, "Herzl, the Scramble, and a Meeting That Never Happened," 113.

20. Cited in Alroey, "Journey to New Palestine," 47.

21. Alroey, "Journey to New Palestine," expands substantially on this point.

22. Zangwill's essentially English vision for the future of Zionism has often been represented as his major weakness within the Russian- and Polish-dominated Zionist Organization, and it does help to explain his eventual marginality within mainstream Zionism; but given subsequent British control over not only Palestine but much of the rest of the Arab Middle East as well, it also explains the staying power and far-reaching influence of his vision for Jewish national identity and the solution of resettlement. See David Glover, "Imperial Zion: Israel Zangwill and the English Origins of Territorialism," in Bar-Yosef and Valman, *Jews in Late Victorian and Edwardian Culture,* 134.

23. See Erik Zurcher, *Turkey: A Modern History,* 3rd ed. (London: Tauris, 2004), especially chs. 8 and 9, for a useful overview of this process.

24. Cited in Stephen P. Ladas, *The Exchange of Minorities: Bulgaria, Greece and Turkey* (New York: Macmillan, 1932), 18–19.

25. Ladas, *Exchange of Minorities,* 21–22.

26. Theodora Dragostinova, "Navigating Nationality in the Emigration of Minorities between Bulgaria and Greece, 1919–1941," *East European Politics and Societies* 23, 2 (2009): 192.

27. Ibid.

28. League of Nations, *Memorandum on the Mission and Work of the Mixed Commission on Greco-Bulgarian Emigration* (Geneva: League of Nations, 1929), 11.

29. For a detailed look at the implications of the exchange, see Theodora Dragostinova, *Between Two Motherlands: Nationality and Emigration among the Greeks of Bulgaria, 1900–1949* (Ithaca, N.Y.: Cornell University Press, 2011).

30. League of Nations Council, *The Question of Exchange of Populations between Turkey and Greece* (Geneva: League of Nations, 1922), 6. Emphasis added. The term "racial minorities" recurs several times in Nansen's presentation of the idea to the League Council.

31. Although they also determined that "the Greek Orthodox religion was in a sense the external link of union between the two parts of the Greek nation, the free and the unredeemed." See Ladas, *Exchange of Minorities,* 379–81.

32. Ibid., 383.

33. For useful overviews of these encounters, see Akçam, *Young Turks' Crime against Humanity*; Zurcher, *Turkey*; and Naimark, *Fires of Hatred.*

34. Renee Hirschon, "'Unmixing Peoples' in the Aegean Region," in *Crossing the Aegean: An Appraisal of the 1923 Compulsory Exchange between Greece and Turkey,* ed. Renee Hirschon (New York: Berghahn Books, 2003), 14–15.

35. Great Britain, Parliamentary Papers, *Turkey No. 1 (1923) Lausanne Conference on Near Eastern Affairs, 1922–1923* (Cmd. 1814) (London: HMSO, 1923), 117.

36. Roland Huntford, "Fridtjof Nansen and the Unmixing of Greeks and Turks in 1924," Nansen Memorial Lecture (Oslo: Norwegian Academy of Science and Letters, 1999), 16. On the generally positive reception of the exchange, see especially Donald Bloxham, "The Great Unweaving: The Removal of Peoples in Europe, 1875–1949," in *Removing Peoples: Forced Removal in the Modern World,* ed. Richard Bessel and Claudia Haake (Oxford: Oxford University Press, 2009), 205–6.

37. Susan Pedersen has explored the ways in which this support for Zionist colonization represented an exception to the Permanent Mandates Commission's general opposition to settler colonialism. See her "Settler Colonialism at the Bar of the League of Nations," in *Settler Colonialism in the Twentieth Century,* ed. Caroline Elkins and Susan Pedersen (London: Routledge, 2005), 113–34.

38. League of Nations, Permanent Mandates Commission, *Report on the Work of the Ninth Session of the Commission* (Geneva: League of Nations, 1926), 14.

39. League of Nations, Permanent Mandates Commission, *Report on the Work of the Fourth Session of the Commission* (Geneva: League of Nations, 1924), 12.

40. Pedersen, "Settler Colonialism at the Bar of the League of Nations," 128.

41. "The Establishment in Palestine of the Jewish National Home," memorandum submitted by the Zionist Organisation to the Secretary-General of the League of Nations, October 1924, 12–13.

42. PMC minutes of the 32nd Session, July 30–August 18, 1937.

43. John Hope Simpson's *The Refugee Question* (Oxford: Clarendon Press, 1939) estimated that there were approximately 205,000 Armenian refugees in 1924, of whom 31.7 percent were in Syria and Lebanon; by 1936–37, the number had grown to about 225,000, of whom a higher proportion (nearly 50%) were in Syria

and Lebanon. Aleppo represented the most significant concentration of Armenian refugees, with more than 40,000 already there in 1919.

44. Republique française, Ministere des Affaires étrangeres, *Rapport sur la situation de la Syrie et du Liban (juillet 1922-juillet 1923)* (Paris: Imprimerie nationale, 1923), 19–22. Alternative estimations which place the Armenian numbers a bit higher can be found in Greenshields, "Settlement of Armenian Refugees in Syria and Lebanon," 60–61.

45. Altug, "Sectarianism in the Syrian Jazira," 74–75. Altug emphasizes that there were many victims of these policies besides Armenians, and that non-Armenian refugees and victims were poorly tracked such that numbers are still uncertain.

46. These League estimates for global Armenian refugee numbers were considerably higher than those offered in other sources; see, for instance, Simpson, *Refugee Question*, which suggested a number of about 205,000 in 1924.

47. League of Nations, *Scheme for the Settlement of Armenian Refugees: General Survey and Principal Documents* (Geneva: League of Nations, 1927), 68.

48. Ibid., 69.

49. "Minutes of Plenary Meeting of the Assembly, September 12, 1925," in League of Nations, *Scheme for the Settlement of Armenian Refugees,* 176–77.

50. Ibid., 181. This scheme met with considerable skepticism in Britain, where it was viewed as little more than a plan to hand over large sums of money in development assistance to the Bolsheviks—a view the Soviet government seems to have shared.

51. See Richard Hovannisian, *The Republic of Armenia*, vol. 2: *From Versailles to London, 1919–1920* (Berkeley: University of California Press, 1993), 300.

52. Peter Gatrell, "Displacing and Re-placing Population in the Two World Wars: Armenia and Poland Compared," *Contemporary European History* 16, 4 (2007): 515.

53. Ibid.

54. "Report by M. Carle on the Present Position of Armenian Refugees in Syria, 1925," in League of Nations, *Scheme for the Settlement of Armenian Refugees,* 77.

55. Ibid., 80.

56. This policy, ironically, led later to some of these refugees placed in Alexandretta becoming refugees for a second time when the sanjak became part of Turkey in the late 1930s. See Sarah Shields, *Fezzes in the River: Identity Politics and European Diplomacy in the Middle East on the Eve of World War II* (Oxford: Oxford University Press, 2011), chs. 5–7.

57. For details on this, see especially White, "Refugees and the Definition of Syria."

58. *Al-Yawm,* October 14, 1931, cited and discussed in ibid., 11–12. White points out that fears that the French might partition Syria were by no means far-fetched in this period, when territorial negotiations over Alexandretta were looming and partition was being discussed as a real political possibility across the region.

59. Migliorino, *(Re)constructing Armenia in Lebanon and Syria,* 57.

60. Ibid., 60–61.

61. On the extensive discussion about whether the benefits of control over Iraq justified British military expenditures there, which became a major public debate in

the context of the 1919 negotiations and the 1920 Iraqi revolt against the imposition of British authority and sporadically reemerged in the subsequent decade, see particularly Keith Jeffery, *The British Army and the Crisis of Empire* (Manchester: Manchester University Press, 1984); Jafna Cox, "A Splendid Training Ground: The Importance to the Royal Air Force of Its Role in Iraq, 1919–32," *Journal of Imperial and Commonwealth History* 13, 2 (1985): 157–84; Silverfarb, *Britain's Informal Empire in the Middle East*; Priya Satia, "The Defense of Inhumanity: Air Control and the British Idea of Arabia," *American Historical Review* 111, 1 (2006): 16–51; and David Omissi, "Britain, the Assyrians and the Iraq Levies, 1919–1932," *Journal of Imperial and Commonwealth History* 17, 3 (1989): 301–22. Several of these works explore the decision taken by the British in the context of the revolt to depend heavily on the newly formed Royal Air Force to maintain control over Iraq via the strategy of mass bombing of civilian targets, in cooperation with small local levies (which in northern Iraq were almost entirely Assyrian) and the Iraqi army working on the ground.

62. The specifics of the negotiations within the Permanent Mandates Commission are covered in detail in Susan Pedersen, "Getting Out of Iraq—in 1932: The League of Nations and the Road to Normative Statehood," *American Historical Review* 115, 4 (2010): 975–1000. On this move from mandate status to a highly circumscribed independence, see also Tripp, *History of Iraq*, chs. 2 and 3; Peter Sluglett, *Contriving King and Country: Britain in Iraq* (London: Tauris, 2007), ch. 5; and Dodge, *Inventing Iraq*, 30–41.

63. *Al-Istiqlal*, February 19, 1931.

64. Intelligence Report, April 1931, CO 730/162/8.

65. A. F. Paulus to H. Rassam, September 5, 1930, CO 730/162/8.

66. *Al-Istiqlal*, April 13, 1931. Emphasis added.

67. *Sada al-'Ahd*, April 22, 1931.

68. For a detailed and nuanced look at the politics among Iraqi Jews and the range of Iraqi nationalist positions vis-à-vis the Baghdadi Jewish community, see especially Orit Bashkin, *New Babylonians: A History of the Jews in Modern Iraq* (Stanford, Calif.: Stanford University Press, 2012), especially ch. 6. Bashkin points out that while these sorts of hostile commentaries did appear, most newspapers were not printing such diatribes, and that in fact much of the information being propagated in 1940s Iraq about the Yishuv and Zionism was reasonably accurate and did not seek to implicate or target Iraqi Jews.

69. Mar Shimun to the League of Nations, October 23, 1931, LNA R2318 6A/22528/655. Similar Kurdish claims can be seen in Rappard, "Report on the Various Petitions Emanating from Kurdish Sources," June 22, 1931, LNA R2316 6A/22413/655.

70. Cited in Pedersen, "Getting Out of Iraq—in 1932," 99.

71. "Special Report of the Commission to the Council on the Proposal of the British Government with Regard to the Emancipation of Iraq," PMC minutes, October 26–November 13, 1931, 222.

72. Stafford, "Iraq and the Problem of the Assyrians," 165.

73. "Petition," in *Iraq Administration Reports 1914–1932*, vol. 10, ed. Robert L. Jarman (Slough: Archive Editions, 1992), 475–76.

74. Donabed, *Reforging a Forgotten History*, 100.

75. Yusuf Malek, *The British Betrayal of the Assyrians* (Chicago: Assyrian National Federation and Assyrian National League of America, 1935), 221. Malek saw this position as a self-interested one, claiming that the Iraqi government had essentially bought off some Assyrian leaders with the promise of material returns and positions of influence.

76. Donabed, *Reforging a Forgotten History*, 106.

77. Stafford, *Tragedy of the Assyrians*, 168.

78. Elie Kedourie, *The Chatham House Version and Other Middle Eastern Studies* (New York: Praeger, 1970), 247.

79. The Save the Children Fund, along with the pro-Armenian Lord Mayor's Fund, provided some funding that was used along with Iraqi government money to set up a new Assyrian refugee camp in Mosul for survivors of the Simele massacre in 1933. For details on the camp, which at its height housed 1,500 people, see D. B. Thomson, "The Assyrian Refugee Camp," speech delivered to meeting of the Save the Children Fund on February 21, 1934, reprinted in *Journal of the Royal Central Asian Society* 21, 2 (1934): 269–76.

80. Raphael Lemkin, *Lemkin on Genocide*, ed. Steven L. Jacobs (Lanham, Md.: Lexington Books, 2011).

81. See chapter 5 for further details on this kind of diaspora activism and its international audience.

82. Petition from Dohuk villagers to Major Thomson, June 26, 1933, LNA R3923 4/7290/3314.

83. Mar Shimun to League Secretary General, October 8, 1933, LNA R3923 4/7290/3314.

84. Ibid.

85. Bashkin, *Other Iraq*, 52.

86. Michael Eppel, *The Palestine Conflict in the History of Modern Iraq, 1928–1948* (London: Frank Cass, 1994), 54–55.

87. Cited in Bassam Tibi, *Arab Nationalism: Between Islam and the Nation-State*, 3rd ed. (New York: St. Martin's Press, 1997), 122. Tibi views al-Husri's Arab nationalist approach as owing a great deal to the influence of nineteenth-century German Romantic thought.

88. Simon, *Iraq between the Two World Wars*, 31.

89. Al-'Askari, *Soldier's Story*, 241. For a gloss on al-'Askari's broader views of Iraqi nationalism, see Muhammad, *Ja'far al-'Askari*, 71–140.

90. Khaldun al-Husry, "The Assyrian Affair of 1933 [II]," *International Journal of Middle East Studies* 5, 3 (1974): 353.

91. This episode has attracted more scholarly attention than any other in post-1918 Assyrian history, though recent literature on it is not extensive. Early British chroniclers of the Assyrians tended to present the massacre as a straightforward example of Iraqi Arab/Kurdish brutality; see the accounts in Stafford, *Tragedy of the*

Assyrians, and "Iraq and the Problem of the Assyrians," as well as Sykes, "Summary of the History of the Assyrians in Iraq"; Ernest Main, "Iraq and the Assyrians, 1923–1933," *Journal of The Royal Central Asian Society* 20, 4 (1933): 664–674; and Philip Mumford, "Kurds, Assyrians, and Iraq," *Journal of the Royal Central Asian Society* 20, 1 (1933): 110–19, among others. These accounts relate closely to the interpretations of local and (especially) diaspora Assyrian writings, which tend to present the community as a coherent and ancient national entity for whom the 1933 massacre represented the callous abandonment of the British and the culmination of many centuries of persecution; see, for instance, Mar Eshai Shimun's own *The Assyrian Tragedy* (privately published, 1988); Yusuf Malek, *British Betrayal of the Assyrians;* Paul Shimmon, *The Assyrian Tragedy* (Annemasse, France: n.pub., 1934); and more recently, Solomon (Sawa) Solomon, *Chapters from Modern Assyrian History* (privately published, 1996). An Arab-oriented interpretation of the massacre can be found in Khaldun al-Husry's two articles, "The Assyrian Affair of 1933 [I] and [II]," *International Journal of Middle East Studies* 5, 2–3 (1974): 161–76 and 344–60, which present a version of events more sympathetic to the cause of Iraqi Arab nationalism and the Iraqi army. More recent scholarly accounts have tended to examine the *longue durée* of Assyrian history, placing both the community and the massacre in a frame of long-standing nationhood and persecution; for examples, see the work of Sargon Donabed, *Remnants of Heroes: The Assyrian Experience: The Continuity of the Assyrian Experience from Kharput to New England* (Chicago: Assyrian Academic Society Press, 2003), and *Reforging a Forgotten History,* which contains a useful overview of the massacre based partly on oral histories. Perhaps the best introduction to the relevant issues and the colonial context of the massacre is still Zubaida, "Contested Nations."

92. Susan Pedersen notes that Britain had successfully rejected the suggestion that a League commissioner be placed on the ground in Iraq, arguing that signing on to a minorities protection agreement like the ones already extant for Poland and other central and eastern European nations would not represent a violation of sovereignty. See *Guardians,* 282.

93. Minutes of committee meeting, September 17, 1935, LNA C1533 20A/80694/19093.

94. Ibid.

95. Save the Children brochure, July 1935, enclosed in LNA C1533 20A/80532/19093.

96. *Times,* June 15, 1935, reproduced in LNA C1533 20A/80532/19093.

97. Tawfiq al-Swaidy to Chairman of Committee for the Settlement of the Assyrians, January 17, 1934, LNA R3925 4/7955/3314.

98. Memo on "Settlement of the Assyrians of Iraq," Secretariat of the Committee for the Settlement of the Assyrians, October 24, 1933, LNA C1530 20A/80619/18766. The report goes on to note that this estimate of the total Assyrian population probably represented an understatement, with figures from other sources putting the population at about thirty thousand.

99. Borberg to French Minister of Foreign Affairs, November 26, 1934, LNA C1531 20A/80619/18766.

100. Proceedings at meeting of Members of the Company, July 20, 1933, LNA C1490 20A/80611/17038.

101. Note on Parana Plantation Ltd., June 2, 1933, LNA C1490 20A/80611/17038.

102. Summary of article in "A Noite," November 2, 1933, LNA C1533 20A/80617/19093.

103. Report of the Commission appointed to examine proposals for the settlement of Assyrians in Brazil, n.d. 1934, LNA R3934 4/10815/7582.

104. Report by Browne on the work of the Commission, March 26, 1934, LNA R3933 4/9765/7582.

105. Report of the Commission appointed to examine proposals for the settlement of Assyrians in Brazil, n.d. 1934, LNA R3934 4/10815/7582.

106. Ibid.

107. Memo on "Settlement of the Assyrians of Iraq," Secretariat of the Committee for the Settlement of the Assyrians, October 24, 1933, LNA C1530 20A/80619/18766.

108. "Status of Assyrians Emigrating to Brazil," March 16, 1934, LNA R3934 4/10189/7582.

109. The League collected dozens of newspaper articles on this, all extremely hostile to Assyrian settlement and to immigration in general. See the clippings in LNA C1490 20A/80625/17038 from various dates in 1934.

110. "Memo on the Possibilities of Assyrian Settlement in the Rupunini District of British Guiana," September 1934, LNA R3945 4/20316/13763.

111. Ibid.

112. Report by the Committee [for the Settlement of the Assyrians] to the Council on the action taken in regard to the project for settling the Assyrians in British Guiana, May 18, 1935, LNA R3945 4/18170/13763.

113. Ibid.

114. Yacob Malik Ismiel, Malik Baite, Yoko Shlimun, Malik Warda, Rais Eshi, Rais Iskhaq, Malik Marozlr, Tooma Markhmoora, Yoshia Eshi, Malik Selim, Shamasha Ismail, Rais Mikhail to Minister of Interior Baghdad, July 23, 1933, LNA R3923 4/6523/3314.

115. Sanders and [illegible] to Information Section of the League, December 28, 1935, LNAR 3940 4/20968/11757.

116. Ibid.

117. Minutes of meeting of financial subcommittee appointed by Assyrian Committee, October 9, 1935, LNA R3928 4/20492/3314.

118. Report of the Committee of the Council on the Settlement of the Assyrians of Iraq, July 2, 1926, LNA R3926 4/9022/3314.

119. Minutes of meeting of financial subcommittee appointed by Assyrian Committee, October 9, 1935, LNA R3928 4/20492/3314. White, "Refugees and the Definition of Syria," 19, has higher figures derived from the French sources.

120. Alexis Leger to LN Secretary-General, June 23, 1936, LNA R3926 4/9022/3314.

121. "Settling the Assyrians," *Times,* June 6, 1936; cited in White, "Refugees and the Definition of Syria."

122. For a total of about 1,450 Assyrian settlers. See "Note from the French Government on the Existing Assyrian Settlement on the Khabur," September 10, 1935, LNA R3938 4/192691/11757.

123. Cited in White, "Refugees and the Definition of Syria," 20.

124. An impossibility, since there were no similar colonial corporations but rather a combination of Syrian state land and privately owned parcels, the holders of which were well aware of the money to be made in holding firm on pricing. See "Memo on the Session of the Assyrian Committee," July 21–22, 1937, LNA T161/758.

125. Ibid.

126. Bayard Dodge, "The Settlement of the Assyrians on the Khabbur," *Journal of the Royal Central Asian Society* 27, 3 (1940): 310.

127. Isaac Steinberg, *Australia—The Unpromised Land: In Search of a Home* (London: V. Gollancz, 1948), 115.

128. Alexander Mintz to Delegate of Australia at Evian, July 1938, FO 919/5.

129. Ibid.

130. Markus Lewinson to Refugees Relief Committee, 1938, FO 919/5.

131. Geoff War to Chief Rabbi of Vienna, July 2, 1938, FO 919/5.

132. Immanuel Veliskovsky, "Plan for the Solution of the Emigration Problem," July 1, 1938, CO 919/5.

133. "The Nansen International Office for Refugees—Nobel Lecture," Nobelprize.org, www.nobelprize.org/nobel_prizes/peace/laureates/1938/nansen-lecture .html.

134. Cited and discussed in Mark Mazower, *No Enchanted Palace: The End of Empire and the Ideological Origins of the United Nations* (Princeton, N.J.: Princeton University Press, 2009), 111–13. Mazower points out that in Roosevelt's development of the wartime M-Project, which explored mass migration and resettlement as a solution to a wide variety of global problems, "the fate of the Jews, peace in Europe, and the development of the Middle East were interconnected." The M-Project has been seriously underresearched, but for one overview; see Greg Robinson, "FDR's M Project: Building a Better World through [Racial] Science," *Critique Internationale* 2 (2005), 65–82.

135. Cited in Alroey, "Zionism without Zion?" 23.

136. For an especially trenchant examination of the concept of *terra nullius* (no-man's land), focusing on its application in Australia, see Sven Lindqvist, *Terra Nullius: A Journey through No One's Land* (New York: New Press, 2007). The ongoing relevance of this concept is also usefully discussed in Lorenzo Verancini, *The Settler Colonial Present* (Houndmills, Basingstoke: Palgrave Macmillan, 2015), especially ch. 3.

137. On this process, see Mazower, *Hitler's Empire,* especially ch. 3.

CHAPTER 4

1. McCarthy, *Population of Palestine*, 10. Numbers have been rounded.

2. The literature on British policy, Zionist development, and Palestinian nationalism during the mandate years is extensive. On the development of separate political and economic spheres for Arabs and Jews, see particularly Charles Smith, *Palestine and the Arab-Israeli Conflict*, 8th ed. (Boston: Bedford/St. Martin's Press, 2013); Rashid Khalidi, *The Iron Cage: The Story of the Palestinian Struggle for Statehood* (Boston: Beacon Press, 2006); and Assaf Likhovski, *Law and Identity in Mandate Palestine* (Chapel Hill: University of North Carolina Press, 2006). On Labor Zionism and its efforts (not always successful) to enforce all-Jewish enclaves in Palestine, see particularly Zachary Lockman, *Comrades and Enemies: Arab and Jewish Workers in Palestine, 1906–1948* (Berkeley: University of California Press, 1996); Gershon Shafir, *Land, Labor, and the Origins of the Israeli-Palestinian Conflict, 1882–1914* (Cambridge and New York: Cambridge University Press, 1989); Zeev Sternhell, *The Founding Myths of Israel: Nationalism, Socialism, and the Making of the Jewish State* (Princeton, N.J.: Princeton University Press, 1998); and Mark LeVine, *Overthrowing Geography: Jaffa, Tel Aviv, and the Struggle for Palestine, 1880–1948* (Berkeley: University of California Press, 2001).

3. James Gelvin, *The Israel-Palestine Conflict: One Hundred Years of War*, 3rd ed. (Cambridge: Cambridge University Press, 2014), 93.

4. On the revolt of 1936–39, see especially Ted Swedenburg, *Memories of Revolt: The 1936–1939 Rebellion and the Palestinian National Past* (Minneapolis: University of Minnesota Press, 1995); Matthew Hughes, "From Law and Order to Pacification: Britain's Suppression of the Arab Revolt in Palestine, 1936–39," *Journal of Palestine Studies* 39, 2 (2010): 6–22; Laila Parsons, "Soldiering for Arab Nationalism: Fawzi al-Qawuqji in Palestine," *Journal of Palestine Studies* 36, 4 (2007): 33–48; and Kenneth Stein, "The Intifada and the 1936–39 Uprising: A Comparison," *Journal of Palestine Studies* 19, 4 (1990): 64–85. Some more general accounts that include discussions of the revolt can be found in Weldon Matthews, *Confronting an Empire, Constructing a Nation: Arab Nationalists and Popular Politics in Mandate Palestine* (London: Tauris, 2006); Bayan al-Hut, *Qiyadat wa-al-mu'assasat al-siyasiyya fi Filastin, 1917–1948* (Beirut: Mu'assasat al-dirasat al-filastiniyya, 1981); and Ann Mosely Lesch, *Arab Politics in Palestine, 1917–1939: The Frustration of a National Movement* (Ithaca, N.Y.: Cornell University Press, 1979).

5. On the history of French involvement in the Mount Lebanon region and the specifics of the French mandate in Lebanon, see particularly Akram Khater, *Inventing Home: Emigration, Gender, and the Middle Class in Lebanon, 1870–1920* (Berkeley: University of California Press, 2001); Kais Firro, *Inventing Lebanon: Nationalism and the State under the Mandate* (London: Tauris, 2002); Asher Kaufman, *Reviving Phoenicia: The Search for Identity in Lebanon* (London: Tauris, 2004); Ussama Makdisi, *The Culture of Sectarianism: Community, History, and Violence in Nineteenth-Century Ottoman Lebanon* (Berkeley: University of California Press,

2000); Jennifer Dueck, *The Claims of Culture at Empire's End: Syria and Lebanon under French Rule* (Oxford and New York: Oxford University Press, 2010); and Khoury, *Syria and the French Mandate*. Older but still useful literature includes Longrigg, *Syria and Lebanon under French Mandate*; Kamal Salibi, *The Modern History of Lebanon* (New York: Praeger, 1965); and Philip Hitti, *A Short History of Lebanon* (London: Macmillan, 1965).

6. See Longrigg, *Syria and Lebanon under French Mandate*, 116n2, who points out that the patriarch had received guarantees about some form of Maronite autonomy from both Clemenceau and Pichon when he visited Paris in 1919.

7. A political reality that some scholars have suggested constituted a reason for drawing Lebanon's borders to include so many non-Christians; see, for instance, William Cleveland and Martin Bunton, *A History of the Modern Middle East,* 5th ed. (Boulder, Colo.: Westview Press, 2012), 209.

8. Simon Jackson, "The Wartime Origins of French Mandate Syria," in *France in an Era of Global War, 1914–1945,* ed. Ludivine Broch and Alison Carrol (Houndmills, Basingstoke: Palgrave Macmillan, 2014), 134. In another example of ethnically separatist colonial practices, the French also divided the Légion d'Orient into two different corps to separate Syrian volunteers from Armenians.

9. Jackson, "Wartime Origins of French Mandate Syria," 138. The history of the Armenian section of the Légion is dealt with in Donald Bloxham, *The Great Game of Genocide: Imperialism, Nationalism, and the Destruction of the Ottoman Armenians* (Oxford: Oxford University Press, 2005); and N. E. Bou-Nacklie, "Les Troupes Spéciales: Religious and Ethnic Recruitment, 1916–46," *International Journal of Middle East Studies* 25, 4 (1993): 645–60.

10. Yusef Sawda, *Fi Sabil Lubnan* (Beirut: Dar Lahad Khater, 1988).

11. For further discussion of the decision to separate Lebanon from Syria, see Carol Hakim, *The Origins of the Lebanese National Idea* (Berkeley: University of California Press, 2013), 213–60.

12. Meir Zamir, "Smaller and Greater Lebanon—The Squaring of a Circle?" *Jerusalem Quarterly* 23 (1982): 40; and "Emile Eddé and the Territorial Integrity of Lebanon," *Middle Eastern Studies* 14, 2 (1978): 232–35. Maronite reservations about the Greater Lebanon plan are also discussed in Laura Zittrain Eisenberg, *My Enemy's Enemy: Lebanon in the Early Zionist Imagination, 1900–1948* (Detroit: Wayne State University Press, 1994), 48–51.

13. Abraham Mitri Rihbany chronicled his experiences at the peace conference in his book *Wise Men from the East and from the West* (Boston and New York: Houghton Mifflin, 1922), parts of which had been published earlier in *Harper's* magazine.

14. Faris Nimr and Ya'qub Sarruf edited the newspapers *al-Muqattam* and *al-Muqtataf,* both published in Cairo.

15. Khalil Sa'adih, "Kitab Maftuh 'ila al-Suriyyin wa-l-lubnaninyyin wa-l-filistiniyyin," *al-Majalla,* November 15, 1918; cited in Stacy Fahrenthold, "Transnational Modes and Media: The Syrian Press in the *Mahjar* and Emigrant Activism during World War I," *Mashriq and Mahjar* 1 (2013): 45.

16. Hakim, *Origins of the Lebanese National Idea*, 232.

17. Ibid., 255.

18. Saad Eskandar, "Southern Kurdistan under Britain's Mesopotamian Mandate: From Separation to Incorporation, 1920–23," *Middle Eastern Studies* 37, 2 (2001): 154. Guiditta Fontana makes the argument that the British were consciously interested in creating ethnically homogenous territories during this early period of negotiations over Mesopotamia, a goal they abandoned by the mid-1920s as strategic and economic concerns took precedence. See her article "Creating Nations, Establishing States: Ethno-Religious Heterogeneity and the British Creation of Iraq in 1919–23," *Middle Eastern Studies* 46, 1 (2010): 1–16.

19. On the trajectory of Kurdish nationalism during this period, see particularly McDowall, *Modern History of the Kurds*, as well as Mahir Aziz, *Kurds of Iraq: The Ethnonationalism and National Identity in Iraqi Kurdistan* (London: Tauris, 2011); Tripp, *History of Iraq*; M. R. Izady, "Kurds and the Formation of the State of Iraq, 1917–1932," in Spector and Tejirian, *Creation of Iraq*, 95–109; and Othman Ali, "The Kurds and the Lausanne Peace Negotiations, 1922–23," *Middle Eastern Studies* 33, 3 (2006): 521–34.

20. On this, see especially Shields, "Mosul Questions"; Schofield, "Laying It Down in Stone"; as well as Joseph, "Turko-Iraqi Frontier and the Assyrians." For more details on the Mosul proposals and resolution, see chapter 2.

21. Robert Schaeffer, *Warpaths: The Politics of Partition* (New York: Hill and Wang, 1990), 7. The question of the definition of partition (which is generally agreed to be a twentieth-century phenomenon) has been debated extensively in political science literature, much of which is concerned primarily with the question of whether or not partition is ever a justifiable approach to ethnonational conflict. For some especially prominent arguments within this discussion, see Brendan O'Leary, "Analysing Partition: Definition, Classification, and Explanation," *Political Geography* 26 (2007): 886–908, and "Debating Partition: Justifications and Critiques," *Working Papers in British-Irish Studies* 78 (2006); Nicholas Sambanis, "Partition as a Solution to Ethnic War: An Empirical Critique of the Theoretical Literature," *World Politics* 52, 4 (2000): 437–83; Chaim Kaufmann, "When All Else Fails: Ethnic Population Transfers and Partitions in the Twentieth Century," *International Security* 23, 2 (1998): 120–56; Nicholas Sambanis and Jonah Schulhofer-Wohl, "What's in a Line? Is Partition a Solution to Civil War?" *International Security* 34, 2 (2009): 82–118; and Radha Kumar, "The Troubled History of Partition," *Foreign Affairs* 76, 1 (1997): 22–34. Historians, by and large, have not interested themselves in the concept of comparative partition to the same degree as political scientists.

22. The only example thus far of this definition of partition had occurred outside the Middle East, though within the confines of the British empire (and following a long and bloody anticolonial revolt): the 1920 Government of Ireland Act creating Northern and Southern Ireland, the latter of which seceded from the United Kingdom two years later to become the Irish Free State. For some useful comparative examinations of Ireland and Palestine, see T. G. Fraser, *Partition in Ireland, India, and Palestine: Theory and Practice* (New York: St Martin's Press, 1984); and Joe

Cleary, *Literature, Partition and the Nation State: Culture and Conflict in Ireland, Israel and Palestine* (Cambridge: Cambridge University Press, 2002).

23. This draft mandate for Mesopotamia was never implemented; following the revolt of 1920, the British and the League decided on a strategy of installing the Hashemite monarchy with British backing rather than putting into place an explicitly colonial administration like those constructed in Palestine, Syria, and Lebanon. See Tripp, *History of Iraq*, ch. 2.

24. League of Nations, *Mandates: Final Drafts of the Mandates for Mesopotamia and Palestine, for the Approval of the Council of the League of Nations* (London: HMSO, 1921), 5–6

25. League of Nations, *Mandat pour la Syria et le Liban*, 4.

26. League of Nations, *Mandate for Palestine* (London: HMSO, 1922), 8. Emphasis added.

27. Ibid., 8. This proposed "Jewish agency" did not come into existence until 1929 and was separate from the Va'ad Leumi, the elected assembly for the Yishuv.

28. Ibid.

29. On the British response and the gradual intensification of the military campaign against the revolt, see particularly Jacob Norris, "Repression and Rebellion: Britain's Response to the Arab Revolt in Palestine of 1936–39," *Journal of Imperial and Commonwealth History* 36, 1 (2008): 25–45.

30. Including G. K. Chesterton, who approved the idea on essentially anti-Semitic grounds. For a detailed overview of pre-1937 partition discussions in British circles, see Penny Sinanoglou, "British Plans for the Partition of Palestine, 1929–1938," *Historical Journal* 52, 1 (2009): 131–52, which argues for a long history of the concept of partition prior to the Peel Commission's proposals.

31. Ibid., 142.

32. Ibid., 145.

33. Palestine Royal Commission, *Summary of the Report of the Palestine Royal Commission, with Extracts* (London: HMSO, 1937), 2.

34. Ibid., 10.

35. William Robert Wellesley Peel, and Palestine Royal Commission, *Summary of the Report*, 368.

36. Many scholars have remarked on the predominance of this image; see, for instance, Peter Gatrell, *The Making of the Modern Refugee* (Oxford: Oxford University Press, 2013), 121.

37. Palestine Royal Commission, *Summary of the Report*, 13.

38. Ibid.

39. Ibid., 14.

40. Peel, and Palestine Royal Commission, *Summary of the Report*, 361.

41. Cited in Aaron S. Klieman, "The Resolution of Conflicts through Territorial Partition: The Case of Palestine," *Comparative Studies in Society and History* 22, 2 (1980): 284.

42. Permanent Mandates Commission, *Minutes of the Thirty-Second (Extraordinary) Session,* July 30–August 18, 1937, reprinted in Aaron S. Klieman, *The Rise of Israel: The Partition Controversy, 1937* (New York: Garland, 1987), 103, 106.

43. Amery address to House of Commons, July 21, 1937, *Parliamentary Debates: House of Commons Official Report,* vol. 326 (London: HMSO, 1937), 2275.

44. Ameen Rihani, *The Fate of Palestine: A Series of Lectures, Articles, and Documents about the Palestinian Problem and Zionism* (Beirut: Rihani Printing and Publishing House, 1967), 72–73.

45. These problems are all pointed out in Mustafa Kabha, "Palestinians and the Partition Plan," in *The Two-State Solution: The UN Partition Resolution of Mandatory Palestine—Analysis and Sources,* ed. Ruth Gavinson (London: Bloomsbury, 2013), 31.

46. On the Istiqlal Party's genesis and positions, see Matthews, *Confronting an Empire, Constructing a Nation,* especially ch. 8.

47. *Al-Liwa',* July 9, 1937.

48. For recollections of the Arab Higher Committee's members' and other Palestinian political elites' reaction to the partition plan, see especially Izzat Darwaza, *Mudhakkirat Muhammad Izzat Darwaza: Sijill hafil bi-masirat al-haraka al-arabiyya wal-qadiyya al-filastiniyya khilal qarn min al-zaman 1887–1984* (Beirut: Dar al-Gharb al-Islami, 1993), vol. 3. Arab reactions are also discussed in some detail in al-Hut, *Qiyadat,* 760ff.

49. *Filastin,* October 18, 1937.

50. AHC memo to Peel Commission, reprinted in Gavinson, *Two-State Solution,* 70.

51. On this point, see especially Norris, "Repression and Rebellion."

52. As Natasha Wheatley has put it, "Despite their dissent, Arab Palestinians assumed that the system possessed some power, and sought to manipulate it as best they could . . . [via] a hard-nosed, methodical, even positivist internationalism." See her "Mandatory Interpretation," 208–9.

53. Notes on MacDonald meeting with Husayni, Alami, and Tannus, June 1939, CO 733/353/7.

54. This was in part a consequence of the sectarianizing nature of the mandate itself, which through the 1920s had sought to institutionalize communal difference by making religious identification the basis for legal, political, and economic access to the state. For details on this process, see Robson, *Colonialism and Christianity in Mandate Palestine,* especially ch. 2.

55. Ilan Pappé, "Hajj Amin and the Buraq Revolt," *Jerusalem Quarterly* 19 (2003), 10.

56. For Hajj Amin al-Husayni's own recollections of his activities during this era, see his memoirs, *Mudhakkirat al-Hajj Muhammad Amin al-Husayni,* ed. 'Abd al-Karim al-'Umar (Damascus: Al-Ahali, 1999).

57. Criminal Investigation Department Report, January 30, 1935, CO 371/18957.

58. Ibid.

59. Ibid.

60. Cemal Ayedin, "The Question of Orientalism in Pan-Islamic Thought: The Origins, Content, and Legacy of Transnational Muslim Identities," in *From Orientalism to Postcolonialism: Asia, Europe, and the Lineages of Difference,* ed. Sucheta Mazumdar, Vasant Kaiwar, and Thierry Labnica (London: Routledge, 2009), 107–28.

61. Izzat Tannous, *The Palestinians: A Detailed Documented Eyewitness History of Palestine under British Mandate* (New York: I.G.T., 1988), 183.

62. Ibid., 179.

63. George Mansur to MacDonald, October 25, 1939, CO 733/410/22. Emphasis added.

64. Arab National League memo, "Stop the Bloodshed in the Holy Land," reprinted in Tannous, *Palestinians,* 207–8.

65. For a useful critique of some of the literature on Arab anti-Semitism, see Alexander Flores, "The Arabs as Nazis? Some Reflections on 'Islamofascism' and Arab Anti-Semitism," *Die Welt des Islams* 52 (2012): 450–70.

66. Cited in Itzhak Galnoor, *The Partition of Palestine: Decision Crossroads in the Zionist Movement* (Albany: State University of New York Press, 1995), 57.

67. Galnoor suggests that Weizmann was already considering partition as a possible path forward as early as 1936, prior to the formation of the Peel Commission, and that his apparent reluctance in talks with the commission was intended merely to strengthen his hand when the discussion came down to specifics. He was also interested in prolonging the debate as long as possible, with the idea that ongoing immigration could only strengthen the Jewish position vis-à-vis the British and the Arabs if the final territorial decisions were postponed.

68. Yossi Katz, *Partner to Partition: The Jewish Agency's Partition Plan in the Mandate Era* (London and Portland, Ore.: Frank Cass, 1998), 85–87. The longer history of Zionist transfer plans for the Palestinians is explored in detail in Nur Masalha, *Expulsion of the Palestinians: The Concept of "Transfer" in Zionist Political Thought, 1882–1948* (Washington, D.C.: Institute for Palestine Studies, 1992).

69. Masalha, *Expulsion of the Palestinians.*

70. Cited in Galnoor, *Partition of Palestine,* 63.

71. Vladimir Jabotinsky addressing House of Lords, February 11, 1937, reprinted in Walter Laqueur and Barry Rubin, eds., *The Israel-Arab Reader: A Documentary History of the Middle East Conflict,* 5th ed. (New York: Penguin, 1995), 52–53.

72. Resolution of Zionist Congress, August 1937, reprinted in Galnoor, *Partition of Palestine,* 207–8.

73. Elie Kedourie, "The Bludan Congress on Palestine, September 1937," *Middle Eastern Studies* 17, 1 (1981): 107.

74. The main source of information on the Congress is the lengthy report by the British Consul in Damascus, Colonel Gilbert MacKereth, September 15, 1937, FO 371/20814. Kedourie reproduced this document in its entirety in his brief examination, "Bludan Congress," 109–25.

75. Memorandum on the Bludan Congress, September 15, 1937, FO 371/20814.

76. Annex 2, Report of the Political Committee, Memorandum on the Bludan Congress, September 15, 1937, FO 371/20814.

77. Ibid.

78. Annex 4, Report of the Propaganda Committee, Memorandum on the Bludan Congress, September 15, 1937, FO 371/20814.

79. Annex 5, "Description of a Violently Anti-Jewish Pamphlet Printed in Cairo for the Palestine Defence Committee There, Which Was Given to Each of the Persons Attending the Bludan Congress," Memorandum on the Bludan Congress, September 15, 1937, FO 371/20814. I have been unable to locate an extant Arabic copy of this text; it is possible that the translation made by colonial officials glossed this in terms of European-style anti-Semitism. It is also worth noting that this did in fact reflect actual tactics on the part of the Zionists to weaken Arab nationalism by appealing to various minorities, including the Kurds, the Druze, and the Maronites; see Hillel Cohen, *Army of Shadows: Palestinian Collaboration with Zionism, 1917–1948*, trans. Haim Watzman (Berkeley: University of California Press, 2008), 165–68; and Eisenberg, *My Enemy's Enemy*.

80. Report on Parliamentary Congress on Palestine, October 8, 1938, FO 371/21881.

81. Ibid.

82. See chapter 3.

83. PMC Minutes of the 32nd Session, July 30–August 18, 1937.

84. Permanent Mandates Commission, *Minutes of the Thirty-Second (Extraordinary) Session,* July 30–August 18, 1937, United Nations Information System on the Question of Palestine (UNISPAL), http://unispal.un.org/UNISPAL.NSF/0/FD05535118AEF0DE052565ED0065DDF7.

85. For a discussion of the differentiated nature of Jewish and Arab political institutions, see especially Khalidi, *Iron Cage,* 31–64.

86. PMC Minutes of the 32nd Session, July 30–August 18, 1937. This policy was of course deliberate, intended to preempt the emergence of a secular nationalist anti-imperialist movement. For further analysis on this point, see Robson, *Colonialism and Christianity,* especially ch. 2.

87. PMC Minutes of the 32nd Session, July 30–August 18, 1937.

88. Ibid.

89. Ibid.

90. Ibid.

91. Ibid.

92. Ibid.

93. Ibid.

94. Ibid.

95. White Paper, 1939, http://avalon.law.yale.edu/20th_century/brwh1939.asp.

96. On the question of partition in India and Pakistan, see especially Yasmin Khan, *The Great Partition: The Making of India and Pakistan* (New Haven, Conn.: Yale University Press, 2007); and Gyanendra Pandey, *Remembering Partition:*

Violence, Nationalism and History in India (Cambridge: Cambridge University Press, 2001).

97. UN Doc. A/364 Add. 1, 1947, UN Archives (UNA).

98. Memorandum from Lohamei Herut Yisrael (LEHI) to UNSCOP, June 26, 1947; reprinted in Gavinson, *Two-State Solution*, 151–57.

99. David Ben-Gurion address to UNSCOP, July 4, 1947, in United Nations, *Special Committee on Palestine*, vol. 3: *Oral Evidence Presented at Public Meetings* (Lake Success, N.Y.: 1947), 8–23.

100. David Ben-Gurion address to UNSCOP, July 4, 1947.

101. UN Doc. A/364, 1947, UNA; also cited in Linde Lindkvist, *Shrines and Souls: The Reinvention of Religious Liberty and the Genesis of the Universal Declaration of Human Rights* (Lund: Lund University Press, 2014), 184.

102. This replacement of Palestinian voices with Lebanese and Syrian ones essentially reflected and reinforced the Zionist position that Palestinian political commitments could be submerged in a broader Arab context. On this point, see especially Khalidi, *Iron Cage*, 125.

103. Report to the General Assembly of the UN Special Committee on Palestine, September 3, 1947, http://unispal.un.org/UNISPAL.NSF/0/07175DE9FA2D E563852568D3006E10F3.

104. Report of Sub-Committee 2, November 11, 1947, reprinted as United Nations, *The Partition of Palestine 29 Nov 1947: An Analysis* (Beirut: Institute for Palestine Studies, 1967), 32. This subcommittee was made up of the representatives from Afghanistan, Egypt, Iraq, Lebanon, Pakistan, Saudi Arabia, Syria, and Yemen, and its report was composed mainly by Muhammad Zafrullah Khan and Fares al-Khoury.

105. The federal proposal can be found in UN Doc. A/364, 1947, UNA.

106. "Memorandum on Rights of Minorities in Palestine," 1947, Box S-0609–0001, II, UNSCOP Papers, UNA.

107. Report to the General Assembly of the UN Special Committee on Palestine, September 3, 1947.

108. This is a particularly important point to emphasize because many scholars have looked at the emergence of UN policy as a rejection of the League's focus on collective rights via the minorities treaties and the beginnings of a new regime of *individual* human rights; see especially the work of Mark Mazower, "Minorities and the League of Nations in Interwar Europe"; "Strange Triumph of Human Rights"; and "Two Cheers for Versailles," *History Today* 49, 7 (1999): 8–14. In fact, while this shift in emphasis did indeed constitute an important break between the League and the UN, there were other ways in which the UN represented a continuation of League philosophies and policies—like its ongoing interest in "solutions" of ethnic separation and partition, which continued to feature prominently in UN policy through the twentieth century. The Dayton Accords of 1995, for instance, legitimized and formalized the ethnic cleansing and population exchanges that had taken place in Bosnia and Herzegovina during the war. On this point, see especially Lindkvist, *Shrines and Souls,* ch. 6.

109. On the 1948 war and the expulsion of the Palestinians, see especially Benny Morris, *The Birth of the Palestinian Refugee Problem, 1947–1949* (Cambridge: Cambridge University Press, 1987); Benny Morris et al., *The Birth of the Palestinian Refugee Problem Revisited* (Cambridge: Cambridge University Press, 2003); Avi Shlaim, *Collusion across the Jordan: King Abdullah, the Zionist Movement, and the Partition of Palestine* (New York: Columbia University Press, 1988); and Ilan Pappé, *The Ethnic Cleansing of Palestine* (Oxford: Oneworld Press, 2006).

110. As with all such violent transfers, the numbers of dead and displaced people is somewhat uncertain, with estimates of casualties ranging from half a million to two million people and displacements ranging from about twelve million to as many as twenty million throughout the subcontinent. For an investigation, see C. Embdad Haque, "The Dilemma of 'Nationhood' and Religion: A Survey and Critique of Studies on Population Displacement Resulting from the Partition of the Indian Subcontinent," *Journal of Refugee Studies* 8, 2 (1995): 185–209; see also Pandey, *Remembering Partition*, 2.

111. Memo from Howard Wilson to AFSC, "The Future of the Palestine Refugees," March 11, 1949, cited in Benjamin Schiff, *Refugees unto the Third Generation: U.N. Aid to the Palestinians* (Syracuse, N.Y.: Syracuse University Press, 1995), 19.

112. UN General Assembly, Resolution 194 on "The Palestine Question," December 11, 1948, http://unispal.un.org/UNISPAL.NSF/0/C758572B78D1CD0085256BCF0077E51A.

113. For a detailed examination of Israeli attitudes toward Palestinian refugees and the refusal to allow for their return immediately following the war of 1948, see especially Shira Robinson, *Citizen Strangers: Palestinians and the Birth of Israel's Liberal Settler State* (Stanford, Calif.: Stanford University Press, 2013), 68–112.

114. Herbert Kunde to UNRWA acting director, August 3, 1953, cited in Schiff, *Refugees unto the Third Generation*, 35.

115. For further details, see Schiff, *Refugees unto the Third Generation*, 35–47.

116. Ibid., 49.

117. Julie Peteet, *Landscape of Hope and Despair: Palestinian Refugee Camps* (Philadelphia: University of Pennsylvania Press, 2005), 88.

118. UN Resolution 394, December 14, 1950, http://daccess-ods.un.org/TMP/9873545.16983032.html.

119. Though they also declared that those with property destroyed in the context of "normal" military operations should not be compensated. See Michael R. Fischbach, *Records of Dispossession: Palestinian Refugee Property and the Arab-Israeli Conflict* (New York: Columbia University Press, 2003), 85.

120. See Gerard Daniel Cohen, *In War's Wake: Europe's Displaced Persons in the Postwar Order* (Oxford: Oxford University Press, 2012), 128–29.

121. See its statement at www.unrwa.org/who-we-are.

122. This is an especially important point to make because the historiography of the modern Middle East nearly always separates out Israel/Palestine as a case whose modern history is fundamentally different from any other part of the region, and fails to acknowledge the broader regional and imperial context in which partition

arose. Aaron Klieman, for instance, in an article on the origin of the partition concept, locates it in a "predisposition towards compromise found in English culture
and history," bemoaning that "the only difficulty is that such conceptions are not
always present in the mind of foreign negotiators, as became tragically apparent
during the late 1930s in Palestine" ("Resolution of Conflicts through Territorial
Partition," 284).

CHAPTER 5

1. Mark Levene, "Nationalism and Its Alternatives in the International Arena:
The Jewish Question at Paris, 1919," *Journal of Contemporary* History 28, 3 (1993):
513.

2. The most useful exploration of this conflict between Zionists and assimilationists at the peace conference is Levene, *War, Jews, and the New Europe.*

3. Victoria Hattam, *In the Shadow of Race: Jews, Latinos, and Immigrant Politics
in the United States* (Chicago: University of Chicago Press, 2007), 45.

4. Ibid., 45–46.

5. This idea is carefully drawn out in Hattam, *In the Shadow of Race,* particularly
ch. 2, "Fixing Race, Unfixing Ethnicity." See also Abu El-Haj, who notes that
earlier anxieties about the rapid pace of Jewish assimilation into Christian American society that had led many Jewish intellectuals to advocate for understanding
Jewishness as a racial identity now gave way to an assertion that there was no such
thing as a Jewish race, "in order to protect their standing as white.... Scientific
authority was to be brought to bear on the political struggle in an effort to undermine the image of the Jews as nonwhite, in sum, as a lesser race." See *Genealogical
Science,* 71.

6. Hattam, *In the Shadow of Race,* 48; on this point, see also Eric Goldstein, *The
Price of Whiteness: Jews, Race, and American Identity* (Princeton, N.J.: Princeton
University Press, 2007).

7. Louis Brandeis, "A Call to the Educated Jew," *Menorah Journal* 1, 1 (1915): 19.

8. Cited in Hattam, *In the Shadow of Race,* 52.

9. Cited in Melvin Urofsky, *American Zionism from Herzl to the Holocaust*
(Garden City, N.Y.: Anchor, 1976), 220.

10. American Jewish Congress, *Proceedings of Adjourned Session of American
Jewish Congress Including Report of Commission to Peace Conference and of Provi-
sional Organization for Formation of American Jewish Congress* (New York: Ameri-
can Jewish Congress, 1920). See also the discussion in Christian Raitz von Frentz, *A
Lesson Forgotten: Minority Protection under the League of Nations* (New York: St
Martin's Press, 1999).

11. David Hunter Miller, *My Diary at the Conference of Paris,* vol. 4 (New York:
Appeal Printing Company, 1924), 263–64.

12. Petition from "Les Israelites Republique Orientale Uruguay" to Clemenceau,
Mar 11 1919, FO 608/274.

13. Le Congrès des Juifs de Grèce to Peace Conference, March 21, 1919, FO 608/116.

14. Resolution of South African Zionist Conference, January 1919, FO 608/116.

15. Although it bore a certain resemblance to other maximalist national claims being made in the same period, for instance, some visions of a far-flung Greater Syrian state reaching as far as Iraq and the Hijaz. See James Gelvin, *Divided Loyalties: Nationalism and Mass Politics in Syria at the Close of Empire* (Berkeley: University of California Press, 1998), especially ch. 1.

16. James Gidney, *A Mandate for Armenia* (Kent, Ohio: Kent State University Press, 1967), 171.

17. Cited in Paul Helmreich, *From Paris to Sèvres: The Partition of the Ottoman Empire at the Peace Conference of 1919–1920* (Columbus: Ohio State University Press, 1974), 48.

18. On the question of a potential American mandate over Armenia, see especially Donald Bloxham, "The Roots of American Genocide Denial: Near Eastern Geopolitics and the Interwar Armenian Question," *Journal of Genocide Research* 8, 1 (2006): 27–49; Jay Winter, ed., *America and the Armenian Genocide of 1915* (Cambridge: Cambridge University Press, 2004); and Peter Balakian, *The Burning Tigris: The Armenian Genocide and America's Response* (New York: HarperCollins, 2003).

19. Richard Hovannisian, *The Republic of Armenia*, vol. 1: *The First Year, 1918–1919* (Berkeley: University of California Press, 1971), 250.

20. See Helmreich, *From Paris to Sèvres,* 48; and Hovannisian, *Republic of Armenia,* 1: 261.

21. Cited in Mark Malkasian, "The Disintegration of the Armenian Cause in the United States, 1918–1927," *International Journal of Middle East Studies* 16, 3 (1984): 349–365.

22. Telegram from R. Valsoian, Chairman of Armenians of Yonkers, to Peace Conference, April 19, 1919, FO 608/83.

23. Society of Danish Friends of Armenia to Peace Conference, March 3, 1919, FO 608/83.

24. Assemblée en faveur Armenie to Clemenceau, February 11, 1919, FO 608/274.

25. Assemblée Lausanne to Clemenceau, February 1919, FO 608/116.

26. "Armenian, Arab and Jew," *Palestine,* November 24, 1917, cited in Yair Auron, *The Banality of Indifference: Zionism and the Armenian Genocide* (New Brunswick, N.J.: Transaction, 2000), 255.

27. Cited in Auron, *Banality of Indifference,* 256.

28. For a rather tendentious but detailed examination of the ACIA, see Robert George Koolakian, *Struggle for Justice: The Story of the American Committee for the Independence of Armenia, 1915–1920* (Dearborn, Mich.: Armenian Research Center, 2008). It is also discussed in Merrill Peterson, *"Starving Armenians": America and the Armenian Genocide, 1915–1930 and After* (Charlottesville: University of Virginia Press, 2004), 77–81.

29. For a list of the initial members of the ACIA, see American Committee for the Independence of Armenia, *A Report of the Activities: The American Committee for the Independence of Armenia, 1918–1922* (New York: Armenian Press, 1922), 4. Malkasian notes that "Cardashian had indeed succeeded in skimming off the cream of American society for his new organization." See "Disintegration of the Armenian Cause," 352.

30. Theodor Herzl, *The Jewish State,* reprinted in Arthur Hertzberg, ed., *The Zionist Idea: A Historical Analysis and Reader* (Garden City, N.Y.: Doubleday, 1959), 223.

31. James Gerard, "Why America Should Accept Mandate for Armenia," *New York Times,* July 6, 1919.

32. Balakian, *Black Dog of Fate,* 215.

33. Malkasian, "Disintegration of the Armenian Cause," 355–56.

34. Hovannisian, *Republic of Armenia,* 1: 259.

35. See Watenpaugh, *Bread from Stones,* on the Armenian experience in the Syrian refugee camps.

36. Hovannisian, *Republic of Armenia,* 1: 261.

37. Werda, *Flickering Light of Asia.*

38. Ibid.

39. Ibid.

40. Executive Committee of the Assyrian National Association of America, March 29, 1919, FO 608/83.

41. On the question of proving "whiteness" in the American context and the hostile associations surrounding Muslim identity in the early twentieth-century United States, see especially Sarah Gualtieri, *Between Arab and White: Race and Ethnicity in the Early Syrian American Diaspora* (Berkeley: University of California Press, 2009).

42. Executive Committee, Assyrian National Associations of America, memo on "The New Assyria," March 29, 1919, FO 608/274.

43. See Gualtieri, *Between Arab and White.*

44. "Statement of British Policy in the Middle East for Submission to the Peace Conference," February 18, 1919, FO 608/83.

45. Ibid.

46. Avetis Aharonian to Foreign Office, June 19, 1919, FO 608/78.

47. "Statement of British Policy in the Middle East for Submission to the Peace Conference," February 18, 1919, FO 608/83.

48. Memo on Armenian claims, November 21, 1918, CAB 27/37/2525.

49. Memo on "The Claims of the Assyrians," April 19, 1919, FO 608/83.

50. Handbook on Armenia and Kurdistan, May 1919, IOR/P/PS/20/C192, 4.

51. Ibid., 5.

52. Arnold Toynbee, *Armenian Atrocities: The Murder of a Nation* (London: Hodder and Stoughton, 1915), 24.

53. Resolution of the Manchester Council of Christian Congregations, January 12, 1920, FO 608/73.

54. On Arab Christians in Palestine and Syria, see especially Watenpaugh, *Being Modern in the Middle East;* Robson, *Colonialism and Christianity in Mandate Palestine;* and Noah Haiduc-Dale, *Arab Christians in British Mandate Palestine* (Edinburgh: Edinburgh University Press, 2013).

55. Khater's *Inventing Home* deals extensively with this point. It is also empha-sized in Jacob Norris, "Across Confessional Borders: A Microhistory of Ottoman Christians and Their Migratory Paths," in *Minorities and the Modern Arab World: New Perspectives,* ed. Laura Robson (Syracuse, N.Y.: Syracuse University Press, 2016).

56. See Campos, *Ottoman Brothers,* for an examination of these multireligious concepts of citizenship in late Ottoman Palestine.

57. R. Haddad to British Consul General of New York, n.d. [1919], FO 608/105.

58. See, for instance, letter from Palestinians of La Ceiba, Honduras, to Clem-enceau, Lloyd George, and Orlando Paris, January 27, 1919, FO 608/83.

59. See, for instance, letter from Colonie Syrienne dans la Republique Domin-icaine to Clemenceau, March 1919, FO 608/83.

60. Syriens de Paris to Peace Conference, March 1919, FO 608/116.

61. Syria Independence League of Brazil, March 1919, FO 608/116.

62. Levene, "Nationalism and Its Alternatives," 517.

63. Representatives of Society of London Moslems and other signatories to Balfour, March 3, 1919, FO 608/83.

64. "Handbook of Syria and Palestine," 1919, 37–38, IOR PS/20/C195.

65. For a recent overview of immigration policy changes through the twentieth century, see Robert Fleegler, *Ellis Island Nation: Immigration Policy and American Identity in the Twentieth Century* (Philadelphia: University of Pennsylvania Press, 2013), especially ch. 1.

66. Maud Mandel, *In the Aftermath of Genocide: Armenians and Jews in Twentieth-Century France* (Durham, N.C.: Duke University Press, 2003), 42.

67. Cited in Mandel, *In the Aftermath of Genocide,* 44. Mandel points out, however, that there are other instances where Armenians in France were exempted from the kinds of harsh judgments passed on other ethnoreligious groups, perhaps as a consequence both of their Christianity and of their stateless condition which, she argues, rendered them less threatening than other refugee communities still attached to a state outside France.

68. On the broad rejection of Zionism among French Jews before the Second World War, see especially Catherine Nicault, *La France et le Sionisme, 1897–1945: Une recontre manquée?* (Paris: Calmann Levy, 1992); and Nadia Malinovich, "Le Reveil d'Israel: Jewish Identity and Culture in France, 1900–1932" (Ph.D. diss., University of Michigan, 2000).

69. On Cassin's career, see Jay Winter and Antoine Prost, *René Cassin and Human Rights: From the Great War to the Universal Declaration* (New Haven, Conn.: Yale University Press, 2013).

70. Cited in Mandel, *In the Aftermath of Genocide,* 137–38.

71. Robert Silverberg, *If I Forget Thee O Jerusalem: American Jews and the State of Israel* (New York: Morrow, 1970), 141.

72. On evangelical support for Zionism in both Britain and the United States, see especially Lewis, *Origins of Christian Zionism;* on the question of the frequently made comparison between the "pioneer" narrative shared by Americans and the Jewish of the Yishuv, see Hilton Obenzinger, *American Palestine: Melville, Twain, and the Holy Land Mania* (Princeton: Princeton University Press, 1999); and Steven Salaita, *The Holy Land in Transit: Colonialism and the Quest for Canaan* (Syracuse, N.Y.: Syracuse University Press, 2006). For a highly partisan but occasionally useful examination of the American relationship with the idea of Jewish "return," see Oren, *Power, Faith and Fantasy.*

73. Cited in Urofsky, *American Zionism,* 396.

74. See Mark Raider, *The Emergence of American Zionism* (New York: New York University Press, 1998), ch. 6, for a further exploration of both these points.

75. The perpetual debate over the designation of Alexandretta came to a head in the crisis of 1938–39, when France was forced to cede the territory to Turkey. For details, see Shields, *Fezzes in the River.*

76. J. Missakian to Foreign Office, May 16, 1939, FO 371/23281.

77. For a detailed investigation of the internal divisions among French Armenians over support for Soviet Armenia, see especially Mandel, *In the Aftermath of Genocide,* 119–34.

78. Migliorino, *(Re)constructing Armenia,* 62.

79. Ibid., 64.

80. Markar Melkonian, ed., *The Right to Struggle: Selected Writings by Monte Melkonian on the Armenian National Question,* 2nd ed. (San Francisco: Sardarabad Collective, 1993), 123, 131–32.

81. Assyrian Committee in Greece to Secretary General of the LN, August 25, 1934, LNA R3926 4/9656/3314.

82. D.M.K. Javaraud to Sec Gen of LN, September 13, 1933, LNA R3923 4/3314/3314.

83. B.S. Nicolas to Secretary General of LN, 1933, LNA R3923 4/6260/3314.

84. Assyrian National Association of Yonkers, NY to Secretary General of the LN, January 30, 1934, LNA R3923 4/3314/3314.

85. David Perley to Secretary General of the LN, September 7, 1934, R3926 4/9656/3314.

86. Assyrian National League of American in Chicago, August 25, 1934, R3926 4/9656/3314.

87. Ibid.

88. Assyrian National Association of Yonkers, NY to Secretary General of the LN, January 30, 1934, LNA R3923 4/3314/3314.

89. The World Alliance for International Friendship Through the Churches to Secretary General of the LN, 1933, LNA R3923 4/3314/3314.

90. Assyrian National Union to League of Nations, September 8, 1933, LNA R3923 4/3314/3314.

91. Mar Shimun to Secretary General of League, October 25, 1933, LNA C1530 20A/80619/18766.

92. Laycock, *Imagining Armenia,* 159. Laycock connects this view with Lisa Malkki's analysis that relief regimes often blamed refugees themselves, rather than their violent dispersal, for failing to constitute functional political entities: "It is striking how often the abundant literature claiming refugees as its objects of study locates 'the problem' not in the political conditions or processes that produce massive territorial displacements of people, but, rather, within the bodies and minds (and even souls) of people categorized as refugees." See Lisa Malkki, "National Geographic: The Rooting of Peoples and the Territorialisation of National Identity among Scholars and Refugees," *Cultural Anthropology* 7 (1992): 33.

93. Memo on conversation between Mallet and Newcombe, 1919, FO 608/77; cited and discussed in Laycock, *Imagining Armenia,* 196–97.

94. C. Leonard Leese, *Armenia and the Allies* (London: British Armenia Committee, 1920), 14.

95. Werda, *Flickering Light of Asia.*

96. Armen T. Marsoobian, *Fragments of a Lost Homeland: Remembering Armenia* (London: Tauris, 2015), 281.

97. Cited in Urofsky, *American Zionism,* 220. It is perhaps also worth noting that the diasporic focus on the American mandate pinned Armenian nationalist hopes on a state fundamentally uninterested, at this stage, in assuming a new imperial role in the former Ottoman territories, in contrast to the clear British commitment to maintaining control over Palestine.

98. Curzon speech to Eastern Committee, December 2, 1918, CAB 27/24; cited in Hovannisian, *Republic of Armenia,* 1: 269.

99. Minute by Robert Vansittart, 1919, FO 608/79.

100. Malkasian, "Disintegration of the Armenian Cause," 358.

101. Cited in Zvi Ganin, *An Uneasy Relationship: American Jewish Leadership and Israel, 1948–1957* (Syracuse, N.Y.: Syracuse University Press, 2005), 9.

102. Gabriel Sheffer, "The Jewish Diaspora and the Arab-Palestinian-Israeli Conflict," in *Diasporas in Conflict: Peace-Makers or Peace-Wreckers?,* ed. Hazel Smith and Paul Stares (Tokyo: United Nations University Press, 2007), 77.

103. Cited in Ganin, *Uneasy Relationship,* 21.

EPILOGUE

1. Hannah Arendt approaches this point, noting, "Under the most diverse conditions and disparate circumstances, we watch the development of the same phenomena—homelessness on an unprecedented scale, rootlessness to an unprecedented depth. . . . It is as though mankind has divided itself between those who believe in human omnipotence (who think that everything is possible if one knows how to organize masses for it) and those for whom powerlessness has become the major experience of their lives." See *The Origins of Totalitarianism,* rev. ed. (1951; New York: Harcourt, 1973), vii.

2. Both cited in Naimark, *Fires of Hatred,* 110. For an overview of the postwar ethnic cleansing of Germans from eastern Europe, see especially Timothy Snyder, *Bloodlands: Europe between Hitler and Stalin* (New York: Basic Books, 2010), ch. 10.

3. Cited in Bose and Jalal, *Modern South Asia,* 155. The remaking of the remaining communities as "minorities" is discussed briefly in Khan, *Great Partition,* 155, and more extensively in Vazira Fazila-Yacoobali Zamindar, *The Long Partition and the Making of Modern South Asia: Refugees, Boundaries, Histories* (New York: Columbia University Press, 2007), which describes this minoritization as a major aspect of a "long partition" involving not only the initial violence but the bureaucratic process of constructing the two oppositional nation-states in the subsequent years.

4. For a look at the role diasporas have played in various conflict zones across the globe, see especially Hazel Smith and Paul B. Stares, eds., *Diasporas in Conflict: Peace-Makers or Peace-Wreckers?* (Tokyo and New York: United Nations University Press, 2007).

5. United Nations Peacekeeping Force in Cyprus, "UNFICYP Background," www.un.org/en/peacekeeping/missions/unficyp/background.shtml. Some observers have defended the partition itself (not just the UN's role) as a force for peace; see, for instance, the work of political scientist Chaim Kaufmann, who declared in a 2007 article that "the long-term aftermath of the partition must be considered a success from the point of view of human safety." See Chaim Kaufmann, "An Assessment of the Partition of Cyprus," *International Studies Perspective* 8 (2007): 220.

6. On this point, see especially James Kennedy and Liliana Riga, "A Liberal Route from Homogeneity? US Policymakers and the Liberalization of Ethnic Nationalists in Bosnia's Dayton Accords," *Nationalism and Ethnic Politics* 19, 2 (2013): 163–86.

7. For just a few examples of this conversation, see James Stavridis, "It's Time to Seriously Consider Partitioning Syria," *Foreign Policy,* March 9, 2016; Dilip Hiro, "Is Partition a Solution for Syria?" *YaleGlobal Online,* July 31, 2012 (in which Hiro explicitly cites India and Pakistan as a viable and successful example of partition); and Barak Mendelsohn, "Divide and Conquer in Syria and Iraq: Why the West Should Plan for a Partition," *Foreign Affairs,* November 29, 2015.

BIBLIOGRAPHY

ARCHIVAL SOURCES

Central Zionist Archives (CZA), Jerusalem

India Office Records (IOR), British Library, London

Israel State Archives (ISA), Jerusalem

League of Nations Archives (LNA), Geneva

Library of Congress Matson Collection, Washington, D.C.

The National Archives, Kew (TNA)

    Cabinet Papers (CAB)

    Colonial Office (CO)

    Foreign Office (FO)

    Royal Air Force (AIR)

Northcote Papers (NP), British Library, London

United Nations Archives (UNA), New York

United Nations Information System on the Question of Palestine (UNISPAL), http://unispal.un.org/UNISPAL.NSF/udc.htm

PERIODICALS

Filastin (Jaffa)

Al-Istiqlal (Baghdad)

Jornal do Brasil (Rio de Janeiro)

Al-Liwa' (Jerusalem)

Al-Majalla (Buenos Aires)

Menorah Journal (Cambridge, Mass.)

Mirat al-sharq (Jerusalem)

The Near East (London)

New York Times (New York)

Palestine (London)

Sada al-'Ahd (Baghdad)

Times of London (London)

Al-Yawm (Damascus)

WORKS CITED

Abu El-Haj, Nadia. *The Genealogical Science: The Search for Jewish Origins and the Politics of Epistemology.* Chicago: University of Chicago Press, 2012.

Abu Tabikh, Muhsin. *Mudhakkirat al-Sayyid Muhsin Abu Tabikh, 1910–1960.* Beirut: al-Mu'assassa al-'Arabiyya lil-Dirasat wa-al-Nashr, 2001.

Akçam, Taner. *The Young Turks' Crime against Humanity: The Armenian Genocide and Ethnic Cleansing in the Ottoman Empire.* Princeton, N.J.: Princeton University Press, 2012.

Åkermark, Athanasia Spiliopoulou. *Justifications of Minority Protection in International Law.* London: Kluwer Law International, 1996.

Ali, Othman. "The Kurds and the Lausanne Peace Negotiations, 1922–23." *Middle Eastern Studies* 33, 3 (2006): 521–34.

Alroey, Gur. "Angolan Zion: The Jewish Territorial Organization and the Idea of a Jewish State in Western Africa, 1907–1913." *Journal of Modern Jewish Studies* 14, 2 (2015): 179–98.

———. *Bread to Eat and Clothes to Wear: Letters from Jewish Migrants in the Early Twentieth Century.* Detroit: Wayne State University Press, 2011.

———. "Journey to New Palestine: The Zionist Expedition to East Africa and the Aftermath of the Uganda Debate." *Jewish Culture and History* 10, 1 (2008): 23–58.

———. "Mesopotamia—'The Promised Land': The Jewish Territorial Organization Project in the Bilad al-Rafidayn and the Question of Palestine, 1899–1917." *Middle Eastern Studies* 50, 6 (2014): 911–35.

———. "Zionism without Zion? Territorialist Ideology and the Zionist Movement, 1882–1956." *Jewish Social Studies: History, Culture, Society* 18, 1 (2011): 1–32.

Altug, Seda. "Sectarianism in the Syrian Jazira: Community, Land and Violence in the Memories of World War I and the French Mandate (1915–1939)." Ph.D. diss., Utrecht University, 2011.

Amanat, Abbas, Michael Bonine, and Michael Gasper, eds. *Is There a Middle East? The Evolution of a Geopolitical Concept.* Stanford, Calif.: Stanford University Press, 2012.

American Committee for the Independence of Armenia. *A Report of the Activities: The American Committee for the Independence of Armenia, 1918–1922.* New York: Armenian Press, 1922.

American Jewish Congress. *Proceedings of Adjourned Session of American Jewish Congress Including Report of Commission to Peace Conference and of Provisional Organization for Formation of American Jewish Congress.* New York: American Jewish Congress, 1920.

Anghie, Anthony. "Finding the Peripheries: Sovereignty and Colonialism in Nineteenth Century International Law." *Harvard International Law Journal* 40, 1 (1999): 1–80.

Arkush, Allen. "Max Nordau: The Post-Herzl Years." In *The Festschrift Darkei Noam: The Jews of Arab Lands,* ed. Casten Schapkow et al., 235–54. Leiden: Brill, 2015.

Arsan, Andrew. "'This Is the Age of Associations': Committees, Petitions, and the Roots of Interwar Middle Eastern Internationalism." *Journal of Global History* 7, 2 (2012): 166–88.

al-ʿAskari, Jaʿfar Pasha. *A Soldier's Story: From Ottoman Rule to Independent Iraq.* Trans. Mustafa Tariq al-ʿAskari and ed. William Facey and Najdat Fathi Safwat. London: Arabian Publishing, 2003.

Arendt, Hannah. *The Origins of Totalitarianism,* rev. ed. New York: Harcourt, 1973. First published 1951.

Auron, Yair. *The Banality of Indifference: Zionism and the Armenian Genocide.* New Brunswick, N.J.: Transaction, 2000.

Austin, H. H. *The Baqubah Refugee Camp: An Account of Work on Behalf of the Persecuted Assyrian Christians.* London: Faith House, 1920.

Avineri, Shlomo. "Theodor Herzl's Diaries as a Bildungsroman." *Jewish Social Studies* 5, 3 (1999): 1–46.

Ayedin, Cemal. "The Question of Orientalism in Pan-Islamic Thought: The Origins, Content, and Legacy of Transnational Muslim Identities." In *From Orientalism to Postcolonialism: Asia, Europe, and the Lineages of Difference,* ed. Sucheta Mazumdar, Vasant Kaiwar, and Thierry Labnica, 107–28. London: Routledge, 2009.

Aziz, Mahir. *Kurds of Iraq: The Ethnonationalism and National Identity in Iraqi Kurdistan.* London: Tauris, 2011.

Balakian, Peter. *Black Dog of Fate: A Memoir,* 2nd ed. New York: Basic Books, 2009.

———. *The Burning Tigris: The Armenian Genocide and America's Response.* New York: HarperCollins, 2003.

Barkey, Karen, and Mark Von Hagen. *After Empire: Multiethnic Societies and Nation-Building: The Soviet Union and the Russian, Ottoman, and Habsburg Empires.* Boulder, Colo.: Westview Press, 1997.

Bartov, Omer, and Eric D. Weitz, eds. *Shatterzone of Empires: Coexistence and Violence in the German, Habsburg, Russian, and Ottoman Borderland.* Bloomington: Indiana University Press, 2013.

Bar-Yosef, Eitan. "Spying Out the Land: The Zionist Expedition to East Africa, 1905." In *The Jew in Late-Victorian and Edwardian Culture: Between the East End and East Africa,* ed. Eitan Bar-Yosef and Nadia Valman, 183–200. Houndmills, Basingstoke: Palgrave Macmillan, 2009.

Bashkin, Orit. *New Babylonians: A History of the Jews in Modern Iraq.* Stanford, Calif.: Stanford University Press, 2012.

———. *The Other Iraq: Pluralism and Culture in Hashemite Iraq.* Stanford, Calif.: Stanford University Press, 2009.

Batti, Rafa'il. *Al-Sihafa fi al-'Iraq.* Cairo: Jami'at al-Duwal al-'Arabiyya-Muahadat al-Dirasat al-'Arabiyya, 1957.

Bayat, Fadil. *al-Dawla al-'Uthmaniyya fi al-majal al-'Arabi: dirasa tarikhiyya fi al-awda' al-idariyya fi daw' al-watha'iq wa-al-masadir al-'Uthmaniyya hasran.* Beirut: Markaz Dirasat al-Wahdah al-'Arabiyya, 2007.

Bayly, C. A. *Indian Society and the Making of the British Empire.* Cambridge: Cambridge University Press, 1988.

———. "Representing Copts and Muhammadans: Empire, Nation, and Community in Egypt and India, 1880–1914." In *Modernity and Culture from the Mediterranean to the Indian Ocean,* ed. Leila Tarazi Fawaz and C. A. Bayly, 158–203. New York: Columbia University Press, 2002.

Beinin, Joel. "Knowing the 'Other': Arabs, Islam, and the West." In *Doing Race: 21 Essays for the 21st Century,* ed. Hazel Rose Markus and Paula M.L. Moya, 199–215. New York: Norton, 2010.

Belmessous, Saliha. *Assimilation and Empire: Uniformity in French and British Colonies, 1541–1954.* Oxford: Oxford University Press, 2013.

———. "The Problem of Indigenous Claim Making in Colonial History." In *Native Claims: Indigenous Law against Empire, 1500–1920,* ed. Saliha Belmessous. Oxford: Oxford University Press, 2011.

Berman, Nathaniel. "'But the Alternative Is Despair': European Nationalism and the Modernist Renewal of International Law." *Harvard Law Review* 106 (1992–93): 1792–1903.

———. *Passion and Ambivalence: Colonialism, Nationalism, and International Law.* Leiden: Nijhoff, 2012.

Bloxham, Donald. *The Great Game of Genocide: Imperialism, Nationalism, and the Destruction of the Ottoman Armenians.* Oxford: Oxford University Press, 2005.

———. "The Great Unweaving: The Removal of Peoples in Europe, 1875–1949." In *Removing Peoples: Forced Removal in the Modern World,* ed. Richard Bessel and Claudia Haake. Oxford: Oxford University Press, 2009.

———. "The Roots of American Genocide Denial: Near Eastern Geopolitics and the Interwar Armenian Question." *Journal of Genocide Research* 8, 1 (2006): 27–49.

Blumi, Isa. *Ottoman Refugees: Migration in a Post-Imperial World.* London: Bloomsbury Academic, 2013.

Bose, Sugata, and Ayesha Jalal. *Modern South Asia: History, Culture, Political Economy,* 2nd ed. New York: Routledge, 2004.

Bou-Nacklie, N. E. "Les Troupes Spéciales: Religious and Ethnic Recruitment, 1916–46." *International Journal of Middle East Studies* 25, 4 (1993): 645–60.

Brandeis, Louis. "A Call to the Educated Jew." *Menorah Journal* 1, 1 (1915): 19.

Braude, Benjamin, and Bernard Lewis, eds. *Christians and Jews in the Ottoman Empire: The Functioning of a Plural Society,* 2 vols. New York: Holmes and Meier, 1982.

Brett, Michael. "Legislating for Inequality in Algeria: The Senatus-Consulte of 14 July 1865." *Bulletin of the School of Oriental and African Studies* 51, 3 (1988): 440–61.

Brown, Keith. *Loyal unto Death: Trust and Terror in Revolutionary Macedonia.* Bloomington: Indiana University Press, 2013.

Bunton, Martin. "Inventing the Status Quo: Ottoman Land Law during the Palestine Mandate, 1917–1936," *International History Review* 21, 1 (1999): 28–56.

Cabanes, Bruno. *The Great War and the Origins of Humanitarianism, 1918–1924.* New York: Cambridge University Press, 2014.

Callahan, Michael. *Mandates and Empire: The League of Nations and Africa, 1914–1931.* Brighton: Sussex Academic Press, 1999.

Campos, Michelle. *Ottoman Brothers: Muslims, Christians, and Jews in Early Twentieth-Century Palestine.* Stanford, Calif.: Stanford University Press, 2010.

Carmichael, Cathie. *Genocide before the Holocaust.* New Haven, Conn.: Yale University Press, 2009.

Chatterjee, Partha. *The Nation and Its Fragments: Colonial and Postcolonial Histories* Princeton, N.J.: Princeton University Press, 1993.

———. *Nationalist Thought and the Colonial World: A Derivative Discourse?* London: Zed Books, 1986.

Chatty, Dawn. *Displacement and Dispossession in the Modern Middle East.* New York: Cambridge University Press, 2010.

Chevalier, Michel. *Les montangnards chrétiens du Hakkari et du Kurdistan septentrional.* Paris: Departement de Geographie de l'Universite de Paris-Sorbonne.

Clavin, Patricia. *Securing the World Economy: The Reinvention of the League of Nations, 1920–1946.* Oxford: Oxford University Press, 2013.

Cleary, Joe. *Literature, Partition and the Nation State: Culture and Conflict in Ireland, Israel and Palestine.* Cambridge: Cambridge University Press, 2002.

Cleveland, William, and Martin Bunton. *A History of the Modern Middle East,* 5th ed. Boulder, Colo.: Westview Press, 2012.

Coakley, J. F. *The Church of the East and the Church of England: A History of the Archbishop of Canterbury's Assyrian Mission.* Oxford: Clarendon Press, 1992.

Cohen, Gerard Daniel. *In War's Wake: Europe's Displaced Persons in the Postwar Order.* Oxford: Oxford University Press, 2012.

Cohen, Hillel. *Army of Shadows: Palestinian Collaboration with Zionism, 1917–1948.* Trans. Haim Watzman. Berkeley: University of California Press, 2008.

Cohn, Bernard. *Colonialism and Its Forms of Knowledge: The British in India.* Princeton, N.J.: Princeton University Press, 1996.

Courbage, Youssef, and Phillipe Fargues. *Chrétiens et juifs dans l'Islam arabe et turc.* Paris: Fayard, 1992.

de Courtois, Sébastien. *Le génocide oublié: Chrétiens d'orient, les derniers araméens.* Paris: Ellipses, 2002.

Cox, Jafna. "A Splendid Training Ground: The Importance to the Royal Air Force of Its Role in Iraq, 1919–32." *Journal of Imperial and Commonwealth History* 13, 2 (1985): 157–84.

Darwaza, Izzat. *Mudhakkirat Muhammad Izzat Darwaza: Sijill hafil bi-masirat al-haraka al-'arabiyya wal-qadiyya al-filastiniyya khilal qarn min al-zaman 1887–1984.* Beirut: Dar al-Gharb al-Islami, 1993.

Decorzant, Yann. "The League of Nations and the Emergence of a New Network of Economic-Financial Expertise (1914–1923)." *Critique international* 3 (2011): 35–50.

Dodge, Bayard. "The Settlement of the Assyrians on the Khabbur." *Journal of the Royal Central Asian Society* 27, 3 (1940): 301–20.

———. "Foreword." In *The Lions of Marash,* by Stanley Kerr, xi. Albany: State University of New York Press, 1973.

Dodge, Toby. *Inventing Iraq: The Failure of Nation Building and a History Denied.* New York: Columbia University Press, 2003.

Donabed, Sargon. *Reforging a Forgotten History: Iraq and the Assyrians in the Twentieth Century.* Edinburgh: Edinburgh University Press, 2015.

———. *Remnants of Heroes: The Assyrian Experience: The Continuity of the Assyrian Experience from Kharput to New England.* Chicago: Assyrian Academic Society Press, 2003.

Dragostinova, Theodora. *Between Two Motherlands: Nationality and Emigration among the Greeks of Bulgaria, 1900–1949.* Ithaca, N.Y.: Cornell University Press, 2011.

———. "Navigating Nationality in the Emigration of Minorities between Bulgaria and Greece, 1919–1941." *East European Politics and Societies* 23, 2 (2009): 185–212.

Drew, Catriona. "Population Transfer: The Untold Story of Self-Determination." Presentation at Global Fellows Forum, New York University, 2006, www.law.nyu.edu/sites/default/files/upload_documents/gffdrewpaper.pdf

Dueck, Jennifer. *The Claims of Culture at Empire's End: Syria and Lebanon under French Rule.* Oxford and New York: Oxford University Press, 2010.

Edip, Halide. *Turkey Faces West.* New Haven, Conn.: Yale University Press, 1930.

Eisenberg, Laura Zittrain. *My Enemy's Enemy: Lebanon in the Early Zionist Imagination, 1900–1948.* Detroit: Wayne State University Press, 1994.

Eppel, Michael. *The Palestine Conflict in the History of Modern Iraq, 1928–1948.* London: Frank Cass, 1994.

Eskandar, Saad. "Southern Kurdistan under Britain's Mesopotamian Mandate: From Separation to Incorporation, 1920–23." *Middle Eastern Studies* 37, 2 (2001): 153–80.

Fahrenthold, Stacy. "Transnational Modes and Media: The Syrian Press in the *Mahjar* and Emigrant Activism during World War I." *Mashriq and Mahjar* 1 (2013): 32–57.

Fink, Carole. "The League of Nations and the Minorities Question." *World Affairs* 157, 4 (1995): 197–205.

———. *Defending the Rights of Others: The Great Powers, the Jews, and International Minority Protection, 1878–1938*. Cambridge and New York: Cambridge University Press, 2004.

Finkel, Caroline. *Osman's Dream: The Story of the Ottoman Empire 1300–1923*. New York: Perseus, 2005.

Firro, Kais. *Inventing Lebanon: Nationalism and the State under the Mandate*. London: Tauris, 2002.

Fischbach, Michael R. *Records of Dispossession: Palestinian Refugee Property and the Arab-Israeli Conflict*. New York: Columbia University Press, 2003.

Fleegler, Robert. *Ellis Island Nation: Immigration Policy and American Identity in the Twentieth Century*. Philadelphia: University of Pennsylvania Press, 2013.

Flores, Alexander. "The Arabs as Nazis? Some Reflections on 'Islamofascism' and Arab Anti-Semitism." *Die Welt des Islams* 52 (2012): 450–70.

Fontana, Guiditta. "Creating Nations, Establishing States: Ethno-Religious Heterogeneity and the British Creation of Iraq in 1919–23." *Middle Eastern Studies* 46, 1 (2010): 1–16.

Fortna, Benjamin, et al., eds. *State-Nationalism in the Ottoman Empire, Greece and Turkey: Orthodox and Muslims, 1830–1945*. London: Routledge, 2013.

Fraser, T. G. *Partition in Ireland, India, and Palestine: Theory and Practice*. New York: St. Martin's Press, 1984.

Fuccaro, Nelida. *The Other Kurds: Yazidis in Colonial Iraq*. London: Tauris, 1999.

Galnoor, Itzhak. *The Partition of Palestine: Decision Crossroads in the Zionist Movement*. Albany: State University of New York Press, 1995.

Ganin, Zvi. *An Uneasy Relationship: American Jewish Leadership and Israel, 1948–1957*. Syracuse, N.Y.: Syracuse University Press, 2005.

Gatrell, Peter. "Displacing and Re-placing Population in the Two World Wars: Armenia and Poland Compared." *Contemporary European History* 16, 4 (2007): 511–27.

———. *The Making of the Modern Refugee*. Oxford: Oxford University Press, 2013.

Gaunt, David. *Massacres, Resistance, Protection: Muslim-Christian Relations in Eastern Anatolia during World War I*. London: Gorgias Press, 2006.

Gavinson, Ruth, ed. *The Two-State Solution: The UN Partition Resolution of Mandatory Palestine—Analysis and Sources*. London: Bloomsbury, 2013.

Gelvin, James. *Divided Loyalties: Nationalism and Mass Politics in Syria at the Close of Empire*. Berkeley: University of California Press, 1998.

———. *The Israel-Palestine Conflict: One Hundred Years of War*, 3rd ed. Cambridge: Cambridge University Press, 2014.

Gibbons, St Hill, Alfred Kaiser, and Nahum Wilbusch. *Report on the Work of the Commission Sent Out by the Zionist Organization to Examine the Territory Offered by H.M. Government to the Organization for the Purposes of a Jewish Settlement in British East Africa*. London: Wethimer, Lea & Co., 1905.

Gidney, James. *A Mandate for Armenia*. Kent, Ohio: Kent State University Press, 1967.

Gingeras, Ryan. *Sorrowful Shores: Violence, Ethnicity, and the End of the Ottoman Empire, 1912–1923*. Oxford: Oxford University Press, 2009.

Glazier, Jack. *Dispersing the Ghetto: The Relocation of Jewish Immigrants across America*. Ithaca, N.Y.: Cornell University Press, 1998.

Glover, David. "Imperial Zion: Israel Zangwill and the English Origins of Territorialism." In *The Jews in Late Victorian and Edwardian Culture*, ed. Eitan Bar-Yosef and Nadia Valman, 131–43. Houndmills, Basingstoke: Palgrave Macmillan, 2009.

Goldman, Shalom. *Zeal for Zion: Christians, Jews, and the Idea of the Promised Land*. Chapel Hill: University of North Carolina Press, 2009.

Goldstein, Eric. *The Price of Whiteness: Jews, Race, and American Identity*. Princeton, N.J.: Princeton University Press, 2007.

Goldstein-Sabbah, S. "Jewish Education in Baghdad: Communal Space vs. Public Space." In *Modernity, Minority, and the Public Sphere: Jews and Christians in the Middle East*, ed. S. Goldstein-Sabbah and H. Murre-van der Berg. Leiden: Brill, 2016.

Grahl-Madsen, Atle. *The Land Beyond: Collected Essays on Refugee Law and Policy*. Leiden: Brill, 2001.

Grandits, Hannes, et al., eds. *Conflicting Loyalties in the Balkans: The Great Powers, the Ottoman Empire and Nation-Building*. London: Tauris, 2011.

Great Britain, Parliamentary Papers. *Turkey No. 1 (1923) Lausanne Conference on Near Eastern Affairs, 1922–1923* (Cmd. 1814). London: HMSO, 1923.

Greenshields, Thomas. "The Settlement of Armenian Refugees in Syria and Lebanon, 1915–1939." Ph.D. diss., Durham University, 1978.

Grehan, James. *Twilight of the Saints: Everyday Religion in Syria and Palestine*. Oxford: Oxford University Press, 2014.

Gualtieri, Sarah. *Between Arab and White: Race and Ethnicity in the Early Syrian American Diaspora*. Berkeley: University of California Press, 2009.

Haiduc-Dale, Noah. *Arab Christians in British Mandate Palestine*. Edinburgh: Edinburgh University Press, 2013.

Hakim, Carol. *The Origins of the Lebanese National Idea*. Berkeley: University of California Press, 2013.

Hanioğlu, M. Sükrü. "Jews in the Young Turk Movement to the 1908 Revolution." In *The Jews of the Ottoman Empire*, ed. Avigdor Levy, 519–26. Princeton, N.J.: Darwin Press, 1994.

Haque, C. Embdad. "The Dilemma of 'Nationhood' and Religion: A Survey and Critique of Studies on Population Displacement Resulting from the Partition of the Indian Subcontinent." *Journal of Refugee Studies* 8, 2 (1995): 185–209.

Hattam, Victoria. *In the Shadow of Race: Jews, Latinos, and Immigrant Politics in the United States*. Chicago: University of Chicago Press, 2007.

Headlam-Morley, James Wycliffe. *A Memoir of the Paris Peace Conference, 1919*. London: Methuen, 1972.

Helmreich, Paul. *From Paris to Sèvres: The Partition of the Ottoman Empire at the Peace Conference of 1919–1920*. Columbus: Ohio State University Press, 1974.

Hertzberg, Arthur, ed. *The Zionist Idea: A Historical Analysis and Reader*. Garden City, N.Y.: Doubleday, 1959.

Herzl, Theodor. *Diaries of Theodor Herzl*. Ed. Marvin Lowenthal, 2 vols. New York: Dial Press, 1956.

———. *The Jewish State*. New York: Dover, 1988.

Hieronymi, Otto. "The Nansen Passport: A Tool of Freedom of Movement and of Protection." *Refugee Survey Quarterly* 22, 1 (2003): 36–47.

Hirschon, Renee. "'Unmixing Peoples' in the Aegean Region." In *Crossing the Aegean: An Appraisal of the 1923 Compulsory Exchange between Greece and Turkey*, ed. Renee Hirschon. New York: Berghahn Books, 2003.

Hitti, Philip. *A Short History of Lebanon*. London: Macmillan, 1965.

Hovannisian, Richard. *The Republic of Armenia*, vol. 1: *The First Year, 1918–1919*. Berkeley: University of California Press, 1971.

———. *The Republic of Armenia*, vol. 2: *From Versailles to London, 1919–1920*. Berkeley: University of California Press, 1993.

Hughes, Matthew. "From Law and Order to Pacification: Britain's Suppression of the Arab Revolt in Palestine, 1936–39." *Journal of Palestine Studies* 39, 2 (2010): 6–22.

Huntford, Roland. "Fridtjof Nansen and the Unmixing of Greeks and Turks in 1924." Nansen Memorial Lecture. Oslo: Norwegian Academy of Science and Letters, 1999.

al-Husayni, Hajj Amin. *Mudhakkirat al-Hajj Muhammad Amin al-Husayni*. Ed. 'Abd al-Karim al-'Umar. Damascus: Al-Ahali, 1999.

al-Husry, Khaldun. "The Assyrian Affair of 1933 [I] and [II]." *International Journal of Middle East Studies* 5, 2–3 (1974): 161–76 and 344–60.

al-Hut, Bayan. *Qiyadat wa-al-mu'assasat al-siyasiyya fi Filastin, 1917–1948*. Beirut: Mu'assasat al-dirasat al-filastiniyya, 1981.

Hyam, Ronald. *Britain's Imperial Century 1815–1914: A Study of Empire and Expansion*. London: B.T. Batsford, 1976.

Inalcik, Halil. "The Status of the Greek Orthodox Patriarch under the Ottomans." *Turcica* 21–23 (1991): 407–36.

———, et al., eds. *An Economic and Social History of the Ottoman Empire, 1300–1914*, 2 vols. Cambridge: Cambridge University Press, 2004.

Izady, M. R. "Kurds and the Formation of the State of Iraq, 1917–1932." In *The Creation of Iraq, 1914–1921*, ed. Reeva Spector Simon and Eleanor Tejirian, 95–109. New York: Columbia University Press, 2004.

Jackson, Simon. "The Wartime Origins of French Mandate Syria." In *France in an Era of Global War, 1914–1945*, ed. Ludivine Broch and Alison Carrol. Houndmills, Basingstoke: Palgrave Macmillan, 2014.

Jalal, Ayesha. "Exploding Communalism: The Politics of Muslim Identity." In *Nationalism, Democracy and Development: State and Politics in India*, ed. Ayesha Jalal and Sugata Bose. Delhi: Oxford University Press, 1998.

Jarman, Robert L., ed. *Iraq Administration Reports 1914–1932*, vol. 10. Slough: Archive Editions, 1992.

Jeffery, Keith. *The British Army and the Crisis of Empire*. Manchester: Manchester University Press, 1984.

Joseph, J. "The Turko-Iraqi Frontier and the Assyrians." In *The World of Islam: Studies in Honour of Philip K. Hitti*, ed. James Kritzeck and R. Bayly Winder. London: Macmillan, 1959.

Joseph, John. *The Modern Assyrians of the Middle East: Encounters with Western Christian Missions, Archeologists, and Colonial Powers*. Leiden: Brill, 2000.

Kabha, Mustafa. "Palestinians and the Partition Plan." In *The Two-State Solution: The UN Partition Resolution of Mandatory Palestine—Analysis and Sources*, ed. Ruth Gavinson, 29–37. London: Bloomsbury, 2013.

Kadhim, Abbas. *Reclaiming Iraq: The 1920 Revolution and the Founding of the Modern State*. Austin: University of Texas Press, 2012.

Kaplan, Sam. "Territorializing Armenians: Geo-Texts and Political Imaginaries in French-occupied Cilicia, 1919–1922." *History and Anthropology* 15, 4 (2004): 399–423.

Karpat, Kemal. *Ottoman Populations, 1830–1914: Demographic and Social Characteristics*. Madison: University of Wisconsin Press, 1985.

———. *Studies on Ottoman Social and Political History: Selected Articles and Essays*. Leiden: Brill, 2002.

Kasaba, Resat. *A Moveable Empire: Ottoman Nomads, Migrants, and Refugees*. Seattle: University of Washington Press, 2009.

Katz, Yossi. *Partner to Partition: The Jewish Agency's Partition Plan in the Mandate Era*. London and Portland, Ore.: Frank Cass, 1998.

Kaufman, Asher. *Reviving Phoenicia: The Search for Identity in Lebanon*. London: Tauris, 2004.

Kaufmann, Chaim. "An Assessment of the Partition of Cyprus." *International Studies Perspective* 8 (2007): 206–23.

———. "When All Else Fails: Ethnic Population Transfers and Partitions in the Twentieth Century." *International Security* 23, 2 (1998): 120–56.

Kedourie, Elie. "The Bludan Congress on Palestine, September 1937." *Middle Eastern Studies* 17, 1 (1981): 107–25.

———. *The Chatham House Version and Other Middle Eastern Studies*. New York: Praeger, 1970.

Kennedy, James, and Liliana Riga. "A Liberal Route from Homogeneity? US Policymakers and the Liberalization of Ethnic Nationalists in Bosnia's Dayton Accords." *Nationalism and Ethnic Politics* 19, 2 (2013): 163–86.

Khalidi, Rashid. *The Iron Cage: The Story of the Palestinian Struggle for Statehood*. Boston: Beacon Press, 2006.

Khan, Yasmin. *The Great Partition: The Making of India and Pakistan*. New Haven, Conn.: Yale University Press, 2007.

Khater, Akram. *Inventing Home: Emigration, Gender, and the Middle Class in Lebanon, 1870–1920*. Berkeley: University of California Press, 2001.

Khoury, Philip. *Syria and the French Mandate: The Politics of Arab Nationalism, 1920–1945*. Princeton, N.J.: Princeton University Press, 1987.

Kiernan, Ben. *Blood and Soil: A World History of Genocide and Extermination from Sparta to Darfur*. New Haven, Conn.: Yale University Press, 2009.

Klieman, Aaron S. "The Resolution of Conflicts through Territorial Partition: The Case of Palestine." *Comparative Studies in Society and History* 22, 2 (1980): 281–300.

———. *The Rise of Israel: The Partition Controversy, 1937*. New York: Garland, 1987.

Kobrin, Rebecca. *Jewish Bialystok and Its Diaspora*. Bloomington: Indiana University Press, 2010.

Koolakian, Robert George. *Struggle for Justice: The Story of the American Committee for the Independence of Armenia, 1915–1920*. Dearborn, Mich.: Armenian Research Center, 2008.

Kramer, Gudrun. "Moving Out of Place: Minorities in Middle Eastern Urban Societies, 1800–1914." In *The Urban Social History of the Middle East, 1750–1950*, ed. Peter Sluglett, 182–223. Syracuse, N.Y.: Syracuse University Press, 2007.

Kulischer, Eugene M. *Europe on the Move: War and Population Changes, 1917–1947*. New York: Columbia University Press, 1948.

Kumar, Radha. "The Troubled History of Partition." *Foreign Affairs* 76, 1 (1997): 22–34.

Ladas, Stephen P. *The Exchange of Minorities: Bulgaria, Greece and Turkey*. New York: Macmillan, 1932.

Laqueur, Walter, and Barry Rubin, eds. *The Israel-Arab Reader: A Documentary History of the Middle East Conflict*, 5th ed. New York: Penguin, 1995.

Laskier, Michael M. *The Alliance Israélite Universelle and the Jewish Communities of Morocco: 1862–1962*. Albany: State University of New York Press, 1983.

Laycock, Jo. *Imagining Armenia: Orientalism, Ambiguity, and Intervention*. Manchester: Manchester University Press, 2009.

League of Nations. *Decision Relating to the Turco-Irak Frontier, Dec 16 1925*. London: HMSO, 1925.

———. *Mandat pour la Syria et le Liban*. Geneva: League of Nations, 1922.

———. *Mandate for Palestine*. London: HMSO, 1922.

———. *Mandates: Final Drafts of the Mandates for Mesopotamia and Palestine, for the Approval of the Council of the League of Nations*. London: HMSO, 1921.

———. *Memorandum on the Mission and Work of the Mixed Commission on Greco-Bulgarian Emigration*. Geneva: League of Nations, 1929.

———. "Protection of Minorities." Report by the Sixth Committee to the Assembly of the League of Nations, September 20, 1922. Geneva: League of Nations, 1922.

———. *Question de la frontière entre la Turquie et l'Irak; rapport présenté au Conseil par la commission constituée en vertu de la résolution du 30 septembre 1924*. Lausanne: Imprimeries réunies, 1925.

———. *Scheme for the Settlement of Armenian Refugees: General Survey and Principal Documents*. Geneva: League of Nations, 1927.

————, Information Section, LN Secretariat. *The League of Nations and the Protection of Minorities of Race, Language, and Religion.* Geneva: League of Nations, 1927.

————, Permanent Mandates Commission. *Report on the Work of the Ninth Session of the Commission.* Geneva: League of Nations, 1926.

————, Permanent Mandates Commission. *Report on the Work of the Fourth Session of the Commission.* Geneva: League of Nations, 1924.

League of Nations Council. *Protection of Linguistic, Racial or Religious Minorities by the League of Nations: Resolutions and Extracts from the Minutes of the Council.* Geneva: League of Nations, 1929.

————. *The Question of Exchange of Populations between Turkey and Greece.* Geneva: League of Nations, 1922.

Leese, C. Leonard. *Armenia and the Allies.* London: British Armenia Committee, 1920.

Lemkin, Raphael. *Lemkin on Genocide.* Ed. Steven L. Jacobs. Lanham, Md.: Lexington Books, 2011.

Lesch, Ann Mosely. *Arab Politics in Palestine, 1917–1939: The Frustration of a National Movement.* Ithaca, N.Y.: Cornell University Press, 1979.

Levene, Mark. *Genocide in the Age of the Nation State: The Meaning of Genocide.* London: Tauris, 2005.

————. "Herzl, the Scramble, and a Meeting That Never Happened." In *The Jew in Late-Victorian and Edwardian Culture,* ed. Eitan Bar-Yosef and Nadia Valman, 201–20. Houndmills, Basingstoke: Palgrave Macmillan, 2009.

————. "Nationalism and Its Alternatives in the International Arena: The Jewish Question at Paris, 1919." *Journal of Contemporary* History 28, 3 (1993).

————. *War, Jews, and the New Europe: The Diplomacy of Lucien Wolf.* Oxford: Oxford University Press, 1992.

LeVine, Mark. *Overthrowing Geography: Jaffa, Tel Aviv, and the Struggle for Palestine, 1880–1948.* Berkeley: University of California Press, 2001.

Lewis, Donald. *The Origins of Christian Zionism: Lord Shaftesbury and Evangelical Support for a Jewish Homeland.* Cambridge and New York: Cambridge University Press, 2010.

Likhovski, Assaf. *Law and Identity in Mandate Palestine.* Chapel Hill: University of North Carolina Press, 2006.

Lindkvist, Linde. *Shrines and Souls: The Reinvention of Religious Liberty and the Genesis of the Universal Declaration of Human Rights.* Lund: Lund University Press, 2014.

Lindqvist, Sven. *Terra Nullius: A Journey through No One's Land.* New York: New Press, 2007.

Livanios, Dimitris. "Beyond 'Ethnic Cleansing': Aspects of the Functioning of Violence in the Ottoman and Post-Ottoman Balkans." *Southeast European and Black Sea Studies* 8, 3 (2008): 189–203.

Lloyd George, David. *Is It Peace?* London: Hodder and Stoughton, 1923.

Lockman, Zachary. *Comrades and Enemies: Arab and Jewish Works in Palestine, 1906–1948.* Berkeley: University of California Press, 1996.

Longrigg, Stephen. *Syria and Lebanon under French Mandate*. New York: Octagon Books, 1972.

Lust-Okar, Ellen. "Failure of Collaboration: Armenian Refugees in Syria." *Middle Eastern Studies* 32, 1 (1996): 53–68.

Madley, Benjamin. "Patterns of Frontier Genocide, 1803–1910: The Aboriginal Tasmanians, the Yuki of California, and the Herero of Namibia." *Journal of Genocide Research* 6, 2 (2004): 167–92.

Mahmood, Saba. "Religious Freedom, the Minority Question, and Geopolitics in the Middle East." *Comparative Studies in Society and History* 54, 2 (2012): 418–46.

Main, Ernest. "Iraq and the Assyrians, 1923–1933." *Journal of the Royal Central Asian Society* 20, 4 (1933): 664–74.

———. *Iraq from Mandate to Independence*. London: Allen & Unwin, 1935.

Makdisi, Ussama. *Artillery of Heaven: American Missionaries and the Failed Conversion of the Middle East*. Ithaca, N.Y.: Cornell University Press, 2008.

———. *The Culture of Sectarianism: Community, History, and Violence in Nineteenth-Century Ottoman Lebanon*. Berkeley: University of California Press, 2000.

Malek, Yusuf. *The British Betrayal of the Assyrians*. Chicago: Assyrian National Federation and Assyrian National League of America, 1935.

Malinovich, Nadia. "Le Reveil d'Israel: Jewish Identity and Culture in France, 1900–1932." Ph.D. diss., University of Michigan, 2000.

Malkasian, Mark. "The Disintegration of the Armenian Cause in the United States, 1918–1927." *International Journal of Middle East Studies* 16, 3 (1984): 349–65.

Malkki, Lisa. "National Geographic: The Rooting of Peoples and the Territorialisation of National Identity among Scholars and Refugees." *Cultural Anthropology* 7 (1992): 24–44.

Mandel, Maud. *In the Aftermath of Genocide: Armenians and Jews in Twentieth-Century France*. Durham, N.C.: Duke University Press, 2003.

Manela, Erez. *The Wilsonian Moment: Self-Determination and the International Origins of Anticolonial Nationalism*. Oxford: Oxford University Press, 2009.

Mar Eshai Shimun. *The Assyrian Tragedy*. Privately published, 1988.

Marrus, Michael. *The Unwanted: European Refugees from the First World War through the Cold War*. Philadelphia: Temple University Press, 1985.

Marsoobian, Armen T. *Fragments of a Lost Homeland: Remembering Armenia*. London: Tauris, 2015.

Masalha, Nur. *Expulsion of the Palestinians: The Concept of "Transfer" in Zionist Political Thought, 1882–1948*. Washington, D.C.: Institute for Palestine Studies, 1992.

Masters, Bruce. *Christians and Jews in the Ottoman Arab World: The Roots of Sectarianism*. Cambridge: Cambridge University Press, 2001.

Matthews, Weldon. *Confronting an Empire, Constructing a Nation: Arab Nationalists and Popular Politics in Mandate Palestine*. London: Tauris, 2006.

Mazower, Mark. *The Balkans: From the End of Byzantium to the Present Day*. London: Phoenix, 2000.

———. *Hitler's Empire: How the Nazis Ruled Europe.* New York: Penguin, 2008.

———. "An International Civilization? Empire, Internationalism, and the Crisis of the Mid-Twentieth Century." *International Affairs* 82, 3 (2006): 553–66.

———. "Minorities and the League of Nations in Interwar Europe." *Daedalus* 126, 2 (1997): 47–65.

———. *No Enchanted Palace: The End of Empire and the Ideological Origins of the United Nations.* Princeton, N.J.: Princeton University Press, 2009.

———. *Salonica, City of Ghosts: Christians, Muslims, and Jews 1430–1950.* New York: HarperCollins, 2004.

———. "The Strange Triumph of Human Rights, 1933–1950." *Historical Journal* 47, 2 (2004): 379–98.

———. "Two Cheers for Versailles." *History Today* 49, 7 (1999): 8–14.

McCarthy, Justin. *Death and Exile: The Ethnic Cleansing of Ottoman Muslims, 1821–1922.* Princeton, N.J.: Darwin Press, 1995.

———. *The Ottoman Peoples and the End of Empire.* New York: Oxford University Press, 2001.

———. *The Population of Palestine: Population History and Statistics of the Late Ottoman Period and the Mandate.* New York: Columbia University Press, 1990.

McDowall, David. *A Modern History of the Kurds.* London: Tauris, 2003.

Melkonian, Markar, ed. *The Right to Struggle: Selected Writings by Monte Melkonian on the Armenian National Question,* 2nd ed. San Francisco: Sardarabad Collective, 1993.

Metcalf, Thomas. *Ideologies of the Raj.* Cambridge: Cambridge University Press, 1997.

Migliorino, Nicola. *(Re)constructing Armenia in Lebanon and Syria: Ethno-cultural Diversity and the State in the Aftermath of a Refugee Crisis.* New York and Oxford: Berghahn Books, 2008.

Miller, David Hunter. *My Diary at the Conference of Paris,* vol. 4. New York: Appeal Printing Company, 1924.

Mongia, Radhika. "Historicizing State Sovereignty: Inequality and the Form of Equivalence." *Comparative Studies in Society and History* 49, 2 (2007): 384–411.

Montagu, Edwin. "Memorandum on the Anti-Semitism of the Present (British) Government—Submitted to the British Cabinet, August 1917," www.jewishvirtuallibrary.org/jsource/History/Montagumemo.html

Morris, Benny. *The Birth of the Palestinian Refugee Problem, 1947–1949.* Cambridge: Cambridge University Press, 1987.

———, et al. *The Birth of the Palestinian Refugee Problem Revisited.* Cambridge: Cambridge University Press, 2003.

Moses, A. Dirk. "Empire, Colony, Genocide: Keywords and the Philosophy of History." In *Empire, Colony, Genocide: Conquest, Occupation, and Subaltern Resistance in World History,* ed. A. Dirk Moses, 3–54. New York: Berghahn Books, 2008.

Moyn, Samuel. *The Last Utopia: Human Rights in History.* Cambridge, Mass.: Belknap Press, 2010.

Mufti, Aamir. *Enlightenment in the Colony: The Jewish Question and the Crisis of Postcolonial Culture.* Princeton, N.J.: Princeton University Press, 2007.

Muhammad, 'Ala Jasim. *Ja' far al-'Askari was-dawruhu al-siyasi wa-al-'askari fi tarikh al-'Iraq hatta 'am 1936.* Baghdad: Maktabat al-Yaqzah al-'Arabiyya, 1987.

Mumford, Philip. "Kurds, Assyrians, and Iraq." *Journal of the Royal Central Asian Society* 20, 1 (1933): 110–19.

Murre-van den Berg, Heleen. "Chaldeans and Assyrians: The Church of the East in the Ottoman Period." In *The Christian Heritage of Iraq,* ed. Erica Hunter, 146–64. Piscataway, N.J.: Gorgias Press, 2009.

———. "Light from the East (1948–1954) and the De-territorialization of the Assyrian Church in the East." In *Religion Beyond Its Private Role in Modern Society,* ed. Wim Hofstee and Arie van der Kooij, 115–34. Leiden: Brill, 2013.

———, ed. *New Faith in Ancient Lands: Western Missions in the Middle East in the Nineteenth and Early Twentieth Centuries.* Boston and Leiden: Brill, 2005.

Myuhtar-May, Fatme. "Pomak Christianization (Pokrastvane) in Bulgaria during the Balkan Wars of 1912–1913," in *War and Nationalism: The Balkan Wars, 1912–1913, and Their Sociopolitical Implications,* ed. M. Hakan Yavuz and Isa Blumi, 316–60. Salt Lake City: University of Utah Press, 2013.

Naby, Eden. "The Assyrian Diaspora: Cultural Survival in the Absence of a State Structure." In *Central Asia and the Caucasus: Transnationalism and Diaspora,* ed. Touraj Atabaki and Sanjyot Mehendale, 214–30. Abingdon: Routledge, 2005.

Naimark, Norman. *Fires of Hatred: Ethnic Cleansing in Twentieth Century Europe.* Cambridge, Mass.: Harvard University Press, 2001.

Neep, Daniel. *Occupying Syria under the French Mandate: Insurgency, Space, and State Formation.* Cambridge: Cambridge University Press, 2012.

Nicault, Catherine. *La France et le Sionisme, 1897–1945: Une reconte manquée?* Paris: Calmann Levy, 1992.

Norris, Jacob. "Across Confessional Borders: A Microhistory of Ottoman Christians and Their Migratory Paths." In *Minorities and the Modern Arab World: New Perspectives,* ed. Laura Robson. Syracuse, N.Y.: Syracuse University Press, 2016.

———. *Land of Progress: Palestine in the Age of Colonial Development, 1905–1948.* Oxford: Oxford University Press, 2013.

———. "Repression and Rebellion: Britain's Response to the Arab Revolt in Palestine of 1936–39." *Journal of Imperial and Commonwealth History* 36, 1 (2008): 25–45.

Nugent, Walter. *Crossings: The Great Transatlantic Migrations, 1870–1914.* Bloomington: Indiana University Press, 1994.

Obenzinger, Hilton. *American Palestine: Melville, Twain, and the Holy Land Mania.* Princeton, N.J.: Princeton University Press, 1999.

Okkenhaug, Inger Marie. "Christian Missions in the Middle East and the Ottoman Balkans: Education, Reform, and Failed Conversions, 1819–1967." *International Journal of Middle East Studies* 47, 3 (2015): 593–604.

O'Leary, Brendan. "Analysing Partition: Definition, Classification, and Explanation." *Political Geography* 26 (2007): 886–908.

———. "Debating Partition: Justifications and Critiques." *Working Papers in British-Irish Studies* 78 (2006): 1–29.

Omissi, David. "Britain, the Assyrians and the Iraq Levies, 1919–1932." *Journal of Imperial and Commonwealth History* 17, 3 (1989): 301–22.

Oren, Michael. *Power, Faith and Fantasy: America in the Middle East, 1776 to the Present.* New York: Norton, 2007.

Ortayli, Ilber. "Ottomanism and Zionism during the Second Constitutional Period." In *The Jews of the Ottoman Empire,* ed. Avigdor Levy, 527–36. Princeton, N.J.: Darwin Press, 1994.

Owen, Roger. "The Influence of Lord Cromer's Indian Experience on British Policy in Egypt." *St. Antony's Papers* 17 (1965): 109–39.

Palestine Royal Commission. *Summary of the Report of the Palestine Royal Commission, with Extracts.* London: HMSO, 1937.

Pandey, Gyanendra. *The Construction of Communalism in Colonial North India.* Delhi: Oxford University Press, 1990.

———. *Remembering Partition: Violence, Nationalism and History in India.* Cambridge: Cambridge University Press, 2001.

Pappé, Ilan. *The Ethnic Cleansing of Palestine.* Oxford: Oneworld Press, 2006.

———. "Hajj Amin and the Buraq Revolt." *Jerusalem Quarterly* 19 (2003): 6–16.

Parsons, Laila. "Soldiering for Arab Nationalism: Fawzi al-Qawuqji in Palestine." *Journal of Palestine Studies* 36, 4 (2007): 33–48.

Pedersen, Susan. "Getting Out of Iraq—in 1932: The League of Nations and the Road to Normative Statehood." *American Historical Review* 115, 4 (2010): 975–1000.

———. *The Guardians: The League of Nations and the Crisis of Empire.* Oxford: Oxford University Press, 2015.

———. "The Meaning of the Mandates System: An Argument." *Geschichte und Gesellschaft* 32, 4 (2006): 560–82.

———. "Samoa on the World Stage: Petitions and Peoples before the Mandates Commission of the League of Nations." *Journal of Imperial and Commonwealth History* 40, 2 (2012): 231–61.

———. "Settler Colonialism at the Bar of the League of Nations." In *Settler Colonialism in the Twentieth Century,* ed. Caroline Elkins and Susan Pedersen, 113–34. London: Routledge, 2005.

Peel, William Robert Wellesley, and Palestine Royal Commission. *Palestine Royal Commission Report.* London: HMSO, 1937.

Pellew, Jill. "The Home Office and the Aliens Act, 1905." *Historical Journal* 32, 2 (1989): 369–85.

Penslar, Derek. "Zionism, Colonialism, and Postcolonialism." In *Israeli Historical Revisionism: From Left to Right,* ed. Derek Penslar and Anita Shapira, 84–98. Portland, Ore: Frank Cass, 2003.

Perville, Guy. *De l'empire français à la decolonization.* Paris: Hachette, 1991.

Peteet, Julie. *Landscape of Hope and Despair: Palestinian Refugee Camps.* Philadelphia: University of Pennsylvania Press, 2005.

Peterson, Merrill. *"Starving Armenians": America and the Armenian Genocide, 1915–1930 and After.* Charlottesville: University of Virginia Press, 2004.

Petrosian, Vahram. "The Assyrians of Iraq." *Iran and the Caucasus* 10, 1 (2006): 114–47.

Pinsker, Leon. *Autoemancipation.* Trans. D. S. Blondheim. London: Federation of Zionist Youth, 1937.

———. "Autoemancipation!" In *The Zionist Idea: A Historical Analysis and Reader,* ed. Arthur Hertzberg, 178–98. Garden City, N.Y.: Doubleday, 1959.

de Planhol, Xavier. *Minorités en Islam: Geographie politique et sociale.* Paris: Flammarion, 1997.

Porter, Andrew. "Introduction." In *The Oxford History of the British Empire: The Nineteenth Century,* ed. W. Roger Louis and Andrew Porter. Oxford and New York: Oxford University Press, 2009.

Porter, Bernard. *Critics of Empire: British Radicals and the Imperial Challenge.* London: Tauris, 2008.

Preece, Jennifer Jackson. *National Minorities and the European Nation State System.* Oxford: Clarendon Press, 1998.

Provence, Michael. *The Great Syrian Revolt and the Rise of Arab Nationalism.* Austin: University of Texas Press, 2005.

Quataert, Donald. *The Ottoman Empire, 1700–1922.* New York: Cambridge University Press, 2000.

Qureshi, Sadiah. *Peoples on Parade: Exhibitions, Empire, and Anthropology in Nineteenth-Century Britain.* Chicago: University of Chicago Press, 2011.

Raider, Mark. *The Emergence of American Zionism.* New York: New York University Press, 1998.

Raitz von Frentz, Christian. *A Lesson Forgotten: Minority Protection under the League of Nations.* New York: St. Martin's Press, 1999.

Rajagopal, Balakrishnan. "International Law and Third World Resistance." In *The Third World and International Order: Law, Politics and Globalization,* ed. Antony Anghie et al., 145–72. Leiden: Nijhoff, 2003.

Rankin, George. "Custom and the Muslim Law in British India." *Transactions of the Grotius Society* 25 (1939): 89–118.

al-Rasheed, Madawi. *Iraqi Assyrian Christians in London: The Construction of Ethnicity.* Lewiston, N.Y.: Edwin Mellen Press, 1998.

Republique française, Ministere des Affaires étrangeres. *Rapport sur la situation de la Syrie et du Liban (juillet 1922-juillet 1923).* Paris: Imprimerie nationale, 1923.

Riga, Liliana, and James Kennedy. "Tolerant Majorities, Loyal Minorities and 'Ethnic Reversals': Constructing Minority Rights at Versailles, 1919." *Nations and Nationalism* 15, 3 (2009): 461–82.

Rihani, Ameen. *The Fate of Palestine: A Series of Lectures, Articles, and Documents about the Palestinian Problem and Zionism.* Beirut: Rihani Printing and Publishing House, 1967.

Rihbany, Abraham Mitri. *Wise Men from the East and from the West.* Boston and New York: Houghton Mifflin, 1922.

Robinson, Greg. "FDR's M Project: Building a Better World through [Racial] Science." *Critique Internationale* 2 (2005): 65–82.

Robinson, Jacob, et al. *Were the Minorities Treaties a Failure?* New York: Institute of Jewish Affairs, 1943.

Robinson, Shira. *Citizen Strangers: Palestinians and the Birth of Israel's Liberal Settler State.* Stanford, Calif.: Stanford University Press, 2013.

Robson, Laura. "Archeology and Mission: The British Presence in Nineteenth-Century Jerusalem." *Jerusalem Quarterly* 10, 1 (2010): 5–17.

———. *Colonialism and Christianity in Mandate Palestine.* Austin: University of Texas Press, 2011.

———, ed. *Minorities and the Modern Arab World: New Perspectives.* Syracuse, N.Y.: Syracuse University Press, 2016.

———. "Peripheries of Belonging: Military Recruitment and the Making of a 'Minority' in Wartime Iraq." *First World War Studies* 7, 1 (2016): 1–20.

Rodogno, Davide. *Against Massacre: Humanitarian Interventions in the Ottoman Empire, 1815–1914.* Princeton, N.J.: Princeton University Press, 2012.

Rodrigue, Aron. *French Jews, Turkish Jews: The Alliance Israélite Universelle and the Politics of Jewish Schooling in Turkey, 1860–1925.* Bloomington: Indiana University Press, 1990.

———. *Images of Sephardi and Eastern Jewries in Transition: The Teachers of the Alliance Israélite Universelle, 1860–1939.* Seattle: University of Washington Press, 1993.

———. "The Jew as the Original 'Other.'" In *Doing Race: 21 Essays for the 21st Century,* ed. Hazel Rose Markus and Paula M.L. Moya. New York: Norton, 2010.

———. *Jews and Muslims: Images of Sephardi and Eastern Jewries in Modern Times.* Seattle: University of Washington Press, 2003.

———, and Nancy Reynolds. "Difference and Tolerance in the Ottoman Empire." *Stanford Electronic Humanities Review* 5, 1 (1996), www.stanford.edu/group /SHR/5-1/text/rodrigue.html

Ruedy, John. *Modern Algeria: The Origins and Development of a Nation.* Bloomington: Indiana University Press, 2005.

Salaita, Steven. *The Holy Land in Transit: Colonialism and the Quest for Canaan.* Syracuse, N.Y.: Syracuse University Press, 2006.

Salibi, Kamal. *The Modern History of Lebanon.* New York: Praeger, 1965.

Sambanis, Nicholas. "Partition as a Solution to Ethnic War: An Empirical Critique of the Theoretical Literature." *World Politics* 52, 4 (2000): 437–83.

———, and Jonah Schulhofer-Wohl. "What's in a Line? Is Partition a Solution to Civil War?" *International Security* 34, 2 (2009): 82–118.

Satia, Priya. "The Defense of Inhumanity: Air Control and the British Idea of Arabia." *American Historical Review* 111, 1 (2006): 16–51.

Sawda, Yusef. *Fi Sabil Lubnan.* Beirut: Dar Lahad Khater, 1988.

Schaeffer, Robert. *Warpaths: The Politics of Partition.* New York: Hill and Wang, 1990.

Schayegh, Cyrus, and Andrew Arsan, eds. *The Routledge Handbook of the History of the Middle East Mandates*. Abingdon and New York: Routledge, 2015.

Schiff, Benjamin. *Refugees unto the Third Generation: U.N. Aid to Palestinians*. Syracuse, N.Y.: Syracuse University Press, 1995.

Schneer, Jonathan. *The Balfour Declaration: The Origins of the Arab-Israeli Conflict*. New York: Random House, 2010.

Schofield, Richard, ed. *Arabian Boundary Disputes*, vols. 1–20. Cambridge: Cambridge Archive Editions, 1992.

———. "Laying It Down in Stone: Delimiting and Demarcating Iraq's Boundaries by Mixed International Commission." *Journal of Historical Geography* 34, 3 (2008): 397–421.

Schreier, Joshua. *Arabs of the Jewish Faith: The Civilizing Mission in Colonial Algeria*. New Brunswick, N.J.: Rutgers University Press, 2010.

Scott, James C. *Two Cheers for Anarchism: Six Easy Pieces on Autonomy, Dignity, and Meaningful Work and Play*. Princeton, N.J.: Princeton University Press, 2012.

Seker, Nesim. "Demographic Engineering in the Late Ottoman Empire and the Armenians." *Middle Eastern Studies* 43, 3 (2007): 464–65.

Shafir, Gershon. *Land, Labor, and the Origins of the Israeli-Palestinian Conflict, 1882–1914*. Cambridge and New York: Cambridge University Press, 1989.

Shahoian, Levon. *On the Banks of the Tigris*. London: Taderon Press, 2012.

Sharkey, Heather. *American Evangelicals in Egypt: Missionary Encounters in an Age of Empire*. Princeton, N.J.: Princeton University Press, 2013.

Sheffer, Gabriel. "The Jewish Diaspora and the Arab-Palestinian-Israeli Conflict." In *Diasporas in Conflict: Peace-Makers or Peace-Wreckers?* ed. Hazel Smith and Paul Stares. Tokyo: United Nations University Press, 2007.

Shields, Sarah D. *Fezzes in the River: Identity Politics and European Diplomacy in the Middle East on the Eve of World War II*. Oxford: Oxford University Press, 2011.

———. "Mosul Questions: Economy, Identity, and Annexation." In *The Creation of Iraq, 1914–1921*, ed. Reeva Spector Simon and Eleanor Tejirian. New York: Columbia University Press, 2004.

Shimmon, Paul. *The Assyrian Tragedy*. Annemasse, France: n.pub., 1934.

Shlaim, Avi. *Collusion across the Jordan: King Abdullah, the Zionist Movement, and the Partition of Palestine*. New York: Columbia University Press, 1988.

———. *Israel and Palestine: Reappraisals, Revisions, Refutations*. London: Verso, 2009.

Silverberg, Robert. *If I Forget Thee O Jerusalem: American Jews and the State of Israel*. New York: Morrow, 1970.

Silverfarb, Daniel. *Britain's Informal Empire in the Middle East: A Case Study of Iraq, 1929–1941*. New York: Oxford University Press, 1986.

Simon, Reeva Spector. *Iraq between the Two World Wars: The Militarist Origins of Tyranny*, 2nd ed. New York: Columbia University Press, 2004.

———, and Eleanor Tejirian, eds. *The Creation of Iraq, 1914–1921*. New York: Columbia University Press, 2004.

Simpson, John Hope. *The Refugee Question*. Oxford: Clarendon Press, 1939.

Sinanoglou, Penny. "British Plans for the Partition of Palestine, 1929–1938." *Historical Journal* 52, 1 (2009): 131–52.

Skran, Claudia. *Refugees in Interwar Europe: The Emergence of a Regime*. Oxford: Clarendon Press, 1995.

Sluglett, Peter. *Contriving King and Country: Britain in Iraq*. London: Tauris, 2007.

———. "An Improvement on Colonialism? The 'A' Mandates and Their Legacy in the Middle East." *International Affairs* 90, 2 (2014): 413–27.

———, and Nadine Meouchy, eds. *The British and French Mandates in Comparative Perspective*. Leiden: Brill, 2004.

Smith, Charles. *Palestine and the Arab-Israeli Conflict*, 8th ed. Boston: Bedford/St. Martin's Press, 2013.

Smith, Hazel, and Paul B. Stares, eds. *Diasporas in Conflict: Peace-Makers or Peace-Wreckers?* Tokyo and New York: United Nations University Press, 2007.

Snyder, Timothy. *Bloodlands: Europe between Hitler and Stalin*. New York: Basic Books, 2010.

Solomon, Solomon (Sawa). *The Assyrian Levies*. Atour, 2006.

———. *Chapters from Modern Assyrian History*. Privately published, 1996.

Stafford, R. S. "Iraq and the Problem of the Assyrians." *International Affairs* 13, 2 (1934): 159–85.

———. *The Tragedy of the Assyrians*. London: Allen & Unwin, 1935.

Stein, Kenneth. "The Intifada and the 1936–39 Uprising: A Comparison." *Journal of Palestine Studies* 19, 4 (1990): 64–85.

Steinberg, Isaac. *Australia—The Unpromised Land: In Search of a Home*. London: V. Gollancz, 1948.

Sternhell, Zeev. *The Founding Myths of Israel: Nationalism, Socialism, and the Making of the Jewish State*. Princeton, N.J.: Princeton University Press, 1998.

Suny, Ronald, et al., eds. *A Question of Genocide: Armenians and Turks at the End of the Ottoman Empire*. New York: Oxford University Press, 2011.

Swedenburg, Ted. *Memories of Revolt: The 1936–1939 Rebellion and the Palestinian National Past*. Minneapolis: University of Minnesota Press, 1995.

Sykes, Percy. "Summary of the History of the Assyrians." *Journal of the Royal Central Asian Society* 21, 2 (1934): 225–68.

Tannous, Izzat. *The Palestinians: A Detailed Documented Eyewitness History of Palestine under British Mandate*. New York: I.G.T., 1988.

Tejirian, Eleanor H., and Reeva Spector Simon. *Conflict, Conquest, and Conversion: Two Thousand Years of Christian Missions in the Middle East*. New York: Columbia University Press, 2012.

Terunean, Vardan. *Mémoire arménienne: Photographies du camp de réfugiés d'Alep, 1922–1936*. Beirut: Presse de l'Université Saint-Joseph, 2010.

Thompson, Elizabeth. *Colonial Citizens: Republican Rights, Paternal Privilege, and Gender in French Syria and Lebanon*. New York: Columbia University Press, 2000.

Thomson, D. B. "The Assyrian Refugee Camp." *Journal of the Royal Central Asian Society* 21, 2 (1934): 269–76.

Tibi, Bassam. *Arab Nationalism: Between Islam and the Nation-State,* 3rd ed. New York: St. Martin's Press, 1997.

Tignor, Robert. "The 'Indianization' of the Egyptian Administration under British Rule." *American Historical Review* 68 (1963): 636–61.

Toledano, Ehud. *Slavery and Abolition in the Ottoman Middle East.* Seattle: University of Washington Press, 1998.

Toynbee, Arnold. *Armenian Atrocities: The Murder of a Nation.* London: Hodder and Stoughton, 1915.

Travis, Hannibal. "The Assyrian Genocide: A Tale of Oblivion and Denial." In *Forgotten Genocides: Oblivion, Denial, and Memory,* ed. Rene Lemarchand, 123–36. Philadelphia: University of Pennsylvania Press, 2011.

———. *Genocide in the Middle East: The Ottoman Empire, Iraq, and Sudan.* Durham, N.C.: Carolina Academic Press, 2010.

Tripp, Charles. *A History of Iraq,* 2nd ed. Cambridge: Cambridge University Press, 2000.

Tusan, Michelle. *Smyrna's Ashes: Humanitarianism, Genocide, and the Birth of the Middle East.* Berkeley: University of California Press, 2012.

Ulrichsen, Kristian. *The First World War in the Middle East.* London: Hurst, 2014.

United Nations. *The Partition of Palestine 29 Nov 1947: An Analysis.* Beirut: Institute for Palestine Studies, 1967.

United Nations. *Special Committee on Palestine,* vol. 3: *Oral Evidence Presented at Public Meetings.* Lake Success, N.Y.: 1947.

Urofsky, Melvin. *American Zionism from Herzl to the Holocaust.* Garden City, N.Y.: Anchor, 1976.

Verancini, Lorenzo. *The Settler Colonial Present.* Houndmills, Basingstoke: Palgrave Macmillan, 2015.

Vital, David. *A People Apart: The Jews in Europe, 1789–1939.* Oxford: Oxford University Press, 1999.

———. *Zionism: The Formative Years.* Oxford: Clarendon Press, 1982.

Waller, Richard. "Emutai: Crisis and Response in Maasailand, 1883–1902." In *The Ecology of Survival: Case Studies from Northeast African History,* ed. Douglas Johnson and David Anderson, 73–111. Boulder, Colo.: Westview Press, 1988.

Watenpaugh, Keith. *Being Modern in the Middle East: Revolution, Nationalism, Colonialism, and the Arab Middle Class.* Princeton, N.J.: Princeton University Press, 2006.

———. "Between Communal Survival and National Aspiration: Armenian Genocide Refugees, the League of Nations, and the Practices of Interwar Humanitarianism." *Humanity* 5, 2 (2014): 159–81.

———. *Bread from Stones: The Middle East and the Making of Modern Humanitarianism.* Berkeley: University of California Press, 2015.

———. "The League of Nations' Rescue of Armenian Genocide Survivors and the Making of Modern Humanitarianism, 1920–1927." *American Historical Review* 115, 5 (2010): 1315–39.

Weitz, Eric D. "From the Vienna to the Paris System: International Politics and the Entangled Histories of Human Rights, Forced Deportations, and Civilizing Missions." *American Historical Review* 113, 5 (2008): 1313–43.

———. "Self-Determination: How a German Enlightenment Idea Became the Slogan of National Liberation and a Human Right." *American Historical Review* 120, 2 (2015): 462–96.

Weizmann, Chaim. *Trial and Error*. New York: Harper and Brothers, 1949.

Wempe, Sean Andrew. "From Unfit Imperialists to Fellow Civilizers: German Colonial Officials as Imperial Experts in the League of Nations, 1919–1933." *German History* 34, 1 (2016): 21–48.

Werda, Joel. *The Flickering Light of Asia: Or, the Assyrian Nation and Church*. N.pub., 1924, www.aina.org/books/fla/fla.htm#c31

Wheatley, Natasha. "Mandatory Interpretation: Legal Hermeneutics and the New International Order in Arab and Jewish Petitions to the League of Nations." *Past and Present* 227 (2015): 205–48.

White, Benjamin Thomas. *The Emergence of Minorities in the Middle East: The Politics of Community in French Mandate Syria*. Edinburgh: Edinburgh University Press, 2011.

———. "A Grudging Rescue: France, the Armenians of Cilicia, and the History of Humanitarian Evacuations." Unpublished paper, 2015.

———. "Refugees and the Definition of Syria, 1920–1939." *Past and Present* (forthcoming May 2017). doi 10.1093/pastj/gtw048

Wigram, W. *The Assyrians and Their Neighbors*. London: Bell Press, 1929.

Winter, Jay, ed. *America and the Armenian Genocide of 1915*. Cambridge: Cambridge University Press, 2004.

———, and Antoine Prost. *René Cassin and Human Rights: From the Great War to the Universal Declaration*. New Haven, Conn.: Yale University Press, 2013.

Wippman, David. "The Evolution and Implementation of Minority Rights." *Fordham Law Review* 66, 2 (1997): 597–626.

World Zionist Organisation. "The Establishment in Palestine of the Jewish National Home." Geneva: League of Nations, 1924.

Yilmaz, Suhnaz, and Ipek Yosmaoglu. "Fighting the Spectres of the Past: Dilemmas of Ottoman Legacy in the Balkans and the Middle East." *Middle Eastern Studies* 44, 5 (2008): 677–93.

Yosmaoglu, Ipek. *Blood Ties: Religion, Violence, and the Politics of Nationhood in Ottoman Macedonia, 1878–1908*. Ithaca, N.Y.: Cornell University Press, 2014.

———. "Counting Bodies, Shaping Souls: The 1903 Census and National Identity in Ottoman Macedonia." *International Journal of Middle East Studies* 38, 1 (2006): 55–77.

Zamindar, Vazira Fazila-Yacoobali. *The Long Partition and the Making of Modern South Asia: Refugees, Boundaries, Histories*. New York: Columbia University Press, 2007.

Zamir, Meir. "Emile Eddé and the Territorial Integrity of Lebanon." *Middle Eastern Studies* 14, 2 (1978): 232–35.

———. "Smaller and Greater Lebanon—The Squaring of a Circle?" *Jerusalem Quarterly* 23 (1982): 34–52.

Zangwill, Israel. *Speeches, Articles, and Letters of Israel Zangwill*. Westport, Conn.: Hyperion Press, 1976.

Zolberg, Aristide R. "The Formation of New States as a Refugee-Generating Process." In *The Global Refugee Problem: U.S. and World Response. Annals of the American Academy of Political and Social Sciences* 467 (1983): 24–38.

Zubaida, Sami. "Contested Nations: Iraq and the Assyrians." *Nations and Nationalism* 6, 3 (2000): 362–82.

Zurcher, Erik. *Turkey: A Modern History*, 3rd ed. London: Tauris, 2004.

INDEX

Akka, 115, 116*map*

Alami, Musa, 120

Albania, 23, 75. *See also* Balkans; Balkan wars

Aleppo, ii*map,* 36, 51, 59–63, 78–79, 100*map,* 197n43

Alexandretta, 57, 60, 78, 81, 83, 159–161, 197n54, 197n56, 216n75

Algeria, 3, 10–11, 24

Alliance Israélite Universelle (AIU), 11, 26, 142, 157, 171

American Committee for the Independence of Armenia (ACIA), 147, 148, 213n28, 214n29

American Jewish Congress (AJC), 144, 167

Amery, Leo, 53, 90

'Ammun, Daud, 109

Arab Centre, 121–122

Arab revolt (First World War), 50

Arab revolt (Palestine 1936–1939), 123

Armenia, ii*map,* 37, 141, 167; American mandate over, 146, 148, 165; medieval, 37; and philo-Armenian organizations, 37, 79–80, 165; proposed state of, 36, 37, 43, 59, 63, 145–149, 151–152, 155, 159, 165–167; Republic of, 58, 79, 145, 146; Soviet, 60, 79, 80, 148, 160; Turkish and Russian territorial incorporation of, 57. *See also* Armenian genocide

Armenian General Benevolent Union (AGBU), 160*fig.,* 161

Armenian genocide, 4, 35, 46, 145, 153, 170, 186n3, 186n4

Armenians, 2, 4, 5; Allied views of, 10, 19, 37, 38, 44; in diaspora, 39, 141, 142, 145–148, 150–153, 156–157, 159–161, 164, 167; nationalism and, 37- 39; in Ottoman Empire, 16, 22, 40; and refugees, 34, 36, 44–47, 49–64, 78–83, 84, 85, 92, 166; resettlement of, 2, 36, 66, 78–83, 103, 104, 138. *See also* Armenian genocide; Ba'quba

'Askari, Ja'far al-, 50, 89

Assyrian Levies, 47, 50, 51, 54, 85–87, 92

Assyrian National Pact, 86

Assyrians: in diaspora, 5, 141, 142, 148–151, 156, 161–164; genocide of, 186n4; and massacre at Simele, 1, 87–88; as "minorities," 36, 52–54; nationalism and, 38–39, 42–43; and the Ottoman Empire, 39, 42, 46; proposed state for, 36 41, 43–44, 107, 110, 165–167; refugees, 4, 39–56; 66, 78, 83–86, 138; resettlement of, 2, 5, 49, 54–56, 59, 63, 81, 90–100, 104; Western views of, 10; 37, 152, 153, 165–167. *See also* Assyrian Levies; Ba'quba

Austin, H.H., 44, 47. *See also* Ba'quba

Australia, 1, 3, 8, 11, 67, 91, 101–102, 104, 127, 132, 151

Azmi Bey, Khalil, 56

Baghdad, 35, 39, 41*map,* 42, 49, 55, 83, 84, 86, 87, 88, 96, 100*map,* 149

Balfour Declaration, 17, 32, 72, 106, 111, 112, 118, 119, 131, 132, 144, 147. *See also* Zionism